W9-BCU-834

Modern Critical Views

Maya Angelou
Asian American Writers
Jane Austen
James Baldwin
Samuel Beckett
William Blake
The Brontës
Robert Browning
Albert Camus
Lewis Carroll
Willa Cather
Geoffrey Chaucer
Anton Chekhov
Kate Chopin
Samuel Taylor Coleridge
Joseph Conrad
Stephen Crane
Dante
Charles Dickens
Emily Dickinson
John Donne & the 17th-Century Poets
Fyodor Dostoevsky
T. S. Eliot
Ralph Ellison
Ralph Waldo Emerson
William Faulkner
F. Scott Fitzgerald
Sigmund Freud
Robert Frost
George Gordon, Lord Byron
Thomas Hardy
Nathaniel Hawthorne
Ernest Hemingway
Hispanic American Writers
Homer
Langston Hughes
Zora Neale Hurston
Henrik Ibsen
Henry James
James Joyce
Franz Kafka
John Keats
Stephen King
Jamaica Kincaid
D. H. Lawrence
Sinclair Lewis
Gabriel García Márquez
Carson McCullers
Herman Melville
Arthur Miller
Marianne Moore
Toni Morrison
Iris Murdoch
Native American Writers
Joyce Carol Oates
Flannery O'Connor
Eugene O'Neill
George Orwell
Sylvia Plath
Edgar Allan Poe
Contemporary Poets
J. D. Salinger
William Shakespeare–Comedies
William Shakespeare–Histories & Poems
William Shakespeare–Tragedies
George Bernard Shaw
Mary Wollstonecraft Shelley
Percy Bysshe Shelley
Sophocles
John Steinbeck
Henry David Thoreau
Mark Twain
John Updike
Alice Walker
Eudora Welty
Edith Wharton
Walt Whitman
Tennessee Williams
Virginia Woolf
William Wordsworth
Richard Wright
William Butler Yeats

Modern Critical Views

MAYA ANGELOU

Edited and with an introduction by
Harold Bloom
Sterling Professor of the Humanities
Yale University

CHELSEA HOUSE PUBLISHERS
Philadelphia

Printed and bound in the United States of America

10 9 8 7 6 5 4 3 2 1

∞ The paper used in this publication meets the minimum requirements of the American National Standard for Permanence of Paper for Printed Library Materials, Z39.48-1984

Library of Congress Cataloging-in-Publication Data applied for

ISBN 0-7910-4782-2

Contents

Editor's Note

This volume is a selection of the better critical essays that are available concerning the poetry and prose of Maya Angelou. I am grateful to Tenley Williams for her skilled assistance in research and editing. My "Introduction" speculates upon the ultimate relationship between Angelou's sense of self and African American religious tradition. Sidonie Ann Smith begins the chronological sequence of criticism with her meditation upon Angelou's growth in self-awareness throughout *I Know Why the Caged Bird Sings.*

Caged Bird is also the subject of George E. Kent's study of Angelou's relation to other African American autobiographies, while Carol E. Neubauer considers the style of Angelou's *The Heart of a Woman.* Sondra O'Neale examines Angelou's pioneer rule in creating fresh images of African American women throughout her continuing autobiography, after which Selwyn Cudjoe surveys Angelou's achievement in the light of his realization that the mode of memoir is distinctively the African American literary achievement.

Angelou's poetry, to me far more problematic than her prose works, is praised by Priscilla R. Ramsey for its transcendental view of love, while Christine Froula locates Angelou's *Caged Bird* within the literary context of sexual violence against women.

Caged Bird is contrasted to Richard Wright's *Black Boy* by Keneth Kinnamon, after which Joanne M. Braxton, also considering *Caged Bird,* testifies to its powers of transcendence. The complex relation to her audience, shrewdly contrived by Angelou, is studied by Francoise Lionnet, while Mary Jane Lupton traces the mother-son continuity throughout the ongoing autobiography.

In a final essay, Carol E. Neubauer chronicles the creative sense of "the universal majesty of the black woman" in Angelou's career as a poet.

Introduction

Angelou's achievement, more even in her ongoing autobiography than in her verse, has a complex relation to at least two among the principal antecedents of African American memoirs: the slave narrative and the church sermon. Since she is a spellbinder of a storyteller, other elements in African American tradition, including the blues and the oral eloquence of street ways, also enter into her work. Though Angelou is essentially a secular biographer, her extraordinary and persistent sense of self, one that rises both through and above experience, seems to me to go back to the African American paradigm of what I have called the American Religion. What survived of West African spirituality, after the torments of the Middle Passage from Africa to America, was the gnosis that early black Baptists in America spoke of as "the little me within the big me." Though converted to the slaveowners' ostensible Christianity, they transformed that European faith by a radical "knowing" that the "little me" or most inward self did not stem from the harsh space and time of the white world, but emanated ultimately from their unfallen cosmos that preceded the Creation-Fall of the whites. Angelou's pervasive sense that what is oldest and best in her own spirit derives from a lost, black fullness of being is one of the strongest manifestations in African American literature of this ancient gnosis.

I think that this is part of the secret of Angelou's enormous appeal to American readers, whether white or black, because her remarkable literary voice speaks to something in the universal American "little me within the big me." Most Americans, of whatever race or ethnic origin, share the sense that experience, however terrible, can be endured because their deepest self is beyond experience and so cannot be destroyed. Particularly in her best book, *I Know Why the Caged Bird Sings*, Angelous achieves an almost unique tone that blends intimacy and detachment, a tone indeed of assured serenity that transcends the fearful humiliations and outrages that she suffered as a girl. Hundreds of thousands of readers have found in *Caged Bird* an implicit image of the resurrection of their own innermost self, a fragment of divinity that transcended natural birth, and so can never die.

SIDONIE ANN SMITH

The Song of a Caged Bird: Maya Angelou's Quest after Self-Acceptance

I know why the caged bird sings, ah me,
When his wing is bruised and his bosom sore,—
When he beats his bars and he would be free;
It is not a carol of joy or glee,
But a prayer that he sends from his heart's deep core,
But a plea, that upward to Heaven he flings—
I know why the caged bird sings!

"Sympathy"—Paul Laurence Dunbar

A young, awkward girl child dressed in a cut-down faded purple, too-long taffeta gown, stands nervously before an Easter congregation in Stamps, Arkansas, asking, "What you looking at me for?" The next lines refuse to escape forgetfulness, imprinting this one indelibly on the shamefilled silence. Finally the minister's wife offers her the forgotten lines. She grabs them, spills them into the congregation and then stumbles out of the watching church, "a green persimmon caught between [her] legs." Unable to control the pressure of her physical response, she urinated, then laughs "from the knowledge that [she] wouldn't die from a busted head."

But the cathartic laughter never even begins to mute, much less transcend, the real pain that is this experience, the palpable pain that pulses through her long trip down the aisle of that singing church as urine flows

From *Southern Humanities Review* 7:4.

mockingly down her grotesquely skinny, heavily dusted legs. "What you looking at me for?" The question's physical articulation is barely audible; its emotional articulation wails insufferably through the child's whole being, wails her self-consciousness, wails her diminished self-image: "What you looking at me for?"—"What you looking at *me* for?"—over and over until it becomes, "Is something *wrong* with me?" For this child too much is wrong.

The whole way she looks is wrong. She knows it too. That's why they are all looking at her. Earlier as she watches her grandmother make over the white woman's faded dress she revels for one infinitely delicious moment in fantasies of stardom. In a beautiful dress she would be transformed into a beautiful movie star: "I was going to look like one of the sweet little white girls who were everybody's dream of what was right with the world" (4). But between the taffeta insubstantiality of her ideal vision of herself and the raw (fleshy) edges of her substantiality stands the one-way mirror:

> Easter's early morning sun had shown the dress to be a plain ugly cut-down from a white woman's once-was-purple throwaway. It was old-lady-long too, but it didn't hide my skinny legs, which had been greased with Blue Seal Vaseline and powdered with the Arkansas red clay. The age-faded color made my skin look dirty like mud, and everyone in church was looking at my skinny legs. (4)

Wrong dress. Wrong legs. Wrong hair. Wrong face. Wrong color. Wrong. Wrong. Wrong. The child lives in a "black ugly dream," or rather nightmare. But since this life is only a dream, the child knows she will awaken soon into a rightened, a whitened reality.

> Wouldn't they be surprised when one day I woke out of my black ugly dream, and my real hair, which was long and blond, would take the place of the kinky mass that Momma wouldn't let me straighten? My light-blue eyes were going to hypnotize them, after all the things they said about "my daddy must of been a Chinaman" (I thought they meant made out of china, like a cup) because my eyes were so small and squinty. Then they would understand why I had never picked up a Southern accent, or spoke the common slang, and why I had to be forced to eat pigs' tails and snouts. Because I was really white and because a cruel fairy stepmother, who was understandably jealous of my beauty, had turned me into a too-big Negro girl, with nappy black hair, broad feet and a space

> between her teeth that would hold a number-two pencil. (4–5)

In a society attuned to white standards of physical beauty, the black girl child cries herself to sleep at night to the tune of her own inadequacy. At least she can gain temporary respite in the impossible dreams of whiteness. Here in the darkened nights of the imagination, that refuge from society and the mirror, blossoms an ideal self. Yet even the imagination is sometimes not so much a refuge as it is a prison in which the dreamer becomes even more inescapably possessed by the nightmare since the very self she fantasizes conforms perfectly to society's prerequisites. The cage door jangles shut around the child's question: "What you looking at me for?"

In this primal scene of childhood which opens Maya Angelou's *I Know Why the Caged Bird Sings*, the black girl child testifies to her imprisonment in her bodily prison. She is a black ugly reality, not a whitened dream. And the attendant self-consciousness and diminished self-image throb through her bodily prison until the bladder can do nothing but explode in a parody of release (freedom).

In good autobiography the opening, whether a statement of act such as the circumstance of birth or ancestry or the recreation of a primal incident such as Maya Angelou's, defines the strategy of the narrative. The strategy itself is a function of the autobiographer's self-image at the moment of writing, for the nature of that self-image determines the nature of the pattern of self-actualization he discovers while attempting to shape his past experiences. Such a pattern must culminate in some sense of an ending, and it is this sense of an ending that informs certain earlier moments with significance and determines the choice of what experience he recreates, what he discards. In fact the earlier moments are fully understood only after that sense of an ending has imposed itself upon the material of the autobiographer's life. Ultimately, then, the opening moment assumes the end, the end the opening moment. Its centrality derives from its distillation of the environment of the self which generated the pattern of the writer's quest after self-actualization.

In Black American autobiography the opening almost invariably recreates the environment of enslavement from which the black self seeks escape. Such an environment was literal in the earliest form of black autobiography, the slave narrative, which traced the flight of the slave northward from slavery into full humanity. In later autobiography, however, the literal enslavement is replaced by more subtle forms of economic, historical, psychological, and spiritual imprisonment from which the black self still seeks an escape route to a "North." Maya Angelou's opening calls to mind the primal experience which opens Richard Wright's *Black Boy*. Young

Richard, prevented from playing outside because of his sick, "white"-faced grandmother, puts fire to curtains and burns down the house. For this his mother beats him nearly to death. Richard's childhood needs for self-expression culminate in destruction, foreshadowing the dilemma the autobiographer discovers in his subsequent experience. His needs for self-actualization when blocked eventuate in violence. But any attempt at self-actualization is inevitably blocked by society, black and white, which threatens him with harsh punishment, possibly even death. Finally Wright is forced to flee the South altogether with only the knowledge of the power of the word to carry with him. *Black Boy*'s opening scene of childhood rebellion against domestic oppression distills the essence of Wright's struggle to free himself from social oppression.

Maya Angelou's autobiography, like Wright's, opens with a primal childhood scene that brings into focus the nature of the imprisoning environment from which the self will seek escape. The black girl child is trapped within the cage of her own diminished self-image around which interlock the bars of natural and social forces. The oppression of natural forces, of physical appearance and processes, foists a self-consciousness on all young girls who must grow from children into women. Hair is too thin or stringy or mousy or nappy. Legs are too fat, too thin, too bony, the knees too bowed. Hips are too wide or not wide enough. Breasts grow too fast or not at all. The self-critical process is incessant, a driving demon. But in the black girl child's experience of these natural bars are reinforced with the rusty iron social bars of racial subordination and impotence. Being born black is itself a liability in a world ruled by white standards of beauty which imprison the child *a priori* in a cage of ugliness: "What you looking at me for?" This really isn't me. I'm white with long blond hair and blue eyes, with pretty pink skin and straight hair, with a delicate mouth. I'm my own mistake. I haven't dreamed myself hard enough. I'll try again. The black and blue bruises of the soul multiply and compound as the caged bird flings herself against these bars:

> The Black female is assaulted in her tender years by all those common forces of nature at the same time that she is caught in the tripartite crossfire of masculine prejudice, white illogical hate and Black lack of power. (265)

Within this imprisoning environment there is no place for this black girl child. She becomes a displaced person whose pain is intensified by her consciousness of that displacement:

> If growing up is painful for the Southern Black girl, being aware of her displacement is the rust on the razor that threatens the throat.
>
> It is an unnecessary insult. (6)

If the black man is denied his potency and his masculinity, if his autobiography narrates the quest of the black male after a "place" of full manhood, the black woman is denied her beauty and her quest is one after self-accepted black womanhood. Thus the discovered pattern of significant moments Maya Angelou superimposes on the experience of her life is a pattern of moments that race the quest of the black female after a "place," a place where a child no longer need ask self-consciously, "What you looking at me for?" but where a woman can declare confidently, "I am a beautiful, Black woman."

Two children, sent away to a strange place by estranging parents, cling to each other as they travel by train across the Southwestern United States—and cling to their tag: "To Whom It May Concern—that we were Marguerite and Bailey Johnson, Jr., from Long Beach, California, en route to Stamps, Arkansas, c/o Mrs. Annie Henderson" (6). The autobiography of Black America is haunted by these orphans, children beginning life or early finding themselves without parents, sometimes with no one but themselves. They travel through life desperately in search of a home, some place where they can escape the shadow of loneliness, of solitude, of outsiderness. Although Maya and Bailey are traveling toward the home of their grandmother, more important, they are traveling away from the "home" of their parents. Such rejection a child internalizes and translates as a rejection of self: ultimately the loss of home occasions the loss of self-worth. "I'm being sent away because I'm not lovable." The quest for a home therefore is the quest for acceptance, for love, and for the resultant feeling of self-worth. Because Maya Angelou became conscious of her displacement early in life, she began her quest earlier than most of us. Like that of any orphan, that quest is intensely lonely, intensely solitary, making it all the more desperate, immediate, demanding, and making it, above all, an even more estranging process. For the "place" always recedes into the distance, moving with the horizon, and the searcher goes through life merely "passing through" to some place beyond, always beyond.

> Stamps, Arkansas
>
> The town reacted to us as its inhabitants had reacted to all

> things new before our coming. It regarded us a while without curiosity but with caution, and after we were seen to be harmless (and children) it closed in around us, as a real mother embraces a stranger's child. Warmly, but not too familiarly. (7)

Warmth but distance: displacement. The aura of personal displacement is counterpointed by the ambience of displacement within the larger black community. The black community of Stamps is itself caged in the social reality of racial subordination and impotence. The cotton pickers must face an empty bag every morning, an empty will every night, knowing all along that the season would end as it had begun—money-less, credit-less.

The undercurrent of social displacement, the fragility of the sense of belonging, are evidenced in the intrusion of white reality. Poor white trash humiliate Momma as she stands erect before them singing a hymn. Uncle Willie hides deep in the potato barrel the night the sheriff warns them that white men ride after black, any black. The white apparition haunts the life of Stamps, Arkansas, always present though not always visible.

Against this apparition the community shores itself up with a subdued hominess, a fundamental faith in fundamental religion, and resignation. The warmth mitigates the need to resist: or rather, the impossibility of resistance is sublimated in the bond of community.

The people of Stamps adapt in the best way they know: according to Momma Henderson—"realistically"—which is to say that they equate talking with whites with risking their lives. If the young girl stands before the church congregation asking, "What you looking at me for?", the whole black community might just as well be standing before the larger white community and asking that same question. Everything had to be low-key: the less looked at, the better, for the black in a white society. High physical visibility meant self-consciousness within the white community. To insure his own survival the black tried not to be looked at, tried to become invisible. Such a necessary response bred an overriding self-criticism and self-depreciation into the black experience. Maya Angelou's diminished sense of self reflected the entire black community's diminished self-image.

Nevertheless, there is a containedness in this environment called Stamps, a containedness which controls the girl child's sense of displacement, the containedness of a safe way of life, a hard way of life, but a known way of life. The child doesn't want to fit here, but it shapes her to it. And although she is lonely, although she suffers from her feelings of ugliness and abandonment, the strength of Momma's arms contains some of that loneliness.

Suddenly Stamps is left behind. Moving on, the promise of a place. Her mother, aunts, uncles, grandparents—St. Louis, a big city, an even bigger reality, a totally new reality. But even here displacement: St. Louis, with its strange sounds, its packaged food, its modern conveniences, remains a foreign country to the child who after only a few weeks understands that it is not to be her "home." For one moment only the illusion of being in place overwhelms the child. For that moment Mr. Freeman holds her pressed to him:

> He held me so softly that I wished he wouldn't ever let me go. I felt at home. From the way he was holding me I knew he'd never let me go or let anything bad ever happen to me. This was probably my real father and we had found each other at last. But then he rolled over, leaving me in a wet place and stood up. (71)

The orphan hopes, for that infinite moment, that she has been taken back home to her father. She feels loved, accepted. Ultimately Mr. Freeman's strength, his arms, are not succor: they are her seduction. The second time he holds her to him it is to rape her, and, in short minutes, the child becomes even more displaced. The child becomes a child-woman. In court, frightened, the child denies the first time. Mr. Freeman is found dead. The child knows it is because she has lied. What a worthless, unlovable, naughty child! What can she do but stop talking: "Just my breath, carrying my words out, might poison people and they'd curl up and die like the black fat slugs that only pretended. I had to stop talking" (85).

Now total solitude, total displacement, total self-condemnation. Back to Stamps, back to the place of grayness and barrenness, the place where nothing happened to people who, in spite of it all, felt contentment "based on the belief that nothing more was coming to them although a great deal more was due" (86). Her psychological and emotional devastation find a mirror in Stamps' social devastation. Stamps gives her back the familiarity and security of a well-known cage. She climbs back in happily, losing herself in her silent world, surrendering herself to her own worthlessness.

She lives alone in this world for one year until the afternoon when the lovely Mrs. Flowers walks into the store and becomes for Maya a kind of surrogate mother. Mrs. Flowers opens the door to the caged bird's silence with the key of acceptance. For the first time Maya is accepted as an individual rather than as a relation to someone else: "I was liked, and what a difference it made. I was respected not as Mrs. Henderson's grandchild or Bailey's sister but for just being Marguerite Johnson" (98). Such unqualified acceptance allows her to experience the incipient power of her own self-worth.

Inside her germinated this growing consciousness of self-worth and self-importance. Outside, in the life that revolved around her, sat the stagnant air of impotence and frustration. Of this lack of control the child gradually becomes conscious. The older narrator chooses to recreate those moments significant because of their dramatization of this lack of power: the fear attendant upon Bailey's being out late one evening; the church meeting during which the young girl comes to realize that her neighbors used religion as a way of "bask(ing) in the righteousness of the poor and the exclusiveness of the downtrodden" (110). Even the Joe Louis fight which sends a thrill of pride through a black community vicariously winning victory over a white man, becomes a grotesque counterpoint to the normal way of life. Then at the graduation ceremony, during which the exciting expectations of the young graduates and their families and friends are exploded casually by the words of an oblivious and insensitive white speaker, the young girl comes to know already the desperation of impotence:

> It was awful to be Negro and have no control over my life. It was brutal to be young and already trained to sit quietly and listen to charges brought against my color with no chance of defense. We should all be dead. (176)

After the humiliating trip to the white dentist's back door, the child can only compensate for such impotence by fantasizing potency and triumphant success.

One gesture, however, foreshadows Maya's eventual inability to "sit quietly" and is very much an expression of her growing acceptance of her own self-worth. For a short time she works in the house of Mrs. Viola Cullinan, but a short time only, for Mrs. Cullinan, with an easiness that comes from long tradition, assaults her ego by calling her Mary rather than Maya. Such an oversight offered so casually is a most devastating sign of the girl's invisibility. In failing to call her by her name, a symbol of identity and individuality, of uniqueness, Mrs. Cullinan fails to respect her humanity. Maya understands this perfectly and rebels by breaking Mrs. Cullinan's most cherished dish. The girl child is assuming the consciousness of rebellion as a stance necessary for preserving her individuality and affirming her self-worth. Such a stance insures displacement in Stamps, Arkansas.

But now there is yet another move. Once again the train, traveling westward to San Francisco in wartime. Here in this big city everything seems out of place.

> The air of collective displacement, the impermanence of life

> in wartime and the gauche personalities of the more recent arrivals tended to dissipate my own sense of not belonging. In San Francisco, for the first time, I perceived myself as part of something. (205)

In Stamps the way of life remained rigid, in San Francisco it ran fluid. Maya had been on the move when she entered Stamps and thus could not settle into its rigid way of life. She chose to remain an outsider, and in so doing, chose not to allow her personality to become rigid. The fluidity of the new environment matched the fluidity of her emotional, physical, and psychological life. She could feel in place in an environment where everyone and everything seemed out-of-place.

Even more significant than the total displacement of San Francisco is Maya's trip to Mexico with her father. The older autobiographer, in giving form to her past experience, discovers that this "moment" was central to her process of growth. Maya accompanies her father to a small Mexican town where he proceeds to get obliviously drunk, leaving her with the responsibility of getting them back to Los Angeles. But she has never before driven a car. For the first time, Maya finds herself totally in control of her fate. Such total control contrasts vividly to her earlier recognition in Stamps that she as a Negro had no control over her fate. Here she is alone with that fate. And although the drive culminates in an accident, she triumphs.

This "moment" is succeeded by a month spent in a wrecked car lot scavenging with others like herself. Together these experiences provide her with a knowledge of self-determination and a confirmation of her self-worth. With the assumption of this affirmative knowledge and power, Maya is ready to challenge the unwritten, restrictive social codes of San Francisco. Mrs. Cullinan's broken dish prefigures the job on the streetcar. Stamps' acquiescence is left far behind in Arkansas as Maya assumes control over her own social destiny and engages in the struggle with life's forces. She has broken out of the rusted bars of her social cage.

But Maya must still break open the bars of her female sexuality: although she now feels power over her social identity, she feels insecurity about her sexual identity. She remains the embarrassed child who stands before the Easter congregation asking, "What you looking at me for?" The bars of her physical being close in on her, threatening her peace of mind. The lack of femininity in her small-breasted, straight-lined, and hairless physique and the heaviness of her voice become, in her imagination, symptomatic of latent lesbian tendencies. A gnawing self-consciousness still plagues her. Even after her mother's amused knowledge disperses her fears, the mere fact of her being moved by a classmate's breasts undermines any confidence that reassurance had provided. It was only brief respite. Now she knows, knows in her heart, that she is a lesbian. There is only one remedy for such a threatening reality: a man. But even making love with a casual male acquaintance fails to quell her suspicions; the whole affair is such an unenjoyable experience.

Only the pregnancy provides a climatic reassurance: if she can become pregnant, she certainly cannot be a lesbian (certainly a specious argument in terms of logic but a compelling one in terms of emotions and psychology). The birth of the baby brings Maya something totally her own, but, more important, brings her to a recognition of and acceptance of her full, instinctual womanhood. The child, father to the woman, opens the caged door and allows the fully-developed woman to fly out. Now she feels the control of her sexual identity as well as of her social identity. The girl child no longer need ask, embarrassed, "What you looking at me for?" No longer need she fantasize any other reality than her own.

Maya Angelou's autobiography comes to a sense of an ending: the black American girl child has succeeded in freeing herself from the natural and social bars imprisoning her in the cage of her own diminished self-image by assuming control of her life and fully accepting her black womanhood. The displaced child has found a "place." With the birth of her child Maya is herself born into a mature engagement with the forces of life. In welcoming that struggle she refuses to live a death of quiet acquiescence:

> Few, if any, survive their teens. Most surrender to the vague but murderous pressure of adult conformity. It becomes easier to die and avoid conflicts than to maintain a constant battle with the superior forces of maturity. (231)

One final comment: one way of dying to life's struggle is to suppress its inevitable pain by forgetting the past. Maya Angelou, who has since been a student and teacher of dance, a correspondent in Africa, a northern coordinator for the Southern Christian Leadership Council, an actress, writer, and director for the stage and film, had, like so many of us, successfully banished many years of her past to the keeping of the unconscious where they lay dormant and remained lost to her. To the extent that they were lost, so also a part of her self was lost. Once she accepted the challenge of recovering the lost years, she accepted the challenge of the process of self-discovery and reconfirmed her commitment to life's struggle. By the time she, as autobiographer, finished remembering the past and shaping it into a pattern of significant moments, she has imposed some sense of an ending upon it. And in imposing that ending upon it she gave the experience distance and a context and thereby came to understand the past and ultimately to understand herself.

Moreover, she reaffirms her sense of self-worth by making the journey back through her past on its own terms, by immersing herself once again in the medium of her making. Stamps, Arkansas, imprinted its way of life on the child during her formative years: the lasting evidence of this imprint is the sound of it. Her genius as a writer is her ability to recapture the texture of the way of life in the texture of its idioms, its idiosyncratic vocabulary and especially in its process of image-making. The imagery hold the reality, giving it immediacy. That she chooses to recreate the past in its own sounds suggests to the reader that she accepts the past and recognizes its beauty and its ugliness, its assets and its liabilities, its strength and its weakness. Here we witness a return to and final acceptance of the past in the return to and full acceptance of its language, the language a symbolic construct of a way of life. Ultimately Maya Angelou's style testifies to her reaffirmation of self-acceptance, the self-acceptance she achieves within the pattern of the autobiography.

GEORGE E. KENT

Maya Angelou's I Know Why the Caged Bird Sings *and Black Autobiographical Tradition*

Maya Angelou, who spent much of her early life in Arkansas and grew up in California, is the author of three books: the autobiographies *I Know Why the Caged Bird Sings* (1969) and *Gather Together in My Name* (1974); and a volume of poetry, *Just Give Me a Cool Drink of Water 'Fore I Diie* (1971). My concern is with the autobiographies, with primary emphasis upon *I Know Why the Caged Bird Sings.*

I Know Why tells the story of a child's growing to maturity in the small universe of Stamps, Arkansas, in St. Louis, Missouri, and in San Francisco, California. We see Maya (nee Marguerite Johnson) and her brother Bailey shuttled to Grandmother Annie Henderson from the broken home of the mother Vivian Baxter, eventually back to Mother Vivian in St. Louis, then a return to Stamps with Grandmother Henderson, and a final return to California where Maya spends most of her time with her mother but also experiences a calamitous summer with her father, Bailey Johnson, in the southern part of the state. The book is rich in portraits of a wide assortment of blacks, descriptions of the rhythms of their lives and their confrontations with both elemental life and racial relations, and evocations of the patterns of the different environments. Their graphic depiction is always in relationship to the development of the child, but since all the experiences emerge from an imagination which has fully mastered them and, at will, turns them into symbols, they tend to operate on two levels: as mirrors of both the vigor and the unsteadiness of childhood innocence and imagination, and as near

From *African American Autobiography: A Collection of Critical Essays.*

independent vibrations of the spirit of black life. The book ends with Maya's having become an unwed mother, a result of a confused move for sexual identity. Since the book ends with a dramatic episode which emphasizes Maya's beginning to face up to the terrors of motherhood, its resolution is somewhat tentative but complete enough to register the movement into a stance toward life beyond that of childhood.

Gather Together in My Name tells the story of the struggles of young womanhood to create an existence which provides security and love in a very unstable world; its time is the post–World War II period, and it involves settings in San Francisco, Los Angeles, Stamps, Arkansas, and then again various parts of California. On the one side of the tensions is Maya's combination of resourcefulness, imagination, and compulsive innocence; on the other, the intransigence of the world's obstacle courses which impel her into ill-advised love choices, an assortment of jobs ranging from that of short-order cook to setting up a house of prostitution staffed with two lesbians. Finally, in her quest for love and security, she is inveigled into prostitution by the forty-five year old pimp, L. D. Tolbrook, but forcibly argued out of it by her furious brother. Under the pressures of a loveless existence, she sees the decline of her brother into drug addiction and escapes the temptation herself by her new lover's demonstration of the unromantic degradation drugs have inflicted upon him. The book ends with Maya's statement, "I had no idea what I was going to make of my life, but I had given a promise and found my innocence. I swore I'd never lose it again." Technically, the resolution, again, has both tentativeness and a dramatic completeness. However, the feeling it gives is one of abruptness—the sensational character of it registers more fully than the definition of a new stance which it is supposed to impose.

Like *I Know Why*, *Gather Together* presents a wide assortment of personalities and conveys sharp and imaginative insights through them. It is a good book, well worth the doing. But it lacks the feeling of the fully mastered experience, the full measure and imaginative penetration, and the illusion of life vibrating as an entity in itself as well as in relationship to the heroine's own development.

It is thus *I Know Why* which I cite for creating a unique place in black autobiographical tradition. What is that tradition? Like American autobiography, in general, black autobiography has variety: the simple success story of John Mercer Langston's *From the Virginia Plantation to the National Capitol; or, the First and Only Negro Representative in Congress from the Old Dominion* (1894); the somewhat psychological analysis of Katherine Dunham's *A Touch of Innocence* (1959); the public memoir of John Roy

Lynch's *Reminiscences of an Active Life: The Autobiography of John Roy Lynch* (1970); and a varied assortment of autobiographical statements in connection with literary and public matters.

However, a main strand of black autobiographies takes us on a journey through chaos, a pattern established by the narratives of escaped slaves. The pattern takes shape in the first major black autobiography, Gustavus Vassa, *The Interesting Narrative of the Life of Olaudah Equiano, or Gustavus Vassa, the African* (1789). In relationship to later ex-slave statements, Vassa's account can be seen as emphasizing the instability of the black's relationship to all institutions devised to ward off chaos threatening human existence. And it is this instability of relationship to institutions which gives the particular tone and extremity described in much of black autobiography, those of the ex-slave and those born free. Vassa's and other ex-slave autobiographies required the achievement of tenuously held new identities: Vassa's "almost Englishman" and Christian man and usually, with the ex-slave, the combination of a definition implied by the ideals of the enlightenment and Christianity. Thus it is the temperature of urgencies which increases the root uncertainty of existence reflected by a large number of black autobiographies which eventually move from a reflection of the ambiguous dispensations of institutions of the slavery period to the ambiguous dispensations of post-slavery institutions. The autobiographies of Richard Wright (*Black Boy*, 1945), Anne Moody (*Coming of Age in Mississippi*, 1968), Malcolm X's *The Autobiography of Malcolm X* (1965), and others, will illustrate post-slavery journeys of the twentieth century and the persisting ambiguous relationship of blacks to American institutional dispensations.

Up through the early part of the twentieth century, black autobiographies had usually found grounds for a leap of faith and optimism in the complex of ideas known as The American Dream. Booker T. Washington's *Up From Slavery* (1901) is the classic example; it even fits well into the type of success story established by Benjamin Franklin's autobiography, with its emphasis upon common sense and optimism. James Weldon Johnson's *Along This Way: The Autobiography of James Weldon Johnson* (1933) focuses largely upon the public man and ends with a willed optimism: The Black must believe in the American Dream or destroy much that is of value within him. The optimism of such books can be seen as embracing the after-beat of rhythms picked up from those established by the abolitionist perspective in slave narratives. As weapons in the struggle, the narratives absorbed the tenets of Christianity, the ideals of the Enlightenment and of the American Constitution. Things were terrible, but the Great Day would come when the ideals were actualized.

Today the rhythms of the American Dream ideas run in a parallel pattern with a more serious questioning of the Dream itself. Thus Benjamin Mays's *Born to Rebel* (1971) recounts the encounter with nothingness during Mays's youth, but finds grounds for optimism in the fruits of public service. However, Richard Wright's *Black Boy* was the autobiography which began a questioning which shook the fabric of the American Dream, although the autobiography's ending leaves ground for hope of achieving the Dream in the Promised Land of the North. In the process of Wright's questioning, however, the cultural fabric of the black community is torn to shreds and tends to reflect a people teetering upon the brink of nothingness:

> After I had outlived the shocks of childhood, after the habit of reflection had been born in me, I used to mull over the strange absence of real kindness in Negroes, how unstable was our tenderness, how lacking in genuine passion we were, how void of great hope, how timid our joy, how bare our traditions, how hollow our memories, how lacking we were in those intangible sentiments that bind man to man, and how shallow was even our despair. After I had learned other ways of life I used to brood upon the unconscious irony of those who felt that Negroes led so passional an existence! I saw that what had been taken for our emotional strength was our negative confusions, our flights, our fears, our frenzy under pressure. (*Black Boy*, p. 33)

Wright was offended by the degree to which he found a black folk tradition oriented toward mere survival, base submission, and escapism, whereas, as he states in "Blueprint for Negro Writing" (*New Challenge*, Fall, 1937), he wished to mould the tradition into a martial stance. With the help of Marxism, he also wished to create the values by which the race was to live or die, to be not "only against exploiting whites, but against all of that within his own race that retards decisive action and obscures clarity of vision." He decried "a cowardly sentimentality [which had] deterred Negro writers from launching crusades against the evils which Negro ignorance and stupidity have spawned." Thus, from his autobiography and from several works of fiction, there emerges the hero as black rebel-outsider, embattled, particularly after *Uncle Tom's Children*, both with the pretensions of the American Dream and his own folk tradition.

Ralph Ellison's response to Wright's portrait of black life has been mixed. In his essay "Richard Wright's Blues" [*Shadow and Act*, 1964], he seems partly to condone and partly to reinterpret from his own perspective.

Among other things, he notes that the personal warmth of black communal life, in line with Wright's illustrations, "is accompanied by an equally personal coldness, kindliness by cruelty, regard by malice," that the opposite qualities are quickly set off "against the member who gestures toward individuality," and that "The member who breaks away is apt to be more impressed by its negative than by its positive character." He seems to defend the passage I quoted above from *Black Boy*: Wright was rejecting not only the white South in his autobiography but the South within himself—"As a rebel he formulated that rejection negatively, because it was the negative face of the Negro community upon which he looked most often as a child." Embattled himself with Irving Howe in his later essay "The World and the Jug" [*Shadow and Act*, 1964], Ellison at this time rejected the same quotation as having its source in Wright's attempts to see the forms of Negro humanity through the lens of Marxism and in Wright's paraphrase of Henry James's "catalogue of those items of a high civilization which were absent from American life during Hawthorne's day, and which seemed so necessary in order for the novelist to function." However, it must be said that Wright's intense rendering of negative images of black life in such works as *Black Boy* [1945], *Native Son* [1940], *Lawd Today* [1963], and *The Long Dream* [1958], without precluding assists from James and Marxism, would seem to require that we accept his negative remarks as an article of faith and belief. Ellison's earlier remarks, taking into consideration the stance of the rebel, and Wright's own aspiration to launch crusades against ignorance and stupidity seem to come closer to accounting for the degree of negativity in Wright's position. Certainly, another embattled rebel, Anne Moody in *Coming of Age in Mississippi*, seeing black communal life's frequent responses to the incursion of white power, gives off a similar tone of negativity and places beside the American Dream idea a large question mark. Such subsequent landmark autobiographies as Huey P. Newton's *Revolutionary Suicide* [1973] and the earlier *Autobiography of Malcolm X* [1965] seem to complete a rhythm of development away from a middle class consciousness or complex of ideas.

In the attempt to define a major strand of development in a black autobiographical tradition, then, I've outlined the theme of a journey through a highly heated chaos deriving from black life's ambiguous relationship to American institutions, an erosion of faith in the American Dream idea which earlier had provided grounds for optimism, and a controversially developing sense of negativity concerning the quality of black life in America.

I Know Why creates a unique place within black autobiographical tradition, not by being "better" than the formidable autobiographical landmarks described, but by its special stance toward the self, the community, and the universe, and by a form exploiting the full measure of imagination necessary to acknowledge both beauty and absurdity.

The emerging self, equipped with imagination, resourcefulness, and a sense of the tenuousness of childhood innocence, attempts to foster itself by crediting the adult world with its own estimate of its god-like status and managing retreats into the autonomy of the childhood world when conflicts develop. Given the black adult's necessity to compromise with prevailing institutions and to develop limited codes through which nobility, strength, and beauty can be registered, the areas where a child's requirements are absolute—love, security, and consistency—quickly reveal the protean character of adult support and a barely concealed, aggressive chaos.

We can divide the adults' resources, as they appear in the autobiography, into two areas of black life: the religious and blues traditions. Grandmother Henderson, of Stamps, Arkansas, represents the religious traditions; Mother Vivian Baxter, more of the blues-street tradition.

Grandmother's religion gives her power to order her being, that of the children, and usually the immediate space surrounding her. The spirit of the religion combined with simple, traditional maxims shapes the course of existence and the rituals of facing up to something called decency. For Maya and her brother Bailey, the first impact of the blues-street tradition is that of instability: at the ages of three and four, respectively, the children are suddenly shipped to Grandmother when the parents break up their "calamitous" marriage. A note "To Whom It May Concern" identifies the children traveling alone from "Long Beach, California, en route to Stamps, Arkansas, c/o Mrs. Annie Henderson." Angelou generalizes the children's situation as follows: "Years later I discovered that the United States had been crossed thousands of times by frightened Black children traveling alone to their newly affluent parents in Northern cities, or back to grandmothers in Southern towns when the urban North reneged on its economic promises."

Gradually, the children adjust to the new life, becoming an integral part of Grandmother Henderson's General Merchandise Store, Grandmother's church and religion, community school, and general community customs. In Chapters 1–8, we see the techniques by which the author is able to give a full registration of both the beauty and the root absurdity built into the traditions of the folk community. She carefully articulates the folk forms of responding to existence by the use of key symbols and patterns of those involved in religious and blues responses and the joining point between their ways of responding. For example, more than Grandmother Henderson is characterized through the following folk prayer, whose set phrases have accreted through a long tradition of bended knees in homes and small rural churches:

> "Our Father, thank you for letting me see this New Day. Thank you that you didn't allow the bed I lay on last night to be my cooling board, nor my blanket my winding sheet. Guide my feet this day along the straight and narrow, and help me to put a bridle on my tongue. Bless this house, and everybody in it. Thank you, in the name of your Son, Jesus Christ, Amen."

The children are required to avoid impudence to adults, to respect religious piety, and to be obedient. Given the freshness of the childhood imagination, however, many meanings are turned into the absurdity often hovering near the fabric of human rituals. On the grim side, we see the poor giving thanks to the Lord for a life filled with the most meager essentials and a maximum amount of brute oppression. The church rituals create for the poor a temporary transcendence and an articulation of spirit, but their hardships are so graphically awaiting their re-confrontation with the trials of daily existence that the evoked spiritual beauty seems hard-pressed by the pathos of the grotesque. Still, it is from such religious rhythms that Grandmother Henderson possesses the strength to give much order to the children's lives, to set the family in initial order in California, and to provide them with the minimum resources to struggle for a world more attractive. The comic side is reflected through the autonomous imagination of the children: the incongruity between the piety of the shouters and the violence with which the religious gestures of one threatens the minister. Briefly, the author records the joining point between the blues and religious tradition: Miss Grace, the good-time woman, is also conducting rituals of transcendence through her barrelhouse blues for those whose uprush of spirit must have an earthly and fleshly source. The agony in religion and the blues is the connecting point: "A stranger to the music could not have made a distinction between the songs sung a few minutes before [in church] and those being danced to in the gay house."

Despite Grandmother Henderson's strength, the folk religious tradition leaves her with serious limitations. Her giant stature goes to zero, or almost, in any confrontation with the white Southern community, a startling and humiliating experience for the child worshipper of black adult omnipotence. In addition, there is what Ralph Ellison spoke of as a warmth in the folk communal life "accompanied by an equally personal coldness, kindliness by cruelty, regard by malice." It will be recalled that Ellison saw the negative qualities as being activated "against the member who gestures toward individuality." Maya Angelou dramatizes such an action in Chapter 15, a masterful section. Mrs. Bertha Flowers, the town's black intellectual, has ministered to Maya's ever-burgeoning hunger and quest for individuality by giving her a book of poetry, talking to her philosophically about life, and encouraging her to recite poems. Returning to Grandmother Henderson, she happens to say "by the way—." Grandmother gives her a severe beating for using the expression, much to the bewilderment of the child. Later, Grandmother explained that "Jesus was the Way, the Truth and the Light," that "by the way" is really saying "by Jesus," or "by God," and she had no intention of allowing the Lord's name to be taken in vain in her house. In *Gather Together* Grandmother Henderson gives her a severe, protective beating because Maya had endangered her life by responding to whites' abuse of her in the local clothing store by superlative abuse of her own. Thus, regarding folk religious tradition and other aspects of community confrontations with existence, the author imposes the illusion of striking a just balance between spiritual beauty and absurdity.

The confrontation of the self with blues-street tradition takes place while she is with her mother, Vivian Baxter, in St. Louis and California. The author manages the same just balance in portraying it. Because of the different levels of the tradition in which various members of the family are involved, because of the fluid movement some make between it and other traditions, and because of the originality with which the mother's portrait emerges, the exposure is fresh, vivid, lasting. Some of the strict man-woman codes reflected by folk ballads emerge from the character of the mother. Men are able to remain with her only so long as they honor the code, one having been cut and another shot for failure to show proper respect for the mother's prerogatives. In this fast-life area of black tradition, the children receive great kindness and considerable impact from built-in instabilities. Mother Vivian is kind in counseling Maya concerning her sexual confusions, in creating a celebrating atmosphere that children would love, in her matter-of-fact acceptance of Maya's unwed motherhood, and in the strong support she gives to the idea of self-reliance and excellence. She herself is the embodiment of bold aggressiveness and self-reliance. Her philosophy, too, has its brief maxims, involving the acceptance of the chaos swirling through and around "protective" institutions and meeting it with an on-topsmanship derived from the tough and alert self. Thus she believes in preparing for the worst, hoping for the best, and being unsurprised at anything which happens in between. At one point in the sequel autobiography, *Gather Together*, she tells Maya to be the best at anything she chooses to do—even should she choose to be a whore.

But in her fluid existence amidst threatening chaos, one drawback is the requirement of intense absorption in one's own life and in the alertness which makes on-topsmanship possible. Thus, the mother manages well her own relationship to one of her mates, a Mr. Freeman, but Maya finds herself raped by him at the tender age of eight, an act which involves her in ambiguous complicity—but also guilt and lingering shame and confusion. Her sense of innocence is stretched into dubious tenuousness by her instinctual and unconscious complicity. The fast-life tradition, unsatisfied with the actions of the court, provides for Mr. Freeman's murder—and Maya's increased sense of guilt. When she visits her hipsterish father, she suddenly is impelled into a battle with his girlfriend deriving from the girlfriend's jealousy and Maya's ambiguous emotions concerning her mother. In the process, Maya is cut.

Both children are in inner turmoil over their relationship to their beautiful, tough, and coping mother: Maya because of the paradox involved in being the ungainly and awkward daughter of the beautiful mother; Bailey, her brother, because the instability he is put through increases his oedipal ties to her. Chapter 17 is a poignant statement of Bailey's quest for his mother through a movie screen heroine who resembles her. In *Gather Together*, despite his consistent love and protectiveness of his sister Maya, he becomes involved in pimping, and after the loss of a young wife, he begins what seems to be a downward path through drugs. The problem is not that the mother did not love him, but that his earlier hunger was never resolved and her life style and codes helped to prevent his sense of security in relationship to her. Thus *Gather Together* reveals the tough and beautiful mother, who has held her poise in relationship to many men, now attempting to conceal the defeat she experiences in relationship to her son. The tough blues tradition, which is all for individuality, fails precisely where the religious tradition was strong: the provision of stable and predictable conditions.

Thus the author is able to give a just balance to the qualities of both traditions and to reveal the exact point where the universe becomes absurd. A good deal of the book's universality derives from black life's traditions seeming to mirror, with extraordinary intensity, the root uncertainty in the universe. The conflict with whites, of course, dramatizes uncertainty and absurdity with immediate headline graphicness. What intensifies the universalism still more is the conflict between the sensitive imagination and reality, and the imagination's ability sometimes to overcome. Maya and her brother have their reservoir of absurd miming and laughter, but sometimes the imagination is caught in pathos and chaos, although its values are frequently superior. When Grandmother Henderson's response to the insulting rejection by a white dentist to whom she has loaned money is humiliating, Maya finds consolation in the rituals she imagines the Grandmother using. The imaginative reproduction of the preacher's humiliating beating by an overbearing shouter is so productive of laughter that the beating the children receive becomes meaningless. Bailey, the brother, receives a very bitter experience when his imaginative simulation of sexual intercourse with girls while fully clothed suddenly leads to his encounter with a girl who demands reality, inveigles him into an exploitative love affair, and then runs away with a pullman porter.

The major function of the imagination, however, is to retain a vigorous dialectic between self and society, between the intransigent world and the aspiring self. Through the dialectic, the egos maintain themselves, even where tragic incident triumphs. In a sense, the triumph of circumstance for Maya becomes a temporary halt in a process which is constantly renewed, a fact evident in the poetic language and in the mellowness of the book's confessional form.

Finally, since *I Know Why* keeps its eyes upon the root existential quality of life, it makes its public and political statement largely through generalizing statements which broaden individual characters into types: Grandmother Henderson into the Southern mother; Maya into the young black woman, etc. And the after-rhythms of the American Dream can flow in occasionally without gaining the solemnity of a day in court.

The uniqueness of *I Know Why* arises then from a full imaginative occupation of the rhythms flowing from the primal self in conflict with things as they are, but balanced by the knowledge that the self must find its own order and create its own coherence.

CAROL E. NEUBAUER

Displacement and Autobiographical Style in Maya Angelou's The Heart of a Woman

When Maya Angelou started her autobiographical series in 1970 with *I Know Why the Caged Bird Sings*, she naturally chose her childhood as the organizing principle of her first volume. The story of *Caged Bird* begins when the three-year-old Angelou and her four-year-old brother, Bailey, are turned over to the care of their paternal grandmother in Stamps, Arkansas, and it ends with the birth of her son when she is seventeen years old. The next two volumes, *Gather Together In My Name* (1974) and *Singin' and Swingin' and Gettin' Merry Like Christmas* (1976), narrate Angelou's life along chronological lines for the most part, and one would expect that her most recent addition to the autobiographical sequence, *The Heart of a Woman* (1981), would proceed with the account of her career as entertainer, writer, and freedom fighter. In many ways, Angelou meets her readers' expectations as she follows her life forward chronologically in organizing the newest segment in the series. Yet it is interesting to note that at the beginning of *The Heart of a Woman*, as she continues the account of her son's youth, she returns to the story of her own childhood repeatedly. The references to her childhood serve partly to create a textual link for readers who might be unfamiliar with the earlier volumes and partly to emphasize the suggestive similarities between her own childhood and that of her son. Maya Angelou's overwhelming sense of displacement and instability is, ironically, her son's burden too.

The most significant similarity between their childhood years is the

---

From *Black American Literature Forum* 17:3.

condition of displacement in a familial as well as a geographical sense. Both Angelou and Guy, her son, are displaced from their immediate families several times during their youth. They are placed in the care of relatives or family friends and are moved from neighborhood to neighborhood and state to state. In a brief flashback in the second chapter of *The Heart of a Woman*, the writer reminds us of the displacement which characterized her youth and links this aspect of her past with her son's present attitude. When Guy is fourteen, Angelou decides to move to New York. She does not bring Guy to New York until she has found a place for them to live, and when he arrives after a one-month separation, he initially resists her attempts to make a new home for them:

> The air between us [Angelou and Guy] was burdened with his aloof scorn. I understood him too well.
>
> When I was three my parents divorced in Long Beach, California, and sent me and my four-year-old brother, unescorted, to our paternal grandmother. We wore wrist tags which informed anyone concerned that we were Marguerite and Bailey Johnson, en route to Mrs. Annie Henderson in Stamps, Arkansas.
>
> Except for disastrous and mercifully brief encounters with each of them when I was seven, we didn't see our parents again until I was thirteen.

From this and similar encounters with Guy, Angelou learns that the continual displacement of her own childhood is something she cannot prevent from recurring in her son's life.

Rather than a unique cycle perpetuated only within her family, Angelou's individual story presents a clear pattern commonly shared and passed along to new generations continually. In fact she identifies her own situation and the threat of displacement as a common condition among black families in America and acknowledges the special responsibility of the black mother: "She questions whether she loves her children enough—or more terribly, does she love them too much? . . . In the face of these contradictions, she must provide a blanket of stability, which warms but does not suffocate, and she must tell her children the truth about the power of white power without suggesting that it cannot be challenged" (p. 37). Providing stability for the children as the family disintegrates is a virtually impossible task, not only for Angelou but for many women in similar situations. After the dissolution of the family, the single parent is often left with an overwhelming sense of guilt and inadequacy; and, for Angelou, the burden is all the more taxing, because she has been solely responsible for her son from the very beginning of his life.

In *The Heart of a Woman*, Angelou includes numerous anecdotes from Guy's youth which mirror problems she has also faced. These compelling accounts suggest the recurring pattern of displacement and rejection in the relationship between mother and child. Many times Angelou feels that she and her son are skating dangerously "on thin ice!" As a child, Guy expects his mother to offer him constant attention and affection as well as the basic requirements of food and shelter, for which Angelou must often work long hours at more than one job. Her babysitting expenses alone often consume a substantial part of her meager income.

Guy's needs, however, are not simple, and in addition to love, companionship, and the basic necessities, he frequently intimates that his mother should be responsible for order and security on a universal level as well. "My son expected warmth, food, housing, clothes and stability. He could be certain that no matter which way my fortune turned he would receive most of the things he desired. Stability, however, was not possible in my world; consequently it couldn't be possible in his" (p. 123). Angelou's sense of personal failure in caring adequately for Guy lingers for many years. Similarly his sense of disappointment and rejection is reinforced every time his mother brings a new man into their already tenuous relationship or suggests yet another relocation to enhance her professional or economic status.

As Angelou narrates selected events that illustrate the periods of displacement in Guy's life, she adapts elements from both fiction and fantasy. Although she is clearly working within the genre of autobiography, Angelou freely borrows from these two traditionally more imaginative types of writing. On numerous occasions in her earlier volumes, she has employed what has become a rather personalized autobiographical style, a method which integrates ingredients from diverse modes of writing and gracefully crosses over traditionally static generic lines. One of the most memorable uses of fantasy in all of Angelou's writing is found in *Caged Bird* and involves a visit to a racist dentist in Stamps. As a child, she imagines that her grandmother grows to gigantic height and instantly gains superhuman strength to retaliate against the bigoted dentist who refuses to treat Angelou. In *Heart of a Woman*, she combines fiction and fantasy with the more standard biographical or historical mode to capture the subtleties of her relationship with her son and to emphasize the apparent similarities between their lives.

Examples of fictionalization in *Heart of a Woman* are quite varied. They range from rather common techniques such as representational detail in description and reconstructed accounts of actual dialogue, to more specialized devices used to create a sense of history beyond the individual life story and to include other narratives from folklore within her own narrative. Each fictional technique contributes to the overall completeness and credibility of the autobiographical text.

In *Heart of a Woman*, Angelou deliberately strives to capture the individual conversational styles of her relatives and friends. In a sense, her friends and acquaintances become "characters" in the story of her life, and like any good writer of fiction, she attempts to make their conversations realistic and convincing. With some of the people who figure in her autobiography, there is no objective measure for credibility other than the reader's critical appreciation for life itself. If the conversant in question is not well-known beyond the scope of the autobiography, Angelou need only ensure that the dialogue attributed to the individual be consistent with his character as delineated in the text itself. Yet many of her friends and associates were either highly successful celebrities or popular political figures, and the conversations recorded in her life story have points of reference beyond the autobiographical text. In other words, readers can test the degree of verisimilitude in the recorded dialogues with either firsthand knowledge or secondhand sources of information about the celebrities' lives.

It is highly probable, for example, that many of Angelou's readers are already familiar with the rhetorical styles of Martin Luther King, Jr., and Malcolm X, and the popular lyrics of Billie Holiday. In fact the lives of these three people in such accounts as *Why We Can't Wait*, *The Autobiography of Malcolm X*, and *Lady Sings the Blues* have in many ways become part of our contemporary folk history. Angelou adds a personalized quality to her recollections of conversations with these individuals and many others. The record of their conversations in *Heart of a Woman* brings them to life again, because the autobiographer is sensitive to and even somewhat self-conscious about the accurate reconstruction of their individual styles.

Since memory is not infallible, fictionalization comes into play whenever the autobiographer reconstructs or, perhaps more correctly, recreates conversation. While the autobiographer relies on invention, he or she creates the illusion of an infallible memory that records exactly the feel of a place and the words spoken there. Thus, when Angelou narrates visits with Billie Holiday in Laurel Canyon, she takes care to imitate her rather flamboyant verbal style:

> . . . she [Billie Holiday] talked about Hawaii.
> "People love 'the islands, the islands.' Hell, all that shit is a

> bunch of water and a bunch of sand. So the sun shines all the time. What the hell else is the sun supposed to do?"
>
> "But didn't you find it beautiful? The soft air, the flowers, the palm trees and the people? The Hawaiians are so pretty.'
>
> "They just a bunch of riggers. Niggers running around with no clothes on. And that music shit they play. Uhn, uhn." She imitated the sound of a ukulele.
>
> "Naw, I'd rather be in New York. Everybody in New York City is a son of a bitch, but at least they don't pretend they're something else." (p. 9)

As much as Angelou is shocked by the first words that tumble out of the famous entertainer's mouth, she is moved by Holiday's sensitivity in communicating with a precocious young boy who would be offended by any "off-color" phrases. "She carefully avoided profanity and each time she slipped, she'd excuse herself to Guy, saying, 'It's just another bad habit I got'" (p. 13). Holiday and Guy soon develop a balanced rapport and thoroughly enjoy the little time they spend together. Guy exuberantly tells her about his adventures and the books he has read, while she in turn sings her sorrowful songs to him as she relaxes and finds solace in the company of the child. In a sense, the anecdotes about Billie Holiday in *Heart of a Woman* form a tribute to her, for as Angelou admits, "I would remember forever the advice of a lonely sick woman, with a waterfront mouth, who sang pretty songs to a twelve-year-old boy" (p. 17).

In addition to using fictional techniques in the reconstruction of dialogue, Angelou turns to fictionalization to create a sense of history larger than the story of her own life. In her description of her meeting with Malcolm X, for example, Angelou combines the re-creation of credible dialogue with historical references that go beyond her individual life. Again there are points of reference beyond the writer's account that measure its accuracy.

In one scene, Angelou and her close friend Rosa Guy, both representatives of the Cultural Association of Women of African Heritage, decide to call on Malcolm X to ask for his help in controlling a potential riot situation brought about by their United Nations demonstration to protest the death of Lumumba. The following dialogue demonstrates her talent for remembering and recording their conversation as precisely as possible:

> I joined the telling, and we distributed our story equally, like the patter of a long-time vaudeville duo.
>
> "We—CAWAH . . ."

> "Cultural Association of Women of African Heritage."
> "Wanted to protest the murder of Lumumba so we—"
> "Planned a small demonstration. We didn't expect—"
> "More than fifty people—"
> "And thousands came."
> "That told us that the people of Harlem are angry and that they are more for Africa and Africans"
> "than they ever let on . . ." (p. 167)

Face to face with Malcolm X, Angelou and her friend, both extremely articulate women, are reduced to a stammering "vaudeville duo." The stichomythic rhythm in the reconstructed conversation suggests the degree of intimidation that the women experienced in the presence of Malcolm X. The power of his personality causes their initial uneasiness, which soon turns to disappointment as Malcolm X coolly refuses to involve his Muslim followers in public demonstration.

Angelou's unsuccessful interview with the Harlem leader provides a clear contrast with her first meeting with Martin Luther King. The larger historical context of their exchange expands the personal perimeter of her life story. At the time of her first conversation with King, Angelou has been working as Northern Coordinator of the Southern Christian Leadership Conference in New York. She has devoted the previous months to raising funds, boosting membership, and organizing volunteer labor both in the office and in the neighborhoods. When Dr. King pays his first visit to the New York office during her tenure, she does not have advance notice of his presence and rushes into her office one day after lunch to find him sitting at her desk. They begin to talk about her background and eventually focus their comments on her brother, Bailey:

> "Come on, take your seat back and tell me about yourself."
> . . . When I mentioned my brother Bailey, he asked what he was doing now.
>
> The question stopped me. He was friendly and understanding, but if I told him my brother was in prison, I couldn't be sure how long his understanding would last. I could lose my job. Even more important, I might lose his respect. Birds of a feather and all that, but I took a chance and told him Bailey was in Sing Sing.
>
> He dropped his head and looked at his hands. . . .
>
> "I understand. Disappointment drives our young men to some desperate lengths." Sympathy and sadness kept his voice

> low. "That's why we must fight and win. We must save the Baileys of the world. And Maya, never stop loving him. Never give up on him. Never deny him. And remember, he is freer than those who hold him behind bars." (pp. 92–93)

Angelou appreciates King's sympathy, and of course shares his hope that their work will make the world more fair and free. She recognizes the undeniable effects of displacement on Bailey's life and fervently hopes that her son, who has not escaped the pain of displacement, will be spared any further humiliation and rejection.

When Angelou extends her personal narrative to include anecdotes about well-known entertainers or political figures, or observations about significant historical events, she necessarily fictionalizes the story of her past. Fictionalization is clearly at play on both a conscious and an unconscious level in the act of remembering and transcribing key events from her private life, but it becomes virtually inevitable in recording her subjective impressions about a public event or person. Whenever there is more than one account of an event, as there usually is in the public or historical context, comparisons reveal inconsistencies or discrepancies that are the product of varied individual response. Thus fictionalization occurs when Angelou includes other narratives within the narrative of her life. Each borrowed story is usually a sampling of folklore, but is told in a slightly different context to achieve a special effect within the autobiography.

One example of adapting borrowed narratives to illuminate her own story involves the folktale of Brer Rabbit. Several months after Angelou marries the South African freedom fighter Vusumzi Make, they decide to move from their apartment in New York to Cairo to facilitate Make's efforts to raise funds and political support for the cause. When they leave for Egypt with Guy, the family looks forward to a period untroubled by the abusive telephone threats that riddled the domestic peace of their lives together in New York. But although the threatening telephone calls end when they move to Cairo, Angelou finds a different restriction on her life that has little to do with political sanctions of the South African government: As the wife of a well-known activist, she ironically finds her own life less free and is not at liberty to find work for herself, because her husband prefers that she stay at home and devote her time fully to her responsibilities as housewife and mother.

After several months in Cairo, however, the Make family suffers financial restraints, and Angelou takes it upon herself to seek employment without her husband's knowledge. Through the help of a family friend, she is offered the job of Editor of *The Arab Observer*, a Cairo-based news journal with an international scope. Although she has not been trained professionally in journalism, Angelou accepts the position, partly to supplement the family income, but more importantly to meet the challenge of the job. The challenge of being Editor is a significant one, not only because of the demanding and diverse responsibilities but, more critically, because as a black American woman working with a male staff in a country deeply influenced by the Islamic faith, Angelou has to prove herself on more than one level.

The conditions in her office at first are less than friendly. When Angelou gives an account of the relief she experienced when moved from her centrally located desk into a rather secluded library, she borrows a popular tale from Joel Chandler Harris' Brer Rabbit:

> Finally, when the farmer had the rabbit turning at a fast speed, he pointed him toward the briar patch and let go. Brer Rabbit landed on his feet. His eyes were dry and bright. His ears perked up and waved. Brer Rabbit grinned at the farmer, his teeth shining white as buttermilk. He said, "Home, at last. Home at last. Great God Almighty, I'm home at last."
>
> I smiled sweetly as the men shoved and pulled my desk into the library. When they left, and I stood before the crowded book shelves, reading unfamiliar titles and the names of authors unknown to me, still I felt just like Brer Rabbit in the briar patch. (p. 233)

Angelou equates her delight in her move to the library with Brer Rabbit's relief at being tossed into the briar patch by the farmer. Both are victims, in a sense, of their situations yet both use their native wit and resourcefulness to overcome debilitating odds. The books in the library are written in English and are just what Angelou needs to supplement her knowledge of international politics and the Arab world. Moreover, by borrowing the Brer Rabbit narrative, Angelou makes an implicit comparison between her own position as a black American woman in an African, Islamic, male-oriented world and the inhumane conditions of black Americans in slavery. Finally, by including one of the earliest examples of folk literature about blacks in America, Angelou places her own narrative within the ranks of an established folk tradition.

Just as her experiences as a black American in Africa call to mind Brer Rabbit on occasion, so she recalls the stories of several slave heroines while attending an informal gathering of African women in London. All of the women present are the wives of political activists in the struggle to end apartheid and second-class citizenship for black Africans. Although their national backgrounds are quite different, they share the same sense of frustration and ineffectualness in comparison with their husbands, who ironically enjoy more autonomy in the fight for freedom. To ease their sense of uselessness, they gather one day in the home of Mrs. Oliver Tambo, the wife of the leader of the African National Congress. Here the women narrate traditional tales from African folklore. Although Angelou initially feels somewhat estranged from the spontaneous ceremony, she is soon moved to share folktales from the tradition of slave narratives concerning women who led the fight for freedom in America.

Her first story narrates the history of Harriet Tubman, a model of the strong black women at the heart of American history, a woman who fought against devastating odds and suffered extraordinary personal sacrifice to free many of her people. Tubman is, therefore, an appropriate figure to celebrate in an international group of black women. Tubman, Angelou tells them, "stood on free ground, above a free sky, hundreds of miles from the chains and lashes of slavery and said, 'I must go back. With the help of God I will bring others to freedom,' and . . . although suffering brain damage from a slaver's blow, she walked back and forth through the lands of bondage time after time and brought hundreds of her people to freedom" (p. 137). Pleased with the success of her first tale, Angelou follows the inspiring story of Harriet Tubman with an even more dramatic presentation of the heroism of Sojourner Truth. Once again she selects the figure of a fearless black American woman who devoted her life to end slavery and to educate both Northerners and Southerners about the responsibilities of freedom. Sojourner Truth, like Harriet Tubman, is a fitting example of the essential strength of black American women to share with a group of African women celebrating the same heroic characteristics in their ancestors. The anecdote relates an equal rights meeting in the 1800s at which Truth addressed the group and was accused by a white man of being a man dressed as a woman:

> "Ain't I a woman? I have suckled your babes at this breast. " Here she put her large hands on her bodice. Grabbing the cloth she pulled. The threads gave way, the blouse and her undergarments parted and her huge tits hung, pendulously free. She continued, her face unchanging and her voice never faltering, "And ain't I a woman?"
>
> When I finished the story, my hands tugging at the buttons of my blouse, the African women stood applauding, stamping

> their feet and crying. Proud of their sister whom they had not known a hundred years before. (p. 138)

The stories about Sojourner Truth and Harriet Tubman, like the folktale of Brer Rabbit, enlarge the scope of Angelou's autobiography and bring certain historical points of reference to the story of one person's life. Readers come to understand *Heart of a Woman* not only through the avenues of her life opened in the text but through the samplings of folklore that are included as well. Fictionalization comes into play as Angelou adapts these borrowed narratives and anecdotes to illustrate the theme of displacement in her life and her son's.

I have shown that Angelou adapts fictional techniques in *Heart of a Woman* to make her life story fully realistic and convincing, and to supplement the personal scope with the larger historical context. In addition Angelou uses elements of fantasy to illustrate disappointments and defeats she has experienced in life and to reveal the complexity of her relationship with her son. Her use of fantasy can be divided into two types: the narration of a fantasy that ends in illusion and suggests the autobiographer's somewhat ironic stance in examining her past and the narration of a fantasy that becomes reality and emphasizes her inability to protect her son and herself from harmful influences. With both types of fantasy, the writer stresses the importance of imagination when a situation does not measure up to one's expectations.

One of the most important examples of the first type of fantasy concerns Angelou's prospects for marriage at various times in her life. She includes her unrealistic hopes for her impending marriages to demonstrate how firmly she had believed in the American dream of stability through marriage and family. Even in the earlier *Singin' and Swingin' and Gettin' Merry Like Christmas*, Angelou had accounted for her illusory belief that she had finally met the man of her dreams who would give her everything she had always lacked—love, domestic tranquility, security, children, and an attractive house in the suburbs modeled after *Better Homes and Gardens*:

> At last I was a housewife, legally a member of that enviable tribe of consumers whom security made as fat as butter and who under no circumstances considered living by bread alone, because their husbands brought home the bacon. I had a son, a father for him, a husband and a pretty home for us to live in. My life began to resemble a Good Housekeeping advertisement. I cooked well-balanced meals and molded fabulous jello

> desserts. My floors were dangerous with daily applications of wax and our furniture slick with polish.

When Angelou describes her fantasy about marriage and its power to bring normalcy and stability to her life, whether in *Singin' and Swingin'* or *Heart of a Woman*, she uses an ironic point of view to suggest how much she had yet to learn about marriage. Her ironic stance, thereby, fosters understanding on the part of the reader.

In *Heart of a Woman*, Angelou stresses the irony in her present perspective by juxtaposing her fantasized notion of marriage with the way two relationships actually develop. She carefully exposes her illusory hopes and underscores her naïveté with the actual disappointment she experienced. While working in New York, Angelou meets Thomas Allen, a bail bondsman, whom she plans to marry in order to bring stability into her life and a father into Guy's. For some years, she has looked for a strong, honest man who, ideally, would help her shoulder the responsibility of raising Guy. She privately imagines the assumed advantages of marrying Thomas until she has convinced herself of her dream:

> I was getting used to the idea and even liking it. We'd buy a nice house out on Long Island, where he had relatives. I would join a church and some local women's volunteer organizations. Guy wouldn't mind another move if he was assured that it was definitely the last one. I would let my hair grow out and get it straightened and wear pretty hats with flowers and gloves and look like a nice colored woman from San Francisco. (p. 102)

But even before the fantasy becomes an illusion, Angelou begins to distrust her dream-like wishes. Her friends and his family caution them not to marry, and she even feels a "twinge which tried to warn me that I should stop and do some serious thinking" (p. 103).

Angelou, however, ignores this annoying suspicion as long as possible, until, one evening when Allen is at her home for dinner, she suddenly realizes what her real future with him would be like:

> At home, Guy watched television and Thomas read the sports pages while I cooked dinner. I knew that but for my shocking plans, we were acting out the tableau of our future. Into eternity, Guy would be in his room, laughing at *I Love Lucy* and Thomas would be evaluating the chances of an athelete [sic] or a national

> baseball team, and I would be leaning over the stove, preparing food for the "shining dinner hour." Into eternity. (p. 124)

In spite of this rather sobering premonition, Angelou does not make her decision to break her engagement with Thomas, until she meets Vus Make, who convinces her that she would be in a better position to offer her gift of humanism to others if she were married to a South African political figure rather than to a bail bondsman.

Although Vus Make's goals are quite different from Thomas Allen's, Angelou experiences the same belief in a perfect fantasy future with her prospective husband—and its dissolution. Part of her imagined future would provide her with the same domestic security she had hoped would develop from other relationships. "I was getting a husband, and a part of that gift was having someone to share responsibilities and guilt" (p. 131). Yet her hopes are even more idealistic than usual, inasmuch as she imagines herself participating in the liberation of South Africa as Vus Make's wife: "With my courage added to his own, he would succeed in bringing the ignominious white rule in South Africa to an end. If I didn't already have the qualities he needed, then I would just develop them. Infatuation made me believe in my ability to create myself into my lover's desire" (p. 123). In reality Angelou is only willing to go so far in recreating herself to meet her husband's desires and is all too soon frustrated with her role as Make's wife. He does not want her to work, but is unable to support his expensive tastes, as well as his family, on his own. The family is evicted from their New York apartment just before they leave for Egypt, and they soon face similar problems in Cairo. Their marriage dissolves after some months despite Angelou's efforts to hold her own as Editor of *The Arab Observer*. In her autobiography she underscores the illusory nature of her fantasy about marriage to show how her perspective has shifted over the years and how much understanding she has gained about life in general. Fantasy, for Angelou, is a form of truth-telling and a way to present subtle truths about her life to her readers.

The second type of fantasy in *Heart of a Woman* is born out in reality rather than in illusion, as is the case with her expectations for marriage. One of the most important uses of the second kind of fantasy involves a sequence that demonstrates how much Angelou fears for Guy's safety throughout his youth. Although her imagination is more sensitive than are the imaginations of most, the recurrent vision of one's child meeting with unexpected danger is common to most parents. Angelou organizes her repetitive fantasies about Guy into a pattern in her autobiography to explain the guilt and inadequacy she often felt in her role as mother.

Throughout her life, she strives to balance the responsibilities of motherhood and the demands of her career as a professional entertainer and writer. Since she has the primary responsibility for raising Guy without a husband and earning an income adequate to meet their basic needs, Angelou is often faced with an impossible situation. She cannot spend as much time with her son as she would like and hold a full-time job at the same time. Thus she is often caught in a situation for which no solution is satisfactory, and she cannot help but suffer from the paradox of being both a victim and a perpetrator of the cycle of displacement.

The first example of a fantasy which involves a threat to Guy's life relates to his mother's career as a professional singer. Although Angelou has vowed to give up the life of an entertainer permanently, she cannot resist an invitation to perform at the opening of the Gate of Horn in Chicago. She naturally has second thoughts about leaving Guy on his own, but cannot turn down the opportunity to earn enough money in two weeks to pay two months' rent. Before leaving New York, she makes arrangements with her close friend John Killens to watch over Guy, even though he is already quite independent and often resents the implication that he needs care or guidance. She also hires an older black woman to stay at her home and cook for Guy.

As she is checking out of her hotel in Chicago, Angelou is called to the phone to hear Killens' voice tell her that there has been trouble. His first words are enough to awaken her deepest fears and replay an all-too-familiar scenario:

> The dread, closer than a seer's familiar, which lived sucking off my life, was that something would happen to my only son. He would be stolen, kidnapped by a lonely person who, seeing his perfection, would be unable to resist. He would be struck by an errant bus, hit by a car out of control. He would walk a high balustrade, showing his beauty and coordination to a girl who was pretending disinterest. His foot would slip, his body would fold and crumble, he would fall fifty feet and someone would find my phone number. I would be minding my own business and a stranger would call me to the phone.
>
> "Hello?"
>
> A voice would say, "There's been trouble."
>
> My nightmare never went further. I never knew how serious the accident was, or my response. And now real life pushed itself through the telephone. (p. 75)

"Real life," in the form of Killens' voice, assures her that Guy is now safe at his home but does not tell her any related details on the telephone, thus allowing her fantasy to grow. Back in New York, she learns that her son has received a threat from a local gang, because the leader's girlfriend has accused Guy of insulting her. As soon as she returns and has a chance to survey the circumstances, Angelou confronts the gang leader directly and warns him against further contact with her son. Although Guy is never actually harmed by the gang, his mother's fantasized nightmare has been brought a step closer to "real life."

A second segment in the pattern of fantasy concerning danger threatening Guy's life relates to the telephone harassment the Make family experiences before their move to Cairo. Shortly after her marriage to Make, Angelou begins to receive threatening phone calls during the day when neither Vus nor Guy is at home. Most concern her husband and, according to him, are placed by people working for the South African government. Initially Angelou responds to all of the telephone calls as if they were true, but gradually learns to distance herself from the immediate shock and lingering fear. Even changing their telephone number does not put an end to the calls; and, occasionally, the unidentified voice informs her that her son has met with unexpected danger and will not be returning home. These calls, of course, nurture her recurrent fantasy about Guy's safety and show the vulnerability she feels as a mother trying to protect her child from any form of danger:

> One afternoon I answered the telephone and was thumped into a fear and subsequent rage so dense that I was made temporarily deaf.
>
> "Hello, Maya Make?" Shreds of a Southern accent still hung in the white woman's voice.
>
> "Yes? Maya Make speaking." I thought the woman was probably a journalist or a theater critic, wanting an interview from Maya Angelou Make, the actress.
>
> "I'm calling about Guy." My mind shifted quickly from a pleasant anticipation to apprehension.
>
> "Are you from his school? What is the matter?"
>
> "No, I'm at Mid-town Hospital. I'm sorry but there's been a serious accident. We'd like you to come right away. Emergency ward." (p. 193)

Angelou does not stop to think about the recent telephone threats until she arrives at the emergency ward to discover that Guy is not there. A telephone call to his school soon assures her that he is safe in his classroom and that she has been the victim of the South African threats and her own fear for her son's life.

Yet not all threats to Guy's life end as harmlessly as the challenge from the gang and the anonymous phone calls. In Accra, where Angelou and Guy go after her marriage with Vus Make deteriorates, she receives another shocking intrusion from "real life." The difference between this warning of danger and all others in the pattern is that this threat brings fantasy to the level of reality. The threat is neither speculative nor alleged, but real.

Just a few days after their arrival in Ghana, some friends invite Angelou and Guy to a picnic. Although his mother declines, Guy immediately accepts the invitation in a show of independence. On the way home from the day's outing, her son is seriously injured in an automobile accident. Even though he has had very little experience driving, Guy is asked to drive, because his host is too intoxicated to operate the car himself. At the time of the collision, the car is at a standstill.

The pair's return delayed, Angelou, before long, is once again terrified by her recurrent nightmare concerning Guy's safety. This time, however, the fantasy becomes reality:

> Korle Bu's emergency ward was painfully bright. I started down the corridor and found myself in a white tunnel, interrupted by a single loaded gurney, resting against a distant wall. I walked up to the movable table and saw my son, stretched his full length under white sheets. His rich golden skin paled to ash-grey. His eyes closed and his head at an unusual angle.
>
> I took my arm away from Alice's grasp and told Katie to stop her stupid snuffling. When they backed away, I looked at my son, my real life. He was born to me when I was seventeen. I had taken him away from my mother's house when he was two months old, and except for a year I spent in Europe without him, and a month when he was stolen by a deranged woman, we had spent our lives together. My grown life lay stretched before me, stiff as a pine board, in a strange country, blood caked on his face and clotted on his clothes. (p. 263)

Although Angelou has never been to Korle Bu Hospital, the emergency ward is painfully familiar. The crisis becomes all the more urgent because they are as yet unaccustomed to the language and have very little available money. Angelou captures the depth of her fear by calling her injured, immobile son, "my real life," "my grown life." In this sequence of fantasy moving to the level of reality, the autobiographer suggests the vulnerability she felt in her role as a mother with full responsibility for the well-being of her only child. In a new country, estranged from her husband with no immediate prospects for employment, Angelou possesses very little control over her life or her son's safety. After the accident in Ghana, Guy is not only striving for independence from his mother but for life itself.

The complex nature of her relationship with her son is at the heart of this most recent of Angelou's autobiographical volumes. At the end, Guy is seventeen and has just passed the matriculation exams at the University of Ghana. The last scene pictures Guy driving off to his new dormitory room with several fellow university students. The conclusion of *Heart of a Woman* announces a new beginning for Angelou and hope for her future relationship with Guy. In this sense, the newest volume in the series follows the pattern established by the conclusions of the earlier volumes. *Caged Bird* ends with the birth of Guy, *Gather Together* with the return to her mother's home in San Francisco after regaining her innocence through the lessons of a drug addict, and *Singin' and Swingin'* with the reunion of mother and son in a paradisiacal setting of a Hawaiian resort. The final scene of *Heart of a Woman* suggests that the future will bring more balance between dependence and independence in their relationship and that both will have significant personal successes as their lives begin to take different courses. Although Guy has assumed that he has been fully "grown up" for years, they have at last reached a point where they can treat each other as adults and allow one another the chance to live independently. Many of Angelou's victories are reflected in Guy in the last scene, for, although Guy is the same age she is at the end of *Caged Bird*, his young life promises many more opportunities and rewards as a result of his mother's perseverance and her belief "that life loved the person who dared to live it." Moreover, Angelou shares Guy's fresh sense of liberation; she too is embarking on a new period of strength and independence as she begins her life yet again—on her own and in a new land. It is from this position of security that Maya Angelou looks back to record her life story and to compensate for the years of distance and displacement through the autobiographical act.

SONDRA O'NEALE

Reconstruction of the Composite Self: New Images of Black Women in Maya Angelou's Continuing Autobiography

The Black woman is America's favorite unconfessed symbol. She is the nation's archetype for unwed mothers, welfare checks, and food stamps. Her round, smiling face bordered by the proverbial red bandanna is the requisite sales image for synthetic pancakes and frozen waffles "just like Mammy use to make." Only her knowledgeable smile of expertise can authenticate the flavor of corporately fried chicken. When sciolists have need to politicize reactionary measures, they usually fabricate self-serving perceptions of "universal" Black women: ostensibly trading poverty vouchers for mink-strewn Cadillacs, or hugging domestic accouterments in poses of beneficent penury, or shaking a firm bodice as a prostituting Lilith, who offers the most exquisite forbidden sex—all cosmologically craved images of a remote, ambivalent Mother Earth. Regardless of which polemic prevails, these mirrors of the same perverted icon provide the greatest reservoir of exploitable and subconsciously desired meaning in American culture.

That said, if the larger society does not know who Black women are, only who it wants them to be; if even Black men as scholars and thinkers writing in this century could not "free" the images of Black women in the national psyche, it remained for Black woman to accomplish the task themselves. Thus the emergence of Black feminine expression in drama, poetry, and fiction during the seventies was long overdue. Because ebon women occupy so much space on the bottom rung in American polls of economy, opportunity, and Eurocultural measurements of femininity, some of these new writers know that for Black liberation art must do more than serve its own form, that fictional conceptions of depth and integrity are needed to reveal the Black women's identity, and that ethnic women readers are bereft of role models who can inspire a way of escape.

Although Black writers have used autobiography to achieve these ends since the days of slavery, few use the genre today. One who employs only the tools of fiction but not its "make-believe" form to remold these perceptions, one who has made her life her message and whose message to all aspiring Black women is the reconstruction of her experiential "self," is Maya Angelou. With the wide public and critical reception of *I Know Why the Caged Bird Sings* (*C.B.*) in the early seventies, Angelou bridged the gap between life and art, a step that is essential if Black women are to be deservedly credited with the mammoth and creative feat of noneffacing survival. Critics could not dismiss her work as so much "folksy" propaganda because her narrative was held together by controlled techniques of artistic fiction as well as by a historic-sociological study of Black feminine images seldom if ever viewed in American literature.

No Black women in the world of Angelou's books are losers. She is the third generation of brilliantly resourceful females, who conquered oppression's stereotypical maladies without conforming to its expectations of behavior. Thus, reflecting what Western critics are discovering is the focal point of laudable autobiographical literature, the creative thread which weaves Angelou's tapestry is not herself as central subject; it is rather a purposeful composite of a multifaceted "I" who is: (1) an indivisible offspring of those dauntless familial women about whom she writes; (2) an archetypal "self" demonstrating the trials, rejections, and endurances which so many Black women share; and (3) a representative of that collective obsidian army which stepped out of three hundred years of molding history and redirected its own destiny. The process of her autobiography is not a singular statement of individual egotism but an exultant explorative revelation that she *is* because her life is an inextricable part of the misunderstood reality of who Black people and Black women truly are. That "self" is the model which she holds before Black women and that is the unheralded chronicle of actualization which she wants to include in the canon of Black American literature.

I

In *Caged Bird*, one gets a rare literary glimpse of those glamorous chignoned Black women of the twenties and thirties who, refusing to bury their beauty beneath maid trays in segregated Hollywood films or New York's budding but racist fashion industry, adapted their alluring qualities to the exciting, lucrative streetlife that thrived in the Jazz Age during the first third of this century. Buzzing with undertones of settlement of the Black urban North and West, these were the days of open gambling, speakeasies, and political bossism. Angelou's mother and maternal grandmother grandly supported their families in these St. Louis and San Francisco environments in ways that cannot be viewed as disreputable because they were among the few tools afforded Black folk for urban survival. But other than nostalgic mention of performing headliners such as Duke Ellington or Billie Holiday, one does not get a sense of Black life in literary or historic reconstructions of the era. Truthful assessment would show that most Blacks were not poor waifs lining soup kitchen doors during the Depression or, because they were denied jobs in the early years of the war effort, pining away in secondary involvement. The landscape in *Caged Bird* is not that of boardinghouse living among middle-class whites as depicted through eyes of nineteenth-century Howellian boredom, but rather that of colorful and adventurous group living in San Francisco's Fillmore district during the shipbuilding years of World War II.

From her moneyed stepfather, Daddy Clidell, Angelou received a basic ghetto education:

> He owned apartment buildings and, later, pool halls, and was famous for being the rarity "a man of honor." He didn't suffer, as many "honest men" do, from the detestable righteousness that diminishes their virtue. He knew cards and men's hearts. So during the age when Mother was exposing us to certain facts of life, like personal hygiene, proper posture, table manners, good restaurants and tipping practices, Daddy Clidell taught me to play poker, blackjack, tonk and high, low, Jick, Jack and the Game. He wore expensively tailored suits and a large yellow diamond stickpin. Except for the jewelry, he was a conservative dresser and carried himself with the unconscious pomp of a man of secure means. [*C.B.*, pp. 213–14]

Through Clidell she "was introduced to the most colorful characters in the Black underground." And from men with names like "Stonewall Jimmy, Just

Black, Cool Clyde, Tight Coat and Red Leg," she heard of the many Brer Rabbit con games which they hustled on Mr. Charlie. Angelou the narrator, detached from Angelou the child, who absorbed from this parlor banter a Black history unavailable in formal education, is able to philosophize and again structure role models:

> When he finished, more triumphant stories rainbowed around the room riding the shoulders of laughter. By all accounts those storytellers, born Black and male before the turn of the twentieth century, should have been ground into useless dust. Instead they used their intelligence to pry open the door of rejection and not only became wealthy but got some revenge in the bargain. It wasn't possible for me to regard them as criminals or be anything but proud of their achievements.
>
> The needs of a society determine its ethics, and in the Black American ghettos the hero is that man who is offered only the crumbs from his country's table but by ingenuity and courage is able to take for himself a Lucullan feast. [*C.B.*, p. 218]

That same sense of historical but undiscovered Black life is seen in the panorama of the now four-volume autobiography. Whether from vivid recollection of fond fellowships in rural schools contrasted with the bitter remembrance of a segregated system designed to animalize Black students that one finds in *Caged Bird*, or from the startling reminiscences of Black entertainers who managed to evade Hitlerism and form enclaves of Black performers in Europe during the war years (e.g., Josephine Baker, Bernard Hassel, Mabel Mercer, "Brickie" Bricktop, Nancy Holloway, and Cordon Heath) that one finds in *Singin' and Swingin' and Gettin' Merry Like Christmas* (*S. & S.*), or from the poignant view of a Northern perch in both the creative (the Harlem Writers Guild) and the political (Northern Coordinator for the SCLC) thought and action of the Civil Rights Movement, as well as the annexing gravitation to African liberation (protest demonstrations at the UN following Lumumba's death) that one finds in her latest work, *The Heart of a Woman*—Angelou's message is one blending chorus: Black people and Black women do not just endure, they triumph with a will of collective consciousness that Western experience cannot extinguish.

II

If there is one enduring misrepresentation in American literature it is the Black Southern matriarch. When Blacks appeared first in James Fenimore Cooper's novel *The Spy*, the Black woman was silent, postforty, corpulent, and in the kitchen. Cooper's contemporary, Washington Irving, duplicated that perspective, and for much of the period that followed, white American authors more or less kept her in that state. By modern times, given characters such as Faulkner's Molly and Dilsey, the images of nonmulatto Southern Black women had still not progressed. When seen at all they were powerless pawns related only to contexts of white aspirations. But Angelou's depiction of her paternal Grandmother Annie Henderson is a singular repudiation of that refraction. While Mrs. Henderson is dependent on no one, the entire Stamps community is at times totally dependent upon her, not as a pietous but impotent weeping post but as a materially resourceful entrepreneur. When explaining that her family heritage precludes acceptance of welfare, Angelou describes Mrs. Henderson's self-sufficiency:

> And welfare was absolutely forbidden. My pride had been starched by a family who assumed unlimited authority in its own affairs. A grandmother, who raised me, my brother and her two own sons, owned a general merchandise store. She had begun her business in the early 1900's in Stamps, Arkansas, by selling meat pies to saw men in a lumber mill, then racing across town in time to feed workers in a cotton-gin mill four miles away. [*S. & S.*, pp. 13–14.]

Through frugal but nonarrogant management of her finances under the meddlesome eye of jealous and avaricious whites, Mrs. Henderson not only stalwartly provides for her crippled son and two robust grandchildren, she feeds the Black community during the Depression *and* helps keep the white economy from collapse. Angelou aptly contrasts gratitude and its absence from both segments. While holding the reluctant hand of her granddaughter Maya, who was suffering from a painful abcessed tooth, Grandmother Henderson endured contemptuous rejection from the town's white dentist: "Annie, my policy is I'd rather stick my hand in a dog's mouth than in a nigger's." She reminded him:

> "I wouldn't press on you like this for myself but I can't take No. Not for my grandbaby. When you come to borrow my money

> you didn't have to beg. You asked me, and I lent it. Now, it wasn't my policy. I ain't no moneylender, but you stood to lose this building and I tried to help you out." [*C.B.*, p. 184]

No matter that the lordly Black woman saved him from ruin when the power structure to which he belonged would not, he still refused to pull her granddaughter's tooth. The author neither supports nor condemns her grandmother's traditional Christian forbearance. What she does do is illustrate alternative views of a Southern Black woman who would not be subjugated by such unconscionable oppression—essential visions of a "composite self."

Another facet of the unknown Southern Black woman is her majestic octoroon maternal grandmother, Mrs. Baxter, who ruled a ghetto borough in Prohibition-era St. Louis:

> . . . the fact that she was a precinct captain compounded her power and gave her the leverage to deal with even the lowest crook without fear. She had pull with the police department, so the men in their flashy suits and fleshy scars sat with church-like decorum and waited to ask favors from her. If Grandmother raised the heat off their gambling parlors, or said the word that reduced the bail of a friend waiting in jail, they knew what would be expected of them. Come election, they were to bring in the votes from their neighborhood. She most often got them leniency, and they always brought in the vote. [*C.B.*, p. 60]

The only change is the urban setting, the self-reliant woman in control of her environment is the atypical contribution which Angelou makes as a corrective to images of Black women. That the medium is not fiction serves the interest of young readers, who can learn to do likewise.

By far the role model which Angelou presents as having the greatest impact on her own life is her mother, Vivian Baxter, whose quintessence could only be shown by her actions for "to describe my mother would be to write about a hurricane in its perfect power. Or the climbing, falling colors of a rainbow." (*C.B.*, p. 58) With firm velveted command often braced with creative violence, Vivian obviated life's obstacles with anything but sentimentality and she reared Maya to do the same: "She supported us efficiently with humor and imagination. . . . With all her jollity, Vivian Baxter had no mercy. . . . 'Sympathy' is next to 'shit' in the dictionary, and I can't even read." (*C.B.*, p. 201) That meant she refused Maya psychological and, after Guy's birth, financial dependence:

> By no amount of agile exercising of a wishful imagination could my mother have been called lenient. Generous she was; indulgent, never. Kind, yes; permissive, never. In her world, people she accepted paddled their own canoes, pulled their own weight, put their own shoulder to their own plows and pushed like hell. . . . [*G.T.*, p. 7]

But through the four books, Vivian is Angelou's certain rock, an invincible resource from which the mystique of exultant Black feminine character is molded. Tough, a rarefied beauty, Vivian effectively challenged any stereotypical expectations with which the white world or Black men attempted to constrict her being. Her instructions to Angelou are mindful of the pitiful words in Zora Neale Hurston's novel: "The Black woman is the mule of the world," but Vivian insisted that not one ebon sister has to accept that warrant:

> "People will take advantage of you if you let them. Especially Negro women. Everybody, his brother and his dog, thinks he can walk a road in a colored woman's behind. But you remember this, now. Your mother raised you. You're full-grown. Let them catch it like they find it. If you haven't been trained at home to their liking tell them to get to stepping." Here a whisper of delight crawled over her face. "Stepping. But not on you.
>
> "You hear me?"
>
> "Yes, Mother. I hear you." [*G.T.*, p. 128]

At a time in life when most women were expected to surrender in place, to Maya's astonishment, Vivian put her age back fifteen years and took on the merchant marine "because they told me Negro women couldn't get in that union. . . . I told them 'You want to bet?' I'll put my foot in that door up to my hip until women of every color can walk over my foot, get in that union, get aboard a ship and go to sea." (*Heart*, p. 28) This is the essence of Angelou's composite: Black progress has been attained in this country not only because of the leadership of Black men but also because of the unsung spirit of noncompliant Black women. This is the revelation she intends the careful portrayals of major women in her life to celebrate.

Finally the most elusive identity in the accumulative "self" is Angelou. One sees her only through the eyes with which she views the world. Attempts at self-description in the opus are rare. As a child and teenager Angelou was inexorably lonely (". . . I was surrounded, as I had been all my life, by strangers" [*C.B.*, p. 66]). But to describe her as filled with self-loathing as one of the few critical examinations of her work has done is inaccurate: ". . . Maya Angelou expresses the most severe self-hatred derived from her appearance. Beaten down by massive self-loathing and self-shame, she felt her appearance was too offensive to merit any kind of true affection from others." The critic concludes, "Angelou's conception of self caused her to be self-limiting and to lack self-assertion and self-acceptance." The young Angelou of *Caged Bird* could be more poignantly described as in the throes of probing self-discovery, deliberation common to adolescence. A child who was searching for inward panacea, to withstand real—not imagined—rejection, disappointment, and even onslaught from an adult world, the young Angelou had few refuges, among them her brother Bailey and her world of books. In the end, self-education through literature and the arts gave her the additional fortitude and intellectual acumen to be a Baxter-Henderson woman of her own generation.

When the adult Angelou faced the world, the humble requirements of Stamps, Arkansas, the speakeasies of St. Louis, and the shipyard boardinghouses of San Francisco had passed away. Through art she could preserve the tenacious women who survived the crucibles those eras intended but aside from will and determination she could not extract dependable techniques from their experiences. Hence the conclusions of Angelou herself as role model for this present age: if Black women are to "paddle their own canoes" in postindustrial society they must do it through force of intellect. Her own experiential development as traced thus far in the latest work, *The Heart of a Woman*, teaches that no option—marriage, entertainment, any dependent existence—is as much a lasting or consummate reservoir. "I made the decision to quit show business. Give up the skin-tight dresses and manicured smiles. The false concern over sentimental lyrics. I would never again work to make people smile inanely and would take on the responsibility of making them think." (*Heart*, p. 45) That decision is her passport to irrevocable freedom to which the definitiveness of the autobiography attests. Angelou, the developing character, had sounded the vastness of a lifetime of loneliness and ascended as Angelou the writer. Art became an assertive statement for three generations of an evolving self.

III

Unlike her poetry, which is a continuation of traditional oral expression in Afro-American literature, Angelou's prose follows classic technique in non-poetic Western forms. The material in each book while chronologically marking her life is nonetheless arranged in loosely structured plot sequences which are skillfully controlled. In *Caged Bird* the tenuous psyche of a gangly, sensitive, withdrawn child is traumatically jarred by rape, a treacherous act from which neither the reader nor the protagonist has recovered by the book's end. All else is cathartic: her uncles' justified revenge upon the rapist, her years of readjustment in a closed world of speechlessness despite the warm nurturing of her grandmother, her granduncle, her beloved brother Bailey, and the Stamps community; a second reunion with her vivacious mother; even her absurdly unlucky pregnancy at the end does not assuage the reader's anticipatory wonder: isn't the act of rape by a trusted adult so assaultive upon an eight-year-old's life that it leaves a wound which can never be healed? Such reader interest in a character's future is the craft from which quality fiction is made. Few autobiographers however have the verve to seize the drama of such a moment, using one specific incident to control the book but with an underlining implication that the incident will not control a life.

The denouement in *Gather Together in My Name* is again sexual: the older, crafty, experienced man lasciviously preying upon the young, vulnerable, and, for all her exposure by that time, naïve woman. While foreshadowing apprehension guided the reader to the central action in the first work, Maya presses the evolvement in *Gather Together* through a limited first-person narrator who seems to know less of the villain's intention than is obvious to the reader. Thrice removed from the action, the reader sees that L. D. Tolbrook is nothing but a slick pimp, that his seductive sexual refusals can only lead to a calamitous end; that his please-turn-these-few-tricks-for-me-baby-so-I-can-get-out-of-an-urgent-jam line is an ancient inducement for susceptible females, but Maya the actor in the tragedy cannot. She is too much in love. Maya, the author, through whose eyes we see a younger, foolish "self," so painstakingly details the girl's descent into the brothel that Black women, all women, have enough vicarious example to avoid the trap. Again, through using the "self" as role model, not only is Maya able to instruct and inspire the reader but the sacrifice of personal disclosure authenticates the autobiography's integral depth.

Just as the title of *Gather Together* is taken from a New Testament injunction for the travailing soul to pray and commune while waiting patiently for deliverance and the *Caged Bird* title is taken from a poem by the beloved Paul Laurence Dunbar, who gave call to Angelou's nascent creativity, the title of the third work, *Singin' and Swingin' and Gettin' Merry Like Christmas,* is a folkloric title symbolic of the author's long-deserved ascent to success and fulfillment. This volume's plot and tone are lifted above adroit reenactments of that native humor so effective in relieving constant struggle in Black life which is holistically balanced in the first two books. The buoyancy is constant because Maya (who had theretofore been called Marguerite or Ritie all her life) the singer, Maya the dancer, Maya the actress, had shed the fearful image of "typical" unwed Black mother with a dead-end destiny. She knew she was more than that. But the racist and sexist society—which had relegated her to dishwasher, short-order cook, barmaid, chauffeur, and counter clerk; which had denied her entrance into secure employment and higher education in the armed services; and which programmed her into a familiar void when the crush of changing modernity even eradicated the avenues which partially liberated her foremothers—seemed invincible. The culmination of her show business climb is a dual invitation: either to replace Eartha Kitt in the Broadway production of *New Faces* or to join the star-studded cast of *Porgy and Bess*, which began a world tour in 1954. From that climax the settings shift to such faraway places as Rome, Venice, Paris, Yugoslavia, Alexandria, Cairo, Athens, and Milan; and the narrator, character, and reader view life from glorious vistas auspiciously removed from the world of that dejected girl in Stamps, Arkansas.

The step from star, producer, and writer for the benefit show *Cabaret for Freedom* to being northern coordinator for the Southern Christian Leadership Conference provides the focus for her latest excursus, *The Heart of a Woman*. Here also, as with each of the previous installments, the work ends with abrupt suspense. In this way dramatic technique not only centralizes each work, it also makes the series narrative a collective whole. In *Caged Bird* the shock-effect ending is the rash conception of her son when in the concluding action of the book she initiates an emotionless affair to see if the word "lesbian" fits her self-description. With a lofty rhetoric which wisdom hindsights she articulates the anguish of a benumbed pregnant sixteen-year-old:

> . . . For eons, it seemed, I had accepted my plight as the hapless, put-upon victim of fate and the Furies, but this time I had to face the fact that I had brought my new catastrophe upon myself. How was I to blame the innocent man whom I had lured into making love to me? In order to be profoundly dishonest, a person must have one of two qualities: either he is unscrupulously ambitious, or he is unswervingly egocentric. He must believe that for his ends to be served all things and people can justifiably be shifted about, or that he is the center not only

> of his own world but of the worlds which others inhabit. I had neither element in my personality, so I hefted the burden of pregnancy at sixteen onto my own shoulders where it belonged. Admittedly, I staggered under the weight. [*C.B.*, pp. 276–77]

And, after viewing a boyfriend's confessed addiction to heroin, she ends *Gather Together* with an initiate's faith: "The next day I took the clothes, my bags and Guy back to Mother's. I had no idea what I was going to make of my life, but I had given a promise and found my innocence. I swore I'd never lose it again." (*G.T.*, p. 214)

Both of these passages are lucid philosophical treatments of life's vicissitudes but the test of superior autobiography is the language and structure of those mundane, though essential, ordinary moments in life. One of the forms that Angelou uses to guide the reader past these apparent surfaces is precise analogy. When describing one of her daddy's girlfriends, the language is not only symbolic but portends their mutual jealousy:

> Dolores lived there with him and kept the house clean with the orderliness of a coffin. Artificial flowers reposed waxily in glass vases. She was on close terms with her washing machine and ironing board. Her hairdresser could count on absolute fidelity and punctuality. In a word, but for intrusions her life would have been perfect. And then I came along. [*C.B.*, p. 221]

When variously citing the notable absences of men in her life, tone and symbolism are delicately synthesized: "I could moan some salty songs. I had been living with empty arms and rocks in my bed" (*Heart*, p. 67); "Indeed no men at all seemed attracted to me. . . . No, husbands were rarer than common garden variety unicorns" (*S. & S.*, p. 13); and "Charles had taken that journey and left me all alone. I was one emotional runny sore" (*G.T.*, p. 26).

Another aspect of style which prevents ponderous plodding in the narrative is Angelou's avoidance of a monolithic Black language. As first-person narrator, she does not disavow an erudition cultivated from childhood through early exposure to and constant reading of such Western masters as Dostoyevsky, Chekhov, Gorky, Dickens, Dunbar, Du Bois, Shakespeare, Kipling, Poe, Alger, Thackeray, James Weldon Johnson, and even the Beowulf poet. Through direct dialogue the reader gleans that Maya is perfectly capable of more expected ghetto expressiveness but such is saved for appropriate moments of high drama such as when a Brooklyn gang threatens to murder her son Guy:

> "I understand that you are the head of the Savages and you have an arrangement with my son. I also understand that the police are afraid of you. Well, I came'round to make you aware of something. If my son comes home with a black eye or a torn shirt, I won't call the police."
>
> His attention followed my hand to my purse. "I will come over here and shoot Susie's grandmother first, then her mother, then I'll blow away that sweet little baby. You understand what I'm saying? If the Savages so much as touch my son, I will then find your house and kill everything that moves, including the rats and cockroaches."
>
> I showed the borrowed pistol, then slid it back into my purse. For a second, none of the family moved and my plans had not gone beyond the speech, so I just kept my hand in the purse, fondling my security. Jerry spoke, "O.K., I understand. But for a mother, I must say you're a mean motherfucker." [*Heart*, pp. 83–84]

In addition to sparse use of street vernacular, she also does not overburden Black communicants with clumsy versions of homespun Black speech. From Arkansas to Europe, from San Francisco to New York, the only imitative affectation is of her uncle Willie's stuttering, "You know . . . how, uh, children are . . . th-th-these days . . ."; her father's corrective pauses of "er," which reaffirms his pretentious mask, "So er this is Daddy's er little man? Boy, anybody tell you errer that you er look like me?"; and the light badinage of customers in Grandma Henderson's store, "Sister, I'll have two cans of sardines. I'm gonna work so fast today I'm gonna make you look like you standing still. Just gimme a couple them fat peanut paddies." The choice not to let imitations of known variables in Black speech dominate expressiveness is reinforcement of a major premise in the works: the nativistic humanness and potential of Black identity.

The four-volume autobiography effectively banishes several stereotypical myths about Black women which had remained unanswered in national literature. Angelou casts a new mold of Mother Earth—a Black woman who repositions herself in the universe so that she chooses the primary objects of her service. And ultimately that object may even be herself. Self-reconstruction of the "I" is a demanding, complex literary mode which not only exercises tested rudiments of fiction but also departs from the more accepted form of biography. Just as in fiction, the biographer can imagine or improvise a character's motives; but the autobiographer is the one narrator who really knows the truth—as well, that is, as any of us can truly know ourselves.

In divulging that truth Angelou reveals a new totality of archetypal Black woman: a composite self that corrects omissions in national history and provides seldom-seen role models for cultural criteria.

SELWYN R. CUDJOE

Maya Angelou and the Autobiographical Statement

> Slavery is terrible for men; but it is far more terrible for women. Super-added to the burden common to all, *they* have wrongs, and sufferings, and mortifications peculiarly their own.
>
> —Linda Brent, *Incidents in the Life of a Slave Girl*

> I think the most important thing about black people is that they don't think they can control anything except their own persons. So everything black people think and do has to be understood as very personal.
>
> —Hannah Nelson, in *Drylongso*

The Afro-American autobiographical statement is the most Afro-American of all Afro-American literary pursuits. During the eighteenth and nineteenth centuries, thousands of autobiographies of Afro-American slaves appeared expressing their sentiments about slavery, the most cruel of American institutions. The practice of the autobiographical statement, up until the contemporary era, remains the quintessential literary genre for capturing the cadences of the Afro-American being, revealing its deepest aspirations and tracing the evolution of the Afro-American psyche under the impact of slavery and modem U.S. imperialism.

Within this context it is important to note that in its most essential aspect slavery as it appeared does not differ very much from the "formal

---

freedoms" granted to Black people in the contemporary United States, since the full franchise was achieved only with the passage of the Civil Rights Act of 1965. Under slavery the whole person was enslaved; during imperialism, the physical body remained free while Black labor was stolen savagely and Black participation in the social and political affairs of the country remained minimal and peripheral. Yet one essential condition characterized both slavery and imperialism: the violation of the personhood of the Afro-American because he was too helpless to defend himself consistently, and the further degradation of his social being as the nature of the system worked toward his further diminishment.

For Afro-American women this violation and degradation possessed its own peculiarities and, as Linda Brent testified in her autobiography, *Incidents in the Life of a Slave Girl* (1861): "Slavery is terrible for men; but it is far more terrible for women. Superadded to the burden common to all, they have wrongs and sufferings and mortifications peculiarly their own." Such a condition may be called double jeopardy—that is, the special cruelty of being at one and the same time the victim of one's race and of one's sex.

Yet the violation and degradation of Afro-American women remained largely ignored, and the nature of their lives remained, as it were, a closely guarded secret. Indeed, of the thousands of autobiographies which were published in the early years very few were concerned with the condition of the Black woman. This absence continued well into the contemporary era, leading to a spectacle in which one could speak about the autobiographical statement in Afro-American literature without really having to confront the Afro-American woman as Black and as female; as a person and as a presence; as someone autonomous and as someone responsible to a community. As a matter of fact, the Afro-American woman remained an all-pervading absence until she was rescued by the literary activity of her Black sisters in the latter part of the twentieth century. There is nothing in the autobiographical statement that makes it essentially different from fiction except, of course, that which has been erected by convention. Michael Ryan, picking up on the observations of Jacques Derrida, has argued that inherent in the structure of the autobiographical statement is the necessary death of the author as a condition for the existence of the referential machinery. "The writing," he states, "must be capable, from the outset, of functioning independently of the subject, of being repeated in the absence of the subject. Strictly speaking, then, its referent is always 'ideal' of fictional—produced and sustained by convention."

To the degree, however, that the referent is present in the autobiography (it being absent or "ideal" in fiction), there is really nothing in the autobiography that guarantees that it will not be read as fiction or vice versa. In fact, any discussion on the Afro-American autobiography is always likely to raise this question: "Is it really true?" and almost always the author must present strong evidence that the work is unquestionably autobiographical. Indeed, Linda Brent was compelled to call upon others to prove the authenticity of her work. Thus at the end of the autobiography, in a kind of afterword, George W. Lowther is forced to corroborate the "authenticity" of the manuscript: "This narrative contains some incidents so extraordinary, that, doubtless, many persons, under whose eyes it may chance to fall, will be ready to believe that it is colored highly, to serve a special purpose. But, however it may be regarded by the incredulous, I know that it is full of living truths." Obviously, the "truth" of the autobiography is neither self-evident nor independent of extratextual confirmation.

Autobiography and fiction, then, are simply different means of arriving at, or (re)cognizing the same truth: the reality of American life and the position of the Afro-American subject in that life. Neither genre should be given a privileged position in our literary history and each should be judged on its ability to speak honestly and perceptively about Black experience in this land. What accounts for the unique power and longevity of this genre in Afro-American writing and its specific permutations within the larger context of the genre? I will suggest three reasons.

Hannah Nelson, an Afro-American woman of the contemporary era, is reported to have said that it is the intense regard for the personal that distinguishes the Black subject from the white subject in the United States. She argues that "the most important thing about black people is that they don't think they can control anything except their own persons. So everything black people *think* and *do* has to be understood as very personal." (My italics) As a result, the inviolability of the Afro-American's personhood is so closely guarded that any assault or presumed assault upon his/her person is frequently resisted. Such a response to social reality always leads to complaints that Blacks tend to be "too touchy," or "too sensitive" in most of their relations with whites. This fact becomes quite apparent in Maya Angelou's *Singin' and Swingin' and Gettin' Merry Like Christmas*.

In fact, Maya Angelou seems to have captured (and elaborated upon) this point when she responded to Mrs. Callinan's inability to call her by her correct name, thus denying her individuality. "Every person I knew had a hellish horror of being 'called out of his name.' It was a dangerous practice to call a Negro anything that could be loosely construed as insulting because of the centuries of their having been called riggers, jigs, dirges, blackbirds, crows, boots and spooks." (*C.B.* p. 91) In fact this sanctity of the person and Mrs. Cullinan's reluctance to grant Angelou her individuality leads to one of the most poignant moments in the text when, in wreaking revenge on Mrs. Cullinan for her indifference and cruelty, Angelou drops some of Mrs. Cullinan's most treasured heirlooms (her casserole and green glass cups) and shocks Mrs. Cullinan into (re)cognition of her personhood. Recounting the incident, Angelou gives her side of the story:

> She actually wobbled around on the floor and picked up shards of the cups and cried, "Oh, Momma. Oh, dear Gawd. It's Momma's china from Virginia. . . . That clumsy nigger. Clumsy little black nigger.,"
>
> Old speckled-face leaned down and asked, "Who did it, Viola? was it Mary? Who did it?" . . . I can't remember whether her action preceded her words, but I know that Mrs. Cullinan said, "Her name's Margaret, goddamn it, her name's Margaret!" And she threw a wedge of the broken plate at me. . . .
>
> Mrs. Cullinan was right about one thing. My name wasn't Mary. [*C.B.*, pp. 92–93]

The realm of the personal, then, is very important, as is its presumed violation.

In her discussion with Professor Gwaltney, Nelson goes on to make another important observation about the difference between Black people and white people, particularly in the area of speech ("speech" used here to refer not so much to the manner of speaking to someone but to its capacity to transmit experience): "Our speech is most directly personal, and every black person assumes that every other black person has a right to a personal opinion. In speaking of great matters, *your personal experience is considered evidence.* With us, distant statistics are certainly not as important as the actual experience of a sober person." (My italics) The speech of the Afro-American, then, is accorded an unusually high degree of importance and acts as an arena where a sense of one's personal and social liberation can be realized. The inordinate amount of weight which the personal assumes may account in part for the strength of the Afro-American autobiographical statement in our literature.

The unique weight of the "personal" and the integrity of the word or speech can better be perceived, in our discussion of the peculiarity of the Afro-American autobiographical statement, as one of the most important means of negotiating our way out of the condition of enslavement and as a means of expressing the intensity with which Afro-American people experience their *violation* and *denigration.* The capacity of speech to convey the intensely lived experience and the closely guarded manner in which the personal is held give to the Afro-American autobiographical statement its special position of authority in Afro-American letters.

As a direct result of this condition, the Afro-American autobiographical statement as a form tends to be bereft of any *excessive subjectivism* and *mindless egotism.* Instead, it presents the Afro-American as reflecting a much more *impersonal* condition, the autobiographical subject emerging as an almost random member of the group, selected to tell his/her tale. As a consequence, the Afro-American autobiographical statement emerges as a *public* rather than a *private* gesture, *me-ism* gives way to *our-ism* and superficial concerns about *individual subject* usually give way to the collective *subjection* of the group.

The autobiography, therefore, is objective and realistic in its approach and is presumed generally to be of service to the group. It is never meant to glorify the exploits of the individual, and the concerns of the collective predominate. One's personal experiences are presumed to be an authentic expression of the society, and thus statistical evidences and sociological treatises assume a secondary level of importance. Herein can be found the importance of the autobiographical statement in Afro-American letters.

It may be argued that the autobiographical statement ruled supreme because of the absence of the novel, which came into full flowering with Richard Wright's *Native Son* (1940). But the predominant place which the autobiographical statement assumed cannot be so reduced since it could be argued that the power of the word (i.e., of speech) and the compelling images evoked by the autobiography has much of its origin in African mythology and its relationship to the spiritual culture of Afro-Americans. Janheinz Jahn in his work *Muntu* (p. 132) testifies to the centrality of the word, Nommo, in African thought. The notion that "the force, responsibility and commitment of the word, and the awareness that the word alone alters the word" (p. 133), seems to have its origin in African culture.

The reverence for the word in traditional African thought and its transformative power in the changed historical conditions of America demanded that the word be used as a weapon and a shield from the cruel reality of American life. The capacity for speech (that is, the capacity to "rap") assumed a primary place in the culture of Afro-Americans; a necessary though not a sufficient condition for liberation.

Thus, where avenues of struggle were closed to the African subject in the diaspora, s/he could recoil him/herself and utilize the nommo as an extended arena in which to continue the struggle for personal and social liberation. In both a metaphorical and a literal sense, speech and language became instruments of liberation in Afro-American thought, and the magical incantation of the word and its power for transformation gave sustenance and hope to Afro-Americans in their darkest hours. As an expression and reflection of the Afro-American experience, the autobiographical statement becomes that strange rite through which the complex consciousness and historical unfoldment of a people stand revealed. It is of and from this experience that Maya Angelou speaks.

In my article "What I Teach and Why" (*Harvard Educational Review*, August 1980), I suggested that the 1970s were an important decade for Afro-American literature because it was a time when we saw the influx of prose writings by Afro-American women writers who expressed themselves in the novel, the short story and the autobiography. While the decade began with the work of Toni Morrison's *The Bluest Eye* (1970), Maya Angelou, *I Know Why the Caged Bird Sings* (1970), Louise Meriwether's *Daddy Was a Numbers Runner* (1970), and Alice Walker's *The Third Life of Grange Copeland* (1970), it ended with Michele Wallace's *Black Macho and the Myth of the Superwoman* (1979) and Mary Helen Washington's anthology *Midnight Birds* (1980).

Throughout the decade, however, there was a subtle distancing of the Afro-American women writers from their male counterparts, particularly in the manner in which they treated the *subjectivity* of their major protagonists; the manner in which these female protagonists were freed, not so much from the other, but from their own menfolk; the bold attempt to speak for the integrity of their selfhood and to define their being in their own terms; and their special need to speak about feminine concerns among themselves. Jeanne Nobles in her work *Beautiful, Also, Are the Souls of My Black Sisters* (1978) argues that the Black women writers of the 1970s "bypass[ed] the popular theme of black reactions to a racist society" (p. 188), while Gwendolyn Brooks confirmed these sentiments when she claimed that these Black writers were "biking to themselves" rather than to others. Mary Helen Washington, in her introduction to *Midnight Birds* (p. xv), would celebrate the fact that the works of Black female writers represented "an open revolt against the ideologies and attitudes that impress [Blackl women into servitude."

Because of limitations on the part of male writers, the female characters who were portrayed never really realized their womanhood (i.e. their essences as autonomous subjects) in the mainstream of Afro-American literature. They were depicted at a surface level of reality that worked as a statement of the condition of the Black female: they never really seemed to have lives worthy of emulation. They invariably seemed to live for others, for Black men or white; for children, or for parents; bereft, always it appeared, of an autonomous self.

It is in response to these specific concerns that Maya Angelou offered her autobiographical statements, presenting a powerful, authentic and profound signification of the condition of Afro-American womanhood in her quest for understanding and love rather than for bitterness and despair. Her work is a triumph in the articulation of truth in simple, forthright terms.

I Know Why the Caged Bird Sings (hereafter referred to as *Caged Bird*) explores growing up Black and female in the American South during the second quarter of this century. It recounts the life of the subject from the age of three to sixteen, the first ten years of which she lived in Stamps, Arkansas, the last three in Los Angeles and San Francisco. The world to which Angelou introduces us is embroidered with *humiliation*, *violation*, *displacement*, and *loss*. From the outset Angelou sounds the pervading themes when she declares: "If growing up is painful for the Southern Black girl, being aware of her displacement is the rust on the razor that threatens the throat. It is an unnecessary insult." (*C.B.*, p. 3) From this introduction she wends her way to the end of her work, where she concludes: "The Black female is assaulted in her tender years by all those common forces of nature at the same time that she is caught in the tripartite crossfire of *masculine prejudice*, *white illogical hate* and *Black lack of power*." (*C.B.*, p. 231)

This is the burden of the work: to demonstrate the manner in which the Black female is violated, by all of the forces above, in her tender years and to demonstrate the "unnecessary insult" of Southern girlhood in her movement to adolescence.

Southern life, as Angelou demonstrates, is one of harshness and brutality. It is exemplified by the conditions under which the workers of Stamps lived, the fear engendered by the Ku Klux Klan, the wanton murder of Black folks (which led Mother Henderson to send Maya and her brother Bailey to their mother in California), the racial separation of the town, and the innumerable incidents of denigration which made life in the South an abomination against God and man. Not that moments of happiness were entirely absent from her childhood life, but such moments came, as Thomas Hardy characterized them in *The Mayor of Casterbridge*, as but "the occasional episode[s] in a general drama of pain."

Such cruelty led to a well-defined pattern of behavior on the part of the South's citizens and the adoption of certain necessary codes if one was to exist in that part of the country. As Angelou points out: "The less you say to white folks (or even powhitetrash) the better." (*C.B.*, p. 22) The insults of the powhitetrash had to be accepted and the spiritual and emotional manner in which the whites tried to debase the Blacks had to be fended off at each moment of existence.

As the text charts Angelou's movement from *innocence* to *awareness*, from childhood to an ever quickening sense of adolescence, there were certain ideological apparatuses, inserted into the social fabric, which Angelou had to overcome in order to maintain a sense of relative liberation and autonomy. It is the virtue of Angelou and the strength of the statement that, as she develops, she is able to detect the presence of these apparatuses, to challenge them and to withstand their pervasive and naturalizing tendencies.

In this country, as in any other capitalist country, religion, education, and sports are supposed to function in certain ideological ways so that the subject accepts certain well-defined practices. Thus, while religion is designed to keep the Afro-American in an oppressed condition, here Black people subverted that institution and used it to assist them to withstand the cruelty of the American experience.

The fight between Joe Louis and Primo Camera was intended to act as a pacifier, as entertainment for Blacks, and to help demonstrate how far they had progressed in the society. "See! A Black boy can now step in the same ring as a white boy." However, the match, as all such events tend to do, turned out to be a tableau in which Black America came face to face with white America, in a struggle of equals. A re-creation of the real drama of American life therefore is played out in the boxing ring: Angelou describes the scene which takes place in her grandmother's store on that night of the fight:

> Babies slid to the floor as women stood up and men leaned toward the radio.
>
> "Here's the referee. He's counting. One, two, three, four, five, six, seven . . . Is the contender trying to get up again?"
>
> All the men in the store shouted, "NO."
>
> —eight, nine, ten." There were a few sounds from the audience, but they seemed to be holding themselves in against tremendous pressure.
>
> "The fight is all over, ladies and gentlemen. Let's get the microphone over to the referee . . . Here he is. He's got the Brown Bomber's hand, he's holding it up . . . Here he is . . ."
>
> Then the voice, husky and familiar, came to wash over us—"The winnah, and still heavyweight champeen of the world . . . Joe Louis."
>
> Champion of the world. A Black boy. Some Black mother's son. He was the strongest man in the world. People drank Coca-Colas like ambrosia and ate candy bars like Christmas. Some of the men went behind the Store and poured white lightning in their soft-drink bottles, and a few of the bigger boys followed them. Those who were not chased away came back blowing

> their breath in front of themselves like proud smokers.
>
> It would take an hour or more before the people would leave the Store and head for home. Those who lived too far had made arrangements to stay in town. It wouldn't do for a Black man and his family to be caught on a lonely country road on a night when Joe Louis had proved that we were the strongest people in the world. [*C.B.*, pp. 114–15]

Singing and perhaps swinging like Christmas, Angelou may have asked the forgiveness of the Italians for this act of celebration when she arrived in Italy some years later. When she was a girl in Arkansas, however, the struggle between the colors continued and the people participated in this life-and-death battle, projecting all of their pent-up emotions onto that boxing match coming over the radio. The sports arena became just another part of the turf where the struggle for justice is carried on in this country.

One of the most poignant moments of ideological unveiling comes when Angelou describes her graduation exercises of 1940 at Lafayette County Training School. As she listens to the condescending and racist manner in which Mr. Edward Donleavy, the featured speaker, insulted the intelligence of her class, hearing the approving "amens" of her elders as he made his invidious comparisons with Central, the white school of the area, Angelou, a young sensitive Black female, could only think: "It was awful to be Negro and have no control over my life. It was brutal to be young and already trained to sit quietly and listen to charges brought against my color with no chance of defense. We should all be dead. I thought I should like to see us all dead, one on top of the other." (*C.B.*, p. 153)

And here the sense of collective responsibility, a sensibility charged by the disparagement of the group, is reflected. In the impotence of childhood there is nothing she can do, but the charges which have been leveled against her people will not be soon forgotten.

Indeed, the act colors the texture of her world; she realizes the emptiness of the sentiments which were expressed in the valedictory address: "I am master of my fate, I am captain of my soul." Observing the inherent falsehood of the statement "To be or not to be," she could only observe in ironic tones: "Hadn't he heard the whitefolks? We couldn't be, so the question was a waste of time." (*C.B.*, p. 154) It is out of this web of reality that she takes her first, fumbling steps toward her social development in Stamps, Arkansas.

According to the text, then, the major crime of the society is that it attempts to reduce all Negroes to a sense of impotence and nothingness. This is the internal "rust" which threatens the "personhood" of Black people (young and old) in all of America. It is the inherent homicidal tendency of an oppressive and racist society which pushes these young people to the brink of spiritual waste and physical destruction. For Maya, such a milieu becomes the point of departure from which she struggles to salvage a sense of dignity and personhood, the necessary prerequisite before any sense of femaleness can be expressed.

Like Linda Brent, Maya Angelou understands that to be Black and female is to be faced with a special quality of violence and violation. This peculiarity is brought into sharp focus when Maya goes to live with her mother and is subsequently raped by her mother's boyfriend. When she is faced with this catastrophe, her first reaction is to withdraw into herself. Yet because of the strength of her individual will, she is able to work herself back to a point where she can function in a seemingly productive manner in her social world. Nevertheless, the rape of this eight-year-old by an almost impotent adult Black male—who, it would seem, was unable to enjoy a relatively mature and respectful relationship with an adult Black woman—can be seen as symbolic of only one aspect of this internal dimension of Black life.

Earlier, I suggested that the works of the Black women writers of this period (either at the autobiographical or the novelistic level) were meant to examine more particularly the shortcomings of Black people at the level of their domestic lives. It is almost as if Angelou wants to suggest that the power, the energy, and the honesty which characterized our examination of our relationship with our oppressor (i.e., at the external level) must now be turned inward in an examination of some of the problems which seem to have inhibited our own level of social development and our quest for liberation. In other words, the problem of Afro-American liberation is to be seen as both an internal and an *external* reality, the former of which must be our exclusive concern. It is this internal probing which characterizes this work (*C.B.*) and marks the writings of the Black female writer.

One cannot, however, simply read the shortcomings of Black life back into the text and forget the complicity of white society, which is the major causative agent of Black denigration. On the larger canvas from which this life is drawn, the villain is to be recognized as a society which reduces men to impotence, women to lives of whoredom, and children to victimization by their fathers' lust and impotence. Indeed, it is the perception of what constitutes femininity and beauty which leads Maya into a sexual liaison that eventually produces an unplanned pregnancy. Certainly at the age of sixteen she was not prepared financially or emotionally to take care of a child.

But to argue for the cruelty and brutality of the society does not deny the episodes of beauty which relieve the monotony of life in Stamps or the violence of California. Nor can one deny the progressive tendency of the religious life of Stamps's Black community. It is to argue, however, that the cruelty so overwhelms the sensibility of the Black person in the South that it makes it very difficult for him/her to exist in the society. For a Black woman it further demonstrates the pain which growth and awareness demand. As Angelou says: "Without willing it, I had gone from being ignorant of being ignorant to being aware of being aware. And the worst part of my awareness was that I didn't know what I was aware of." (*C.B.*, p. 230) This realization of her status is bought at a price: her subjection to the tripartite force of which she speaks (masculine prejudice, white illogical hate, and Black powerlessness).

One of the shortcomings of the text revolves around the manner in which the story is told from the point of view of an adult, who imposes the imagination, logic, and language of an adult upon the work and thus prevents the reader from participating in the unfolding of childhood consciousness as it grows into maturity. The tone of the work is even and constant, which causes the text to be almost predictable in its development. The rationalization of later years tends almost to destroy the flow of the text. Indeed many times one is forced to question the authenticity of her response to incidents in her life.

Such an occasion occurs when Angelou offers what she considers an ethical response to the dehumanization and exploitation of Blacks. Speaking of the "Black underground," she contends:

> It wasn't possible for me to regard them as criminals or be anything but proud of their achievements.
>
> The needs of a society determine its ethics, and in the Black American ghettos the hero is that man who is offered only the crumbs from his country's table but by ingenuity and courage is able to take for himself a Lucullan feast. . . .
>
> Stories of law violations are weighed on a different set of scales in the Black mind than in the white. Petty crimes embarrass the community and many people wistfully wonder why Negroes don't rob more banks, embezzle more funds and employ graft in the unions. "We are the victims of the world's most comprehensive robbery. Life demands a balance. It's all right if we do a little robbing now." [*C.B.*, p. 190–91]

Such attitudes, of course, may extend to most members of the community since so few of us can really compete either legally or equally with our white counterparts. Perhaps the janitor with the robin's-egg-blue Cadillac ought to be laughed at. Yet what makes such an analysis untenable is the fact that ethical postulates in any society usually transcend its mere "needs" if they lead to a reproduction of behavioral patterns that are detrimental to the social development of the group. There is no demonstrable evidence that these people are in fact "heroic" since their activity tends to dehumanize the society and leads to people like Mr. Freeman, her mother's boyfriend, who raped Maya. The inability to transcend the limits which are placed upon Black society by the dominant culture can only lead to the reduction of Black personhood. The characters who are admired are certainly the extensions of Mr. Freeman.

The task of autobiography, then, does not consist in the mere reproduction of naturalistic detail but, because it involves the creative organization of ideas and situations and makes an ethical and moral statement about the society, must generate that which is purposeful and significant for our liberation. In fact the "Principle of Reverse," of which Maya speaks, may help an individual to "get over" initially, precisely because of its essential characteristics, it follows that it can reverse itself and make the apparent victor its victim. Surely, the "Principle of Reverse" may "pry open the door of rejection and [allow] . . . some revenge in the bargain" (*C.B.*, p. 190); it certainly does not and cannot reverse the situation which makes the *violation* and *denigration* of the Black female possible in this society.

The intense solidity and moral center which we observed in *Caged Bird* is not to be found in *Gather Together in My Name* (hereafter referred to as *Gather Together*). The richly textured ethical life of the Black people of the rural South and the dignity with which they live their lives are all but broken as we enter the alienated and fragmented lives which the urban world of America engenders. It is these conditions of alienation and fragmentation which characterize the life of Maya Angelou as she seeks to situate herself in urban California during her sixteenth to nineteenth years.

Gather Together introduces us to a world of prostitution and pimps, con men and street women, drug addiction and spiritual disintegration. Rural dignity gives way to the alienation and destruction of urban life. Maya, the major protagonist, survives, but she is without any sense of purpose and at the end of the work she is forced to concede: "I had no idea what I was going to make of my life, but I had given a promise and found my innocence." (*C.B.*, p. 181) It is as though she had to go to the brink of destruction in order to realize herself; a striking demonstration of how capitalism always and everywhere drives its victim to the end of endurance, so that one must either break under the strains of the society or salvage some dignity from the general confusion.

Gather Together reveals a more selective vision of Afro-American life. In this work, the author writes about one particular kind of Afro-American whom she meets through the kind of work she does. When one considers that Angelou has been a short order cook, a waitress at a nightclub, a madam in charge of her own house of prostitution, a nightclub dancer, a prostitute, and the lover of a drug addict who stole dresses for a living, it becomes apparent that the range of characters whom she encountered during this period of emotional and social upheaval were indeed limited to the declassed elements of the society. And this is what differentiates *Gather Together* from both *Caged Bird* and *Singin' and Swingin' and Gettin' Merry Like Christmas.*

The violation which began in Caged Bird takes on a much sharper focus in *Gather Together.* To be sure, the author is still concerned with the question of what it means to be Black and female in America, but her development is reflective of a particular type of Black woman at a specific moment of history and subjected to certain social forces which assault the Black woman with unusual intensity.

Thus when she arrives in Los Angeles she is aware that even her mother "hadn't the slightest idea that not only was I not a woman, but what passed for my mind was animal instinct. Like a tree or a river, I merely responded to the wind and the tides." (*G.T.*, p. 23) In responding to the indifference of her mother's family to her immaturity, she complains most bitterly, "they were not equipped to understand that an eighteen-year-old mother is also an eighteen-year-old girl." (*G.T.*, p. 27) Yet it is from this angle of vision—that of "a tree in the wind" possessing mostly "animal instinct" to an "unequipped" eighteen-year-old young woman that we must prepare to respond to Angelou's story.

Neither politically nor linguistically innocent, *Gather Together* reflects the imposition of values of a later period in the author's life. Undoubtedly, in organizing the incidents of text in a coherent manner (i.e., having recourse to memorization, selection of incidents, etc.), the fictive principle of which we spoke in our introduction comes fully into play. The fact is that with time the perception of the subject changes, which demonstrates that the autobiographical statement indicates one's *attitudes* toward the fact, rather than the presentation of the facts (i.e., the incidents) as given and unalterable. It is that attitude toward the facts to which critics should respond.

For example, it is difficult for the reader to believe that the young Angelou set out to organize the prostitution of Johnnie Mae and Beatrice because she wanted to take revenge on those "inconsiderate, stupid bitches." (*G.T.*, p. 45) Nor can we, for that matter, accept the fact that she turned tricks for L.D. because she believed that "there was nothing wrong with sex. I had no need for shame. Society dictated that sex was only licensed by marriage documents. Well, I didn't agree with that. Society is a conglomerate of human beings, and that's just what I was. A human being." (*G.T.*, p. 142)

As a justification, it rings too hollow. Society is not a conglomeration merely of human beings. Society is a conglomeration of *social beings* whose acts make them *human* or *nonhuman*. To the degree that those acts *negate* our humanity, they can be considered wrong. To the degree that they *affirm* our humanity they can be considered correct. Such reasoning, though, is only to keep the argument within the context in which Maya Angelou has raised the question.

For me, the importance of the text—its social significance—lies in its capacity to signify to, and from, the larger social context from which it originates. Clearly, *Caged Bird* and *Gather Together* assume their largest meaning or meanings within the context of the larger society. As a consequence, one cannot reduce important attitudes of social behavior by mere strident comments of dissent. Such attitudes and values are derived from the larger social context of Afro-American life. Correspondingly, one questions Angelou's attitude toward Johnnie Mae when she cries out that she has been wounded: "And, ladies, you decided in the beginning that you were going to screw me one way or the other. Look at us now. Who did the screwing?" (*G.T.*, p. 56) It is imperious, but is it correct?

In spite of this imperious attitude, and a certain degree of life-saving pride, Maya is an extremely lonely young woman; a young woman more isolated in bustling California than she was in the quietude of Stamps; a young woman who had to use both that imperious attitude and her life-saving pride to exist. For, as she recounts:

> I had managed in a few tense years to become a snob on all levels, racial, cultural and intellectual. I was a madam and thought myself morally superior to the whores. I was a waitress and believed myself cleverer than the customers I served. I was a lonely unmarried woman and held myself to be freer than the married women I met [*G.T.*, p. 51]

and who, in the middle of the text, is advised by her mother:

> "People will take advantage of you if you let them. Especially Negro women. Everybody, his brother and his dog, thinks he can walk a road in a colored woman's behind. But you remember this, now. Your mother raised you. You're full-grown. Let them catch it like they find it. If you haven't been trained at home to

> their liking tell them to get to stepping." Here a whisper of delight crawled over her face. "Stepping. But not on you." [G.T., p. 108]

Yet precisely because she is drifting through this phase of her life, none of this advice is particularly fruitful to her nor does she seem particularly proud of her activity during those "few tense years" of sixteen through eighteen. Of course, it is not so much that these incidents took place; what is more important is what she made of these incidents in terms of her own social development. While this question cannot be answered here, we hesitate to accept in an unquestioning manner her interpretation of what these events meant to her life.

Finally, two horrendous and dramatic incidents make her realize how much on the brink of catastrophe she had been. The kidnapping of her child (i.e., the near-loss of her child, her most important and significant achievement thus far) and her being saved from a life of drugs by the generosity of Troubadour Martin really gave her that rebirth into innocence; a rebirth at a higher level of dialectical understanding.

Yet in a curious way the book seems not to succeed. Its lack of moral weight and ethical center deny it an organizing principle and rigor capable of keeping the work together. If I may be permitted, the incidents of the book appear merely gathered together in the name of Maya Angelou. They are not so organized that they may achieve a complex level of signification. In fact, it is the absence of these qualities which make the work conspicuously weak.

The language has begun to loosen up and this becomes the work's saving grace. Where there were mere patches of beautiful writing in *Caged Bird*, there is a much more consistent and sustained flow of eloquent and almost honey-dipped writing. The simplicity the speech patterns remains, yet there is a much more controlled use of language. The writing flows and shimmers with beauty; only the rigorous, coherent and meaningful organization of experience is missing.

At the end of the work, the author attempts to recover some of the powerful ideological unfoldment of the society which we encountered in *Caged Bird*. Whereas, however, she presented herself as an integral part of the society in *Caged Bird*, in *Gather Together* she separates herself from the daily life and sufferings of her people and projects a strikingly individual ethos:

> The maids and doormen, factory workers and janitors who were able to leave their ghetto homes and rub against the cold-shouldered white world, told themselves that things were not as bad as they seemed. They smiled a dishonest acceptance at their

> mean servitude and on Saturday night bought the most expensive liquor to drown their lie. Others, locked in the unending maze of having to laugh without humor and scratch without agitation, foisted their hopes on the Lord. They shouted loudly on Sunday morning at His goodness and spent the afternoon preparing the starched uniforms to meet a boss's unrelenting examination. The timorous and the frightened held tightly to their palliatives. I was neither timid nor afraid. [G.T., p. 166]

This kind of distance and assumption weakens the work because it begins to rely almost exclusively on individual exploits rather than to reflect the traditional collective wisdom and/or sufferings of the group. Because of this absence, the work reduces itself at times to a titillating account of a personal life bereft of the context of the larger society. The narrowly private existence of the subject is substituted for the personal universalized (which gives such great power to the Afro-American autobiographical statement), and the importance of *Gather Together* is diminished.

The last scene of *Gather Together*, in which Maya is taken to a room of drug addicts (which symbolically is the outer limits of chaos and destruction) is meant to be contrasted with the opening scene of *Caged Bird* (a striking tableau of innocence) in which Angelou identifies very strongly with all of the cultural conceptions which personify the "ideal" and the "real" and the unattainable nature of the former in American life. The horrifying last scene stands as a foreshadowing of the destruction which awaits those who attempt to achieve those ideals which America presents to her children.

Thus, where she announces at the end of *Caged Bird* that she "had gone from being ignorant of being ignorant to being aware," at the end of *Gather Together* she declares for a certain type of innocence which cannot be really regarded in the same light as that which we found at the beginning of *Caged Bird*. It must be regarded as the (re)discovery of that primal innocence, at a higher level of consciousness, which was was lost in her original encounter with the American dream. The sinking into the slime of the American abyss represents the necessary condition of regeneration and (re)birth into a new and, hopefully, more consciously liberated person. Thus, if *Caged Bird* sets the context for the subject, *Gather Together* presents itself as the necessary purgation through which the initiate must pass in order to (re)capture and to (re)define the social self to function in a relatively healthy manner in white America.

Singin' and Swingin' explores the adulthood of Maya Angelou, again major protagonist, as she moves back into and defines herself more centrally within the mainstream of the Black experience. In this work, she encounters the white world in a much fuller, more sensuous manner, seeking to answer, as she does, the major problem of her works: what it means to be Black and female in America. We would see that this quest, in the final analysis, reduces itself to what it means to be Black and person in America; the urgency of being Black and female collapses into what it means to be Black and person. In order to achieve this, the book is divided into two parts: part one, in which the writer works out her relationship with the white American world, and part two, in which she makes a statement about her own development through her participation in the opera *Porgy and Bess*, and her encounter with Europe and with Africa.

Singin' and Swingin' opens with a scene of displacement in which Angelou feels a sense of being "unanchored" as the family bonds of her youth are torn asunder under the impact of urban life in California Under these new circumstances the author examines her feeling and her relationship with the larger white society as she encounters white people on an intimate personal level for the first time. As the reader will recall, Blacks and whites lived separately in Stamps and the occasion for shared and mutual relations did not exist. Before Angelou can enter into any relationship, though, she must dispense with all the stereotypical notions she has about white people. Indeed it is no longer possible to argue: "It wasn't nice to reveal one's feelings to strangers. And nothing on earth was stranger to me than a friendly white woman." (*S. & S.*, p. 5)

As the autobiography gradually unfolds, she observes that most of the stereotypical pictures which she has of whites are designed to protect her feelings from the cruelty of white hate and indifference. Yet as she grows into adulthood, these notions are punctured and eventually discarded, the biggest test coming when she is forced to make a decision about marrying Tosh, a white man, who is courting her through her son. Part of the difficulty arises from Angelou's awareness that whites had violated her people for centuries and that "Anger and guilt decided before my birth that *Black was Black and white was white* and although the two might share sex, they must never exchange love." (*S. & S.*, pp. 27–28; my italics)

Angelou confronts the problem with a sort of evasion when she tells herself that Tosh "was Greek, not white American; therefore I needn't feel that I had betrayed my race by marrying one of the enemy, nor could white Americans believe that I had so forgiven them the past that I was ready to love a member of their tribe." (*S. & S.*, p. 35) She is not entirely satisfied by the truce she makes with her Blackness and for the rest of her marriage has to contend with the guilt created by her liaison with a white male.

With the end of her marriage, the tears came and the fright that she would be cast into "a maelstrom of rootlessness" (*S. & S.*, p. 44) momentarily embroidered her mind. Soon, however, it gave way to the knowledge that she would be ridiculed by her people in their belief that she was another victim of a "white man [who] had taken a Black woman's body and left her hopeless, helpless and alone." (*S. & S.*, p. 45) At the end of this encounter, however, she would be better prepared to deal with her own life, having gained a certain entrance to the white world and possessing, already, the stubborn realities of Black life.

One of the significant facets of the author's relationship to Tosh revolves around the manner in which she effaces her own identity within the framework of the marriage. But the compromises which she makes to secure a stronger marriage cannot be seen only in the context of the *subject*-ion of wife to husband or Black female to white male. It can also be read as the subjection of the central values of the Black world (and, as a consequence, of the Black woman) to the dominant totality of white values.

In this context, it is to be noted that in spite of the fact that Angelou finds many aspects of white culture objectionable, most of the dominant images of perfection and beauty remain fashioned by the ethos of white society. Yet the tensions which keep the first section of the work together center around the general tendency of her wanting to be absorbed into the larger ambit of American culture (i.e., white culture) and her struggle to maintain a sense of her Black identity.

Against this tension of *absorption* versus *indentity* (i.e., nonabsorption), the writer, as major protagonist, posits her first attempt at an honest relationship with a white person within a structure of antagonism. This encounter occurs when Jorrie and her friends offer Angelou their friendship in a free, and unencumbered manner. Her first response is:

> My God. My world was spinning off its axis, and there was nothing to hold on to. Anger and haughtiness, pride and prejudice, my old back-up team would not serve me in this new predicament. *These whites were treating me as an equal as if I could do whatever they could to. They did not consider that race, height, or gender or lack of education might have crippled me and that I should be regarded as someone invalided.* [*S. & S.*, p. 84; my italics]

This free and equal relationship is significant to her in that it represents an important stage of her evolution toward adulthood.

With her success at the Purple Onion nightclub, another career began for Angelou, one that launched her into a role in the opera *Porgy and Bess.*

As Angelou begins the second phase of her development (i.e., her evolution toward adulthood) her Southern origins became the necessary basis on which she begins to evaluate the major transformations which have taken place in her life thus far. Enjoying the hospitality of her new friend Yanko Varda aboard his yacht, she reveals a dimension of this new awareness:

> I excused myself from the table and went to stand on the deck. The small, exclusive town of Tiburon glistened across the green-blue water and I thought about my personal history. Of Stamps, Arkansas, and its one paved street, of the segregated Negro school and the bitter poverty that causes children to become bald from malnutrition. Of the blind solitude of unwed motherhood and the humiliation of prostitution. Waves slapped at the brightly painted catamaran tied up below me and I pursued my past to a tardy marriage which was hastily broken. And the inviting doors to newer and richer worlds, where the sounds of happiness drifted through closed panels and the doorknobs came off in my hands. [*S. & S.*, p. 124]

The identification of her people's sufferings in the minds of the ordinary European, their immediate identification of her with Joe Louis, the enthusiastic manner in which the Europeans welcomed the *Porgy* cast and the spirituals of her people, led to some of the most revealing moments of her development. The recognition that "Europeans often made as clear a distinction between Black and white Americans as did the most confirmed Southern bigot . . . [in that] Blacks were liked, whereas white Americans were not" (*S. & S.*, pp. 164–65) did much to raise her self-esteem and a recognition of her emergent place in the world.

Her visit to Africa added to that sense of self-worth; her link to the past and herself were complete. In Africa she had found that sense of self-esteem which white America had tried to deny her from the day she was born. She had resumed to her people.

Paradoxically enough, it was in Africa, amid the beggars of Egypt, where she realized the specificity of her Americanness. As she says, "I was young, talented, well-dressed, and whether I would take pride in the fact publicly or not, I was an American." (*S. & S.*, p. 230) Yet the manner in which she and her Black colleagues resisted the sights and practices of enslavement of their fellow Blacks in Egypt demonstrated an identity of common suffering and fraternal solidarity which identified them with the larger community of Africa and its diaspora.

It is, however, the success of *Porgy* which seemed paradigmatic of her evolution as an autonomous and fully liberated person. The pride which she takes in her company's professionalism, their discipline onstage, and the wellspring of spirituality that the opera emoted, all seem to conduce toward an organic harmony of her personal history as it intertwined with the social history of her people. The triumph of *Porgy*, therefore, speaks not only to the dramatic success of a Black company, it speaks, also, to the personal triumph of a remarkable Black woman. *Singin' and Swingin'* is a celebration of that triumph.

In 1970 Maya Angelou produced her first work, a volume concerned with what it meant to be Black and female in America. By 1976 she had enlarged her concerns to address what it meant to be Black and person in America, given the social, political, and economic constraints which militate against any achievement in contemporary America.

PRISCILLA R. RAMSEY

Transcendence: The Poetry of Maya Angelou

ABSTRACT

Maya Angelou's autobiographies present a dislocated self image, one which becomes new and assertive as she transcends the singular self through a wide and compassionate direct assertion of her statements against political injustice. Her love poetry suggests her relationship to a world which can be stultifying, mystifying and oppressive, but one she will not allow to become these things and overwhelm her. The voyage through her life has not been filled with soft and pliable steps each opening into another opportunity for self acceptance and yet she has filled that voyage with fantasy, song, hope and the redefinition of her worlds view through art.

Maya Angelou's physical shifts from Stamps, Arkansas' Lafayette County Public School to the Village Gate's stage in Manhattan and from New York to a teaching podium at Cairo University in Egypt represent an intellectual and psychological voyage of considerable complexity—one of unpredictably erratic cyclic movement. She has chronicled some of this voyage in her three autobiographies: *I Know Why the Caged Bird Sings* [1], a bestseller (in 1970),

Gather Together in My Name (1974) [2], and *Singin' and Swingin' and Gettin' Merry Like Christmas* (1976) [3]. Her final and most recent autobiography is *The Heart of a Woman* (1982) [4]. Additionally she has written three collections of poetry: *Oh Pray My Wings Are Gonna Fit Me Well* (1975) [5], *And Still I Rise* (1971) [6], and *Just Give Me a Cool Drink of Water 'fore I Die* (1971) [7].

In addition to her full length creative writing there have been so many additional accomplishments characterized by so much variety one can only speak of them superficially in this limited space. After acting in "Cabaret for Freedom," she wrote the original television screen play for "Georgia, Georgia." Angelou performed on the stage in Genet's "The Blacks" and Sophocles' "Ajax." Additionally, she explored the parallels between American life and African tradition in a ten-part series she wrote for national television in the 1960's. She worked as a journalist for national newspapers in both Ghana and Cairo.

The public achievements have been many and yet the private motivation out of which her writing generates extends beyond the mere search for words as metaphors for purely private experience. Her poetry becomes both political and confessional. Significantly, one sees in her autobiographies a role-modeling process—one paradigmatic for other women—while not allowing the didactic to become paramount in either the poetry or the autobiographies.

Her autobiographies and poetry reveal a vital need to transform the elements of a stultifying and destructive personal, social, political and historical milieu into a sensual and physical refuge. Loneliness and human distantiation pervade both her love and political poetry, but are counterposed by a glorification of life and sensuality which produces a transcendence over all which could otherwise destroy and create her despair. This world of sensuality becomes a fortress against potentially alienating forces, i.e., men, war, oppression of any kind, in the real world. This essay examines the outlines of this transcendence in selected examples from her love and political poetry with additional thought and experience where relevant, from her autobiographical narratives.

Drawing upon her scholarly and gifted understanding of poetic technique and rhetorical structure in modern Black poetry, Ruth Sheffey explains:

> Genuine rhetoric, indeed all verbal art, coexists with reason, truth, justice. All of the traditions of rational and moral speech are allied to the primitive idea of goodness, to the force of utterance. Because the past is functional in our lives when we neither

> forget it nor try to return to it, the new Black voices must reach the masses in increasingly communal ways, must penetrate those hidden crevices of our beings only recognizable and reachable by poetry [8].

Professor Sheffey speaks here to the fundamental meaning and significance Black poetry holds for its private community. Sheffey's remarks could not more appropriately describe Maya Angelou's poetic voice in terms of motive, content and audience. By way of example consider:

No No No No

No
the two legg'd beasts
that walk like men
play stink finger in their crusty asses
while crackling babies
in napalm coats
stretch mouths to receive
burning tears
on splitting tongues
JUST GIVE ME A COOL DRINK OF WATER 'FORE I DIE

No
the gap legg'd whore
of the eastern shore
enticing Europe to COME
in her
and turns her pigeon shit back to me
to me
Who stoked coal that drove the ships
which brought her over the sinnous cemetery
Of my many brothers

No
the cocktailed afternoons
of what can I do.
In my white rayed pink world.
I've let your men cram my mouth
with their black throbbing hate
and I swallowed after

I've let your mammies
steal from my kitchens
(I was always half-amused)
I've chuckled the chins of
your topsy-haired pickaninnies.
What more can I do?
I'll never be black like you.
(Hallelujah)

No
the red-shoed priests riding
palanquined
in barefoot children country.
the plastered saints gazing down
beneficently
on kneeling mothers
picking undigested beans
from yesterday's shit.

I have waited
toes curled, hat rolled
heart and genitals
in hand
on the back porches
of forever
in the kitchens and fields
of rejections
on the cold marble steps
of America's White Out-House
in the drop seats of buses
and the open flies of war

No More
The hope that
the razored insults
which mercury slide over your tongue
will be forgotten
and you will learn the words of love
Mother Brother Father Sister Lover Friend

My hopes
dying slowly
rose petals falling
beneath an autumn red moon
will not adorn your unmarked graves

My dreams
lying quietly
a dark pool under the trees
will not carry your name
to a forgetful shore
And what a pity

What a pity
that pity has folded in upon itself
an old man's mouth
whose teeth are gone
and I have no pity [7, pp. 38–41].

Once having recited the horrors of capitalistic wars, Angelou continues her narrative focusing then on Black people who were forced, for economic reasons, to "stoke" America's coals. (Her money hungry "gapped legg'd whore" has never beckoned to Blacks as she did to Europe's ethnics promising them her materialistic fruits.) From the beginning, slavery defined a Black involuntary coming, one far alienated from an American dream. Rather than enjoy the dream, Black people were relegated to the drudgery of its death and destruction. Despite the fact that Black men stoked the coals that drew the ships which helped make the "gapped legg'd whore" possible, Black historical victimization cannot be undone "assures" the quasi-liberalized persona's voice in the third stanza. This voice echoes values dramatically different from any we have heard up to this point. For this reason its callousness toward the conditions of Black people dramatizes, all the more, its particular irony: the white liberal voice—whose consolation extends compassion only to the point at which it is convenient—no further.

Her metynomic body imagery functions as poetic referent further chronicling and transporting her prophetic message: stop the assault on Black people and recognize their humanness. As prophecy, her succinct assertions for change beginning with napalmed babies, epitomized in hopeful dreams as the poem progresses—disintegrate ironically into the decayed emptiness of an old man's "gaping mouth."

Again Ruth Sheffey seems relevant to the reading of this poem when she explains:

> The audience must read with the poet's passion and reason, must relish his poignant metaphors, his sensitive ironies, his percussive and passionate repetitions, his urgent suppressions, deletions, the wry humor of his syllables and understatements, his paradoxes—"Have you ever said 'Thank you, sir' for an umbrella full of holes?" [8, p. 107]

The audience, a Black one, cannot help but understand the universal message this poem imports. It is a collectively oriented statement (the persona's "I" operating synedochically for the group), and one of hope, although a hope which ironically collapses at poem's end.

A similar transcendence becomes the ironically complicated prophetic message in:

The Calling of Names

He went to being called a Colored man
after answering to "hey nigger,"
Now that's a big jump,
anyway you figger,
        Hey, Baby, Watch my smoke.
From colored man to Negro.

With the "N" in caps
was like saying Japanese
instead of saying Japs.

        I mean, during the war.

The next big step
was change for true
From Negro in caps to
being a Jew.

        Now, Sing Yiddish Mama.

Light, Yello, Brown

and Dark brown skin,
were o.k. colors to
describe him then,

He was a bouquet of Roses.

He changed his seasons
like an almanac,
Now you'll get hurt
if you don't call him "Black"

Nigguh, I ain't playin' this time [7, p. 43].

As significant referents, words are used to recreate a personal reality, but as verbal discourse they remain very close to the writer's understanding of truth. Maya Angelou brings to the audience her own perceptions of historical change and their relationship to a new reality. With the exception of a long ago Phyllis Wheatley, whose poems speak almost exclusively of God, nature and man, few Black artists have focused their poetic gifts outside history, politics and their changing effects upon Black life. Here Maya Angelou engages in this lifelong tradition of speaking to the concerns of a historical and political Black presence in World War II, Voter and Civil Rights legislation of the fifties; finally the Black Power Movement of the sixties—these events name only a few of the historical and political meanings the synedochic imagery of naming has signalled for Blacks in America.

From the ancient African rituals which gave a child a name harmonious with his or her chi to the derogatory epithets coming out of slavery's master-servant relationships—naming has always held a reality redefining importance for black people. It has reached the level contemporarily with the recreation of one's destiny, an incantation signalling control over one's life. Hence the proliferation of African names with significant meanings.

But as the incantation and the structure of the poem's ideas have evolved out of historical and political event, one hears the old degrading epithets merging into new and more positive meanings.

Her title with its article "the" and preposition "of" signal, perhaps, the only formalizing or distancing aesthetic techniques in the poem. Her emphasis is primarily upon the concrete, the substantive movement back to a derogatory black history and a clearly assertive statement about a more positive future. Like many of the poems in this collection this one also works toward the notion of a positive identity, a positive assertion of what and who

Black people have decided they will be. Her formal rhyme scheme here is one in which the initial stanzas rhyme the second and fourth lines, a rhyming pattern more constricted than in much of her other political poetry. Less metaphorical transformation and less abstraction appear in this poem, however. and while that makes it aesthetically less pleasing, its meaning speaks more directly to the concrete issues of evolving importance to Afro-American history and politics. The abstractions of metaphor perhaps then do not apply here.

A self-defining function continues in "When I Think About Myself." We hear the definitions through a narrative she frequently uses in her poetry: Angelou's persona assumes an ironic distance toward the world. As a result, her relationship to the world loses its direct, i.e., literal quality. She steps back into this distance and can laugh at its characteristics no matter how politically and socially devastating:

When I Think About Myself

When I think about myself
I almost laugh myself to death.
My life has been one big joke.
A dance that's walked
A song that's spoke,
I laugh so hard I almost choke
When I think about myself.

Sixty years in these folks' world
The child I works for calls me girl.
I say "Yes Ma'am" for working's sake
Too proud to break,
I laugh until my stomach ache,
When I think about myself.

My folks can make me split my sides,
I laughed so hard I nearly died,
The tales they tell, sound just like lying,
They grow the fruit,
But eat the rind,
I laugh until I start to crying,
When I think about my folks [7, p. 25].

Out of the emotional distance comes the paradox upon which the persona's insights rest. Dances are walked and songs are spoken reinforcing the dialectical nature of this paradox: an illusion which keeps sacrosanct a much more complicated racial reality.

Both Stephen Henderson's *Understanding the New Black Poetry* and Ruth Sheffey argue that the "I" of Black poetry is not a singular or individualistic referent but a symbol for the ideas of a Black collective. With that point in mind, it becomes clear she is ultimately talking about the ironies of economic oppression which trap Black people provided they allow them, i.e., the ironies to define them rather than their gaining the distance from the oppression to define themselves. An unending tension exists between haves and have-nots—one which the have-nots cannot allow to erupt into open violence and conflict (excluding certain mass exceptions like Watts, New York and Washington in the 1960's). Having once gained an understanding of the absurdity, the have-nots gain superiority in that ironic distance which creates freedom and a partial definition of one's superiority over the oppressor's blind myopia. Perhaps as a further illumination of the ideas generating this poem, Maya Angelou told an illustrative story to George Goodman, Jr. who was reviewing her autobiography, "Caged Bird" for the *New York Times* [9, p. 28]. He remarked that Angelou consistently expressed the sickness of racism like a thread running throughout all her work. Her reply took an illustrative form as she told him about an elderly Black domestic worker in Montgomery, Alabama during Martin Luther King's 1955 Montgomery bus boycotts. The worker solemnly assured her white employer that in spite of the boycotts, she had instructed her husband and children to ride the daily busses. Afterwards, behind the closed, protective doors of the kitchen the employer's liberal, more realistic daughter asked the Black woman why she needed to hide the truth (the Black woman had, in reality, told her family to absolutely stay away from public transportation busses in Montgomery). The elderly maid (a prototype not divorced from this poem's persona by any flight of the imagination) told her, "Honey when you have your head in a lion's mouth, you don't jerk it out. You scratch him behind the ears and draw it out gradually." Like the conclusion of the woman's story, this persona speaks a similarly paradigmatic truth in all its ironic and varied implications. Psychological distance becomes the persona's mightiest weapon, a distance born of years of slowly drawing one's head out of the proverbial lion's mouth.

While Maya Angelou's political poetry suggests the irony of emotional distantiation by using bodily imagery as her objective correlative, her love poetry almost equally as often employs this series of patterns to capture an image, an instant, an emotional attitude. Moreover, fantasy often rounds out the missing parts of the human whole when reality fails to explain fully what she sees. Here in the following poem, "To a Man" she explores this mystery, this distantiation from the understanding of a man:

To a Man

My man is
Black Golden Amber
Changing.
Warm mouths of Brandy Fine
Cautious sunlight on a patterned rug
Coughing laughter, rocked on a whirl of French tobacco
Graceful turns on woolen stilts
Secretive?
A cat s eye.
Southern, Plump and tender with navy bean sullenness
And did I say "Tender?"
The gentleness
A big cat stalks through stubborn bush
And did I mention "Amber"?
The heatless fire consuming itself.
Again. Anew. Into ever neverlessness.
My man is Amber
Changing
Always into itself
New. Now New.
Still itself.
Still [7, p. 6]

If indeed this poem talks about a man and not some more hidden and abstract object we cannot define, then "To a Man" explores the mysteries of a baffling and emotionally distant human being through a persona's fantasy, her worshipping recreation of an artifice rather than of any more luminous understanding of his many selves. And while she does not name him in the poem and he could be reminiscent of any of the men she knew, her description of him evokes a picture of Make, a South African freedom fighter and the man who became her second husband. She recounts this marriage and its end in her final autobiography, *The Heart of a Woman*. Whether a husband or not, his mystery constitutes her poem's ostensible statement, through her persona's particular visual gestalt, i.e., approach. The persona's failure to (penetrate) her subject's overpreoccupation with his own personal style as a wall against intimacy becomes a source of the poem's interesting aesthetic and emotional tension. Her subject cannot be captured, i.e., "understood" and he is cut off from the persona's concentrated engagement by this barrier that she creates—his personal style. The word choices she selects to describe or rather, guess at what she comprehends about him are words suggesting the altering and varying nature of his physical and psychic characteristics. She looks at him seeing only the qualities of an ambiance he creates around himself through the deliberateness of his studied poses. He moves "Cat like." She images his moving dynamism concretely in "woolen stilts" which both regalize and thrust him backward spatially and temporally to a time when he could have been a royal African chieftain dancing on tall stilts.

She magnificently combines the auditory, tactile and visual into the imagery of his " . . . coughing laughter rocked on a whirl of French tobacco" graphically capturing what we take to be—given all she has said before—still, his moving and elegant dynamism. His sight, sound, smell—even his smoke concretized in French rather than in some ordinary domestic. This is no:

Country Lover

Funky blues
Keen toed shoes
High water pants
Saddy night dance
Red soda water
and anybody's daughter [6, p. 4].

A man of expediency, the "Country Lover," clearly he is not the sophisticated and subtle, previous "amber" man.

Like a musical recitative, she repeats in the earlier "To a Man," descriptions framed in rhetorical questions drawing attention all the more to his stolid mystery. In using the repeated rhetorical questions, she counterposes her technique against the traditional way in which modern Black poets use repetition. Modern Black poets use repetitious phrasing for emphasis, clarity and to signal an end to complexity. In Angelou's work the rhetorical questions increase tension and complexity and build upon his opaque mystery. Why?

Some of the explanation might lie in the fact that writers often repeat the issues and conflicts of their own lives throughout much of their art until either concrete conditions or the art brings insight and resolution. Witness

Richard Wright's unending preoccupation with the Communist Party's orthodoxy and demanding control over his work, or Gwendolyn Brooks' mid-career, philosophical redirection after attending the Fisk University Black Writer's Conference. The seeds for a similar obsession lie in her autobiographies and project into Angelou's poetry. She berates herself for her overly romantic ability to place men on pedestals, to create a rose-colored fantasy around them at a distance only to later discover her cognitive error. Her relationships with men in "Caged Bird" and "Gather Together" have this fantasy quality where she overelaborates their personalities in her own mind confusing their concrete behaviors with her day-dream. She does this, sometimes out of her own unconscious desire for their unconditional love—wanting almost a symbiotic object-subject attachment to them. In the final analysis, each of these men exploits her because all are morally and characterologically flawed in ways her own emotional neediness causes her to miss as her fantasy life recreates their personalities. One lover, temporarily stationed close to her home in San Diego, uses her companionship while his naval assignment lasts then leaves her. He returns to his wife. A fast living "sugar daddy" cons her into prostitution to "help" him with a non-existent gambling debt. Again concrete conditions force her into looking beneath the surface he presents. She finds that her "giving" provided pretty dresses for his wife. Nothing more! Finally, when at last she marries, and her fantasies tell her she has found nirvana in the white picket fenced-cottage she has dreamed of she learns its hidden price: she will become prisoner rather than mistress of the house and husband.

In her autobiographies, Angelou presents her flaws head-on not once rationalizing away her own complicity or the details of her own mistakes. The irony and wisdom typical of autobiographies written retrospectively bare the exposed nerves, the humiliating flaws of her experience. But this brutal honesty seems part and parcel for Black female autobiography. A Black psychological self gets created who for all its painful error and insight reveals an enduring depth and strength—one at which readers marvel. Mary Burgher confirms the idea when she says:

> Doubtless Maya Angelou . . . and other Black women autobiographers write about experiences more varied, much harsher, and at times more beautiful than most others encounter. They create incisive and sensitive images of womanhood that remain meaningful to all Black women who struggle to come to terms with the hardships and violence just beneath the surface in the Black experience. "The Caged Bird," like other autobiographies

> of Black women, is a valuable resource to the understanding of Black women because it reveals and symbolizes the Black woman's daring act of remaking her lost innocence into invisible dignity, her never-practiced delicacy into quiet grace, and her forced responsibility into unshouted courage [10] .

Throughout Stephen Butterfield's study of Black autobiography he repeatedly voices statements paralleling Mary Burgher's observation on the important role Black autobiographers play as explorers and purveyors of the Black feminine self and its community [11]. Even Maya Angelou herself reinforced this idea in a newspaper interview when she said:

> "Now I'm going to do what I can to help clear the air in Black America, because as I see it, that's what needs to be done. I'm going to write . . . "Caged Bird" . . . [9, p. 28].

Maya Angelou did in her autobiography just what she promised, she did what "needed to be done," in all its complexity. Given the nature of autobiographical rationalization which critics like Roy Pascal and Stephen Butterfield have pointed out in their work, one which demands a certain tendency to under or overemphasize certain elements for the sake of a unified work of art—despite her compelling honesty—still her autobiographies cannot help but suggest parallels—speculative at best between her poetic themes and her autobiographical. These themes, nevertheless, parallel the pattern of fantasy motivated attachment to men as saviors then the inevitable consequent disillusioning disappointment which one finds both in the autobiographical stories of her life and in the themes of her confessional love poetry.

Erik Erikson provides another possible explanation, and while not an infallible one, it might contribute to further understanding the sources of her romanticism. His discussion of the intricate psychoanalytic dynamics of ego experience sheds some light on Angelou's yearning for undifferentiated attachment to men. First he must ascertain the social nature of our worlds—worlds which include the egos of those most significant to us when he explains:

> They (the egos of others) are significant because on many levels of crude or subtle communication my whole being perceives in them a hospitability to the way in which they order their world and include me—a mutual affirmation, which can be depended upon to activate my being as I can be to activate theirs [12, p. 219].

Unfortunately for Angelou, her fantasy of this ego interaction or mutality is often inaccurate where her perception of men is concerned. She perceives them as the complement of her ego dynamic but far too overwhelmingly so. In other words, she becomes too attached to them too quickly before giving them space and time to prove that, indeed, they are her complements. She is repeatedly hurt by men who are far more experienced than she, who are far more able to see her neediness and exploit it before she is able to see it in herself.

The narcissistic male is always the one most attractive to her and the one most mysterious—ultimately he will always turn out to be the man most destructive to her and her capacity to invest too much of her dependency and need in him too quickly. The wonder which underlies her perceptions in "To a Man" are not surprising provided one has read her autobiographies and identified this common psychic pattern she recurringly illustrates. What she identifies as mystery and wonder are part of the guardedness and distance he sustains—keeping her always at a safe length away from himself. One would expect anger from her rather than wonder.

Anger would have been more appropriate toward his self-protection and yet she does not express anger. Perhaps also the absence of anger affirms the passivity Lillian Arensberg has seen in Angelou's writing [13, pp. 273–291]. We must, however, not overlook another important factor which accounts for what may be occurring here from an aesthetic and artistic rather than a purely psychic point of view. Her persona's opportunity to draw attention to it—rather than to her male subject. Thus, in doing this, she can draw upon her female audience's alleged universal bafflement with the mysterious male psyche. The poem would be better called "To a Woman" in that case, if one accepts this less direct reading of the poem.

Again fantasy subsumes reality in the distance-keeping strategy which provides space for her imaginative elaborations:

Remembrance

Your hands easy
weight, teasing the bees
hived in my hair, your smile at the
slope of my cheek. On the
occasion, you press
above me, glowing, spouting
readiness, mystery rapes
my reason.

When you have withdrawn
yourself and the magic, when
only the spell of your
love lingers between
my breasts, then, only
then, can I greedily consume
your presence [7].

She infuses bodily imagery with the poem's primary work as vehicle of expression concluding finally with the notion that her subject's residual, i.e., his memory (her fantasized version of him) is far preferable to his actual presence. Again full physical and psychological mutality are missing, and she can only experience him within her own grasp of what she rounds but he is in her mind rather than in his physical reality after "the occasion" as she so euphemistically alludes to sex. The bees hived in her hair where mystery rapes her reason signals her chaos, her madness and anxiety toward his impending physical engulfment.

Her persona's fear of physical overwhelming and her wish for estrangement from him counterpoints her earlier "To a Man." What seemed the male's distance keeping desire in the former poem becomes what the female persona wants in the second. In either case, the issue in both is the mistrust of intimacy because men are perceived as engulfing rather than mutual. She desires to maintain psychic boundaries fearing her own vulnerability while paradoxically wanting trusting attachment to men.

Finally, she again raises the recutting psychic remoteness idea, the ambiguity which here defines her only possible conception of love's nature within a changing and undecipherable world:

On Diverse Deviations

When love is a shimmering curtain
Before a door of chance
That leads to a world in question
Wherein the macabrous dance
Of bones that rattle in silence
Of blinded eyes and rolls
Of thick lips thin, denying
A thousand powdered moles,
Where touch to touch is feel
And life a weary whore

I would be carried off, not gently
To a shore,
Where love is the scream of anguish.
And no curtain drapes the door [7, p. 18].

The hyperbolic thousand moles further disguising the already cloaked ambiguous nature of things and the door with its drapes torn away all evoke a naked death. Angelou well could be allusively playing here with the Neo-Classical synonymous relationship between death and consummation.

Furthermore, love as intellectual labyrinth becomes the poem's underlying motif, pervading its progressive movement of ideas. Only at poem's end does the resolution come to this Medea-headed series of ambiguous images synodochically representing love. In the last line, love as the scream of anguish—although terrible in itself—at least becomes something more distinct than all of the varying forms it has taken up to this point.

While Maya Angelou's poetry may not have taken us into every nook and cranny of her long and complex life starting with the Lafayette County Training School—its various movements and insights have nonetheless helped us understand the themes, the issues even some of the conflicts which have pervaded her inner life. Thus, while we could not share the objective events in all their entirety (the autobiographies have helped to partially illuminate these), her various poetic stances have given us some lead into parts of that subjective voyage.

Her autobiographies, the clues they give suggest a self image which as Sidonia Smith points out in her essay, "The Song of the Caged Bird: Maya Angelou's Quest after Self-Acceptance," provides Angelou a strategy for attempting to answer her fundamental and basic questions about the self [14]. Moreover, that self determines the pattern of her writing as Smith also summarily points out. Her autobiographies do indeed present a dislocated self image. But that self image becomes a new and assertive one as she transcends the singular self through a wide and compassionate direct assertion of her statements against political injustice. Her love poetry—on the other hand—suggests her relationship to a world which can be stultifying, mystifying and oppressive, but one she will not allow to become these things and overwhelm her. The voyage through her life has not been filled with soft and pliable steps each opening into another opportunity for self acceptance. Her voyage has instead been anything but that and yet she has filled those voids with fantasy, song, hope and the redefinition of her world's view through art.

CHRISTINE FROULA

The Daughter's Seduction: Sexual Violence and Literary History

> A still, small voice has warned me again to postpone the description of hysteria.
> [FREUD to Fliess, January 1, 1896]

> I felt sorry for mama. Trying to believe his story kilt her.
> [ALICE WALKER'S Celie]

In her speech before the London/National Society for Women's Service on January 21, 1931, Virginia Woolf figured the woman novelist as a fisherwoman who lets the hook of her imagination down into the depths "of the world that lies submerged in our unconscious being. "Feeling a violent jerk, she pulls the line up short, and the "imagination comes to the top in a state of fury":

> Good heavens she cries—how dare you interfere with me. . . . And I—that is the reason—have to reply, "My dear you were going altogether too far. Men would be shocked." Calm yourself. . . . In fifty years I shall be able to use all this very queer knowledge that you are ready to bring me. But not now. You see I go on, trying to calm her, I cannot make use of what you tell me—about women's bodies for instance—their passions—and so on,

> because the conventions are still very strong. If I were to overcome the conventions I should need the courage of a hero, and I am not a hero. . . .
>
> Very well says the imagination, dressing herself up again in her petticoat and skirts. . . . We will wait another fifty years. But it seems to me a pity.

Woman's freedom to tell her stories—and indeed, as this fable shows, to know them fully herself—would come, Woolf went on to predict, once she is no longer the dependent daughter, wife, and servant. Given that condition, Woolf envisioned "a step upon the stair": "You will hear somebody coming. You will open the door. And then—this at least is my guess—there will take place between you and some one else the most interesting, exciting, and important conversation that has ever been heard" (*Pargiters*, xliv).

But that was to be in "fifty years." In 1931, Woolf still felt a silence even within all the writing by women that she knew—even, indeed, within her own. Woolf's fable of silences that go unheard within women's writing points to a violence that is all the more powerful for being nearly invisible. and it interprets women's silence in literary history as an effect of repression, not of absence. In this essay, I will explore the literary history implied by Woolf's fisherwoman image, reading it backward, through Homer and Freud, to elucidate the "conventions" that bound her imagination; and forward, to contemporary works by women that fulfill Woolf's "guess" that women would soon break a very significant silence. Drawing upon feminist analyses of Freud's discovery and rejection of the seduction theory of hysteria, I will argue that the relations of literary daughters and fathers resemble in some important ways the model developed by Judith Herman and Lisa Hirschman to describe the family situations of incest victims: a dominating, authoritarian father; an absent, ill, or complicitous mother; and a daughter who, prohibited by her father from speaking about the abuse, is unable to sort out her contradictory feelings of love for her father and terror of him, of desire to end the abuse and fear that if she speaks she will destroy the family structure that is her only security. By aligning a paradigmatic father-daughter dialogue in Homer's *Iliad* with Freud's dialogue with the hysterics, we can grasp the outline of what I shall call the hysterical cultural script: the cultural text that dictates to males and females alike the necessity of silencing woman's speech when it threatens the father's power. This silencing insures that the cultural daughter remains a daughter, her power suppressed and muted; while the father, his power protected, makes culture and history in his own image. Yet, as the hysterics' speech cured their symptoms, so women, telling stories formerly repressed, have begun to realize the prediction of Woolf's fisherwoman. Maya Angelou's *I Know Why the Caged Bird Sings* (1969) and Alice Walker's *The Color Purple* (1982) exemplify the breaking of women's forbidden stories into literary history—an event that reverberates far beyond their heroes' individual histories to reshape our sense of our cultural past anti its possible future directions.

Cultural Fathers and Daughters: Some Interesting Conversations

What is the fisherwoman's story, the one that got away? The answer I wish to pursue begins with the earliest conversation between man and woman in our literary tradition, that between Helen and Priam in the *Iliad*, book 3. Although readers tend to remember the Helen of the *Iliad* as silent—beauty of body her only speech—the text reveals not Helen's silence but her silenc*ing*. As they stand upon the city wall gazing down at the battlefield, the Trojan king and patriarch Priam asks Helen to point out to him the Greek heroes whose famous names he knows. Her answer exceeds Priam's request:

> "Revere you as I do,
> I dread you, too, dear father. Painful death
> would have been sweeter for me, on that day
> I joined your son, and left my bridal chamber,
> my brothers, my grown child, my childhood friends!
> But no death came, though I have pined and wept.
> Your question, now: yes, I can answer it:
> that man is Agamemnon, son of Atreus,
> lord of the plains of Argos, ever both
> a good king and a formidable soldier—
> brother to the husband of a wanton . . .
> or was that life a dream?"

Helen first invokes her own fear of and reverence for Priam. But this daughterly homage to her cultural father only frames her expression of her longing for her former life and companions. Helen, however, is powerless to escape the male war economy that requires her presence to give meaning to its conflicts, and so she translates her desire for her old life into a death wish that expresses at once culturally induced masochism and the intensity of her resistance to her own entanglement in the warriors' plot. Priam appears to reply only to the words that answer his query:

> The old man gazed and mused and softly cried
> "O fortunate son of Atreus! Child of destiny,
> O happy soul! How many sons of Akhaia
> serve under you! In the old days once I went
> into the vineyard country of Phrygia
> and saw the Phrygian host on nimble ponies,
> . . . .
> And they allotted me as their ally
> my place among them when the Amazons
> came down, those women who were fighting men;
> but that host never equaled this,
> the army of the keen-eyed men of Akhaia.'
>
> [*Iliad*, 74]

Priam seems not to notice Helen's misery as he turns to imaginary competition with the admired and envied Agamemnon. What links his speech to Helen's, however, is the extraordinary fact that the occasion he invokes as his most memorable experience of troops arrayed for battle is a battle against the Amazons. That Amazons come to his mind suggests that, on some level, he *has* heard Helen's desires. Priam's speech recapitulates his conflict with Helen, and hers with Greek culture, as an archetypal conflict between male and female powers. Significantly, Priam does not say which of these forces triumphed. But in leaving the action suspended, he connects past with present, the Amazons' challenge with this moment's conflict between his desires and Helen's who, merely in having desires that would interfere with her role as battle prize, becomes for Priam the Amazon.

What does it mean that Helen should become the Amazon in Priam's imagination? Page duBois and William Blake Tyrrell analyze the Amazon myth as a representation of female power that has escaped the bounds within which Greek culture, specifically the marriage structure, strives to contain it. The Amazon myth, Tyrrell writes, is about daughters, warriors, and marriage. It projects male fear that women will challenge their subordinate status in marriage and with it the rule of the father. In Varro's account of the mythology of Athens's origins, the female citizens of Athens were, under Cecrops, dispossessed of their social and political authority after they banded together to vote for Athena as their city's presiding deity and brought down Poseidon's jealous wrath: "'They could no longer cast a vote, no new-born child would take the mother's name,' . . [and] they are no longer called Athenians but daughters of Athenians." From the Greek woman's lifelong role of daughter, her deprivation of political, economic, and social power, the Amazon myth emerges as "the specter of daughters who refuse their destiny and fail to make the accepted transition through marriage to wife and motherhood" (*Amazons*, 65). Such unruly daughters threatened to be "rivals of men," "opposed or antithetical to the male as father (*Amazons*, 83). Becoming a rival in the male imagination, the daughter also becomes a warrior—as Helen does to Priam, as Clytemnestra does to Apollo when, in the *Eumenides*, he laments that Agamemnon was not cut down by an Amazon instead of by her, as Dido does to Aeneas in his premonitory conflation of her with Penthesilea in *Aeneid*. These allusions suggest that the Amazon figure, a figment of the male imagination, expresses male desire to contain the threat of a female uprising within the arena of the battlefield; that is, to transform the invisible threat of female revolt into a clear and present danger that males might then band together to combat in the regulated violence of war. In linking Helen with the Amazons, Priam dramatizes the threat that female desire poses to the male war culture predicated on its subjugation. Their conversation replicates the larger design of Homer's epic, which, being 'his" story, not hers, turns the tale of a woman's abduction and silencing into the story of a ten-year war between two male cultures. Priam's battle with the Amazons remains suspended in his speech because that battle has not ended. But in this conversation, it is Priam, the cultural father, who triumphs, while Helen's story, by his refusal to hear it, becomes the repressed but discernible shadow of Priam's own.

Helen's exchange with Priam is one skirmish in her culture's war against the Amazons, and a subsequent conversation between Helen and Aphrodite depicts another battle in the form of a cultural daughter's seduction. Here, Helen opposes Aphrodite's demand that she join Paris in bed while the battle rages outside: "'O immortal madness, / why do you have this craving to seduce me? / . . . Go take your place beside Alexandros! / . . . Be / unhappy for him, shield him, till at last / he marries you—or, as he will, enslaves you. / I shall not join him there!'" (*Iliad*, 81–82). Helen passionately and eloquently resists her cultural fate, but Homer's Olympian magic conquers her. Aphrodite silences Helen and enforces her role as object, not agent, of desire by threatening her: "Better not be so difficult. / . . . I can make hatred for you grow / amid both Trojans and Danaäns, / and if I do, you'll come to a bad end" (*Iliad*, 82). The male-authored goddess, embodying the sublimated social authority of Greek culture, forces Helen to relinquish control over her sexuality to the "higher" power of male culture and, like a complicitous mother, presses her to conform to its rule. Helen easily resists being "seduced," angrily thrusting back upon Aphrodite the role of compliant wife/slave that the goddess recommends to her. But this scene makes no distinction between seduction and rape—between being "led astray" and being sexually violated—for Helen can resist sexual complicity only on pain of being cast out altogether from the social world, which is constructed upon marriage. She can be a faithful wife or a "wanton," a "nightmare," a "whore"; she can be a dutiful daughter or an unruly one. But she cannot act out her own desire as Menelaus and Paris, Agamemnon and Akhilleus, Khryses and Hektor, can theirs. Indeed, if wanton in Troy and wife in the bridal chamber are the only choices her culture allows her, she cannot choose even from these. Whereas Paris can propose to settle the dispute by single combat with Menelaus, or the Trojan elders, seeing Helen on the wall, can murmur "let her go [back to Greece] in the ships / and take her scourge from us" (*Iliad*, 73), there is never a question of Helen's deciding the conflict by choosing between the two men.

Although not literally silenced by Aphrodite's metaphysical violence, Helen, surrendering her sexuality, is simultaneously subdued to her culture's dominant text of male desire. "Brother dear," she tells Hektor,

> dear to a whore, a nightmare of a woman!
> That day my mother gave me to the world
> I wish a hurricane blast had torn me away
> to wild mountains, or into tumbling sea
> to be washed under by a breaking wave,
> before these evil days could come! . . .
>
> [*Iliad*, 152]

Helen's will to escape the warriors' marriage plot here turns against the only object her culture permits: herself. She names herself from its lexicon for wayward daughters and passionately imagines death as her only possible freedom. Using the names her culture provides her, weighted with its judgments, Helen loses power even to name herself, her speech confined between the narrow bounds of patriarchal culture and death. That she imagines her death as an entering into the wild turbulence of nature allegorizes the radical opposition of male culture to female nature which the Greek marriage plot enforces: Helen, the Greeks' most exalted image of woman, is also a powerfully expressive subject who must, because of her power, be violently driven back into nature.

Death failing, Helen fulfills her prescribed role by participating in her culture's metaphysical violence against herself: "You [Hektor] are the one afflicted most / by harlotry in me and by his madness, / our portion, all of misery, given by Zeus / that we might live in song for men to come" (*Iliad*,

153). She sacrifices herself upon the altar of patriarchal art, a willing victim who not only suffers but justifies her culture's violence. (Men too suffer the violence of the Greek marriage plot—Helen's "we" includes Hektor—but whereas Hektor resists Andromakhe's pleas and follows his desire for honor into battle, Helen's and Andromakhe's desires are entirely ineffectual.) If the poem, like the war, seems to glorify Helen, in fact she and all the female characters serve primarily to structure the dynamics of male desire in a culture that makes women the pawns of men's bonds *with each other* and the scapegoats for their broken allegiances. The poem's opening scene portrays woman's role in Greek culture as the silent object of male desire, not the speaker of her own. While Agamemnon and Akhilleus rage eloquently over their battle prizes Khryseis and Briseis, the women themselves do not speak at all. They are as interchangeable as their names make them sound, mere circulating tokens of male power and pride—as Akhilleus's apology to Agamemnon upon rejoining the battle confirms: "Agamemnon, was it better for us / in any way, when we were sore at heart, / to waste ourselves in strife over a girl? / If only Artemis had shot her down / among the ships on the day I made her mine, / after I took Lyrnessos!" (*Iliad*, 459).

The *Iliad* suggests that women's silence in culture is neither a natural nor an accidental phenomenon but a cultural achievement, indeed, a constitutive accomplishment of male culture. In Helen's conversations, Homer writes the silencing of woman into epic history as deliberate, strategic, and necessary—a crucial aspect of the complex struggle that is the epic enterprise. In Helen the *Iliad* represents the subjugation of female desire to male rule by means of a continuum of violence, from physical abduction to the metaphysical violence that Greek culture exerts against woman's words and wishes. To a greater extent than we have yet realized, Homer's epic is about marriage, daughters, and warriors. It is about the Amazon.

The *Iliad* is an ancient text, and we have moved very far from the world that produced it—a fact often invoked to distance readers from the violence against women in which the poem participates. But if we set Helen's conversations next to a powerful analogue of our century, Sigmund Freud's dialogues with hysterics and with the phenomenon of hysteria, the paradigmatic force of her "abduction" into the cultural father's script becomes apparent. As the *Iliad* tells the story of a woman's abduction as a male war story, so Freud turned the hysterics' stories of sexual abuse into a tale to soothe a father's ear. And just as Priam's repressed fears seep into his speech in his allusion to the Amazons, so Freud's repression of the daughter's story generates symptomatic moments that "chatter through the fingertips of his psychoanalytic theory.

Freud's conversations with hysterical patients began in the 1880s. At first, Freud, unlike Priam, was able to hear his patients' stories, and he found that in every case, analysis elicited an account of sexual abuse suffered in childhood at the hands of a member of the patient's own family—almost always the father, as he belatedly reported. On this evidence, Freud developed his "seduction theory"—the theory that hysterical symptoms have their origin in sexual abuse suffered in childhood which is repressed and eventually assimilated to later sexual experience. Freud first formulated the seduction theory in a letter to his colleague and confidant Wilhelm Fliess in October 1895, and he presented it to the Vienna psychiatric establishment on April 21, 1896, in a paper titled "The Aetiology of Hysteria." The paper, Freud wrote to Fliess, "met with an icy reception," summed up in Krafft-Ebing's dismissal of it as "a scientific fairytale" (*Origins*, 167n.). For a time Freud pursued the research by which he hoped to prove the seduction theory, writing to Fliess in December 1896: "My psychology of hysteria will be preceded by the proud words: "*Introite et hic dii sunt* [Enter, for here too are gods]" (*Origins*, 172). His pride in his discovery was short-lived, however, for within a year, he would write again to confide "the great secret which has been slowly dawning on me in recent months. I no longer believe in my *neurotica*" (*Origins*, 215). From this point, Freud went on to found psychoanalytic theory upon the oedipal complex.

Historians of psychoanalysis consider Freud's turn from the seduction theory to the oedipal complex crucial to the development of psychoanalysis. Anna Freud wrote that "keeping up the seduction theory would mean to abandon the Oedipus complex, and with it the whole importance of phantasy life. . . . In fact, I think there would have been no psychoanalysis afterwards." But a more critical reading of Freud's abandonment of his seduction theory has emerged from feminist scholarship over the last decade. Several critics have argued—Luce Irigaray from feminist theory, Alice Miller as well as Herman and Hirschman from clinical evidence, Marie Balmary from a psychoanalytic reading of the "text" of Freud's life and work, Florence Rush and Jeffrey Moussaieff Masson from historical evidence, among others—that Freud turned away from the seduction theory not because it lacked explanatory power but because he was unable to come to terms with what he was the first to discover: the crucial role played in neurosis by the abuse of paternal power.

For purposes of the present argument, the issue is best put in terms of credit or authority: the hysterics, Breuer's and his own, confronted Freud with the problem of whose story to believe, the father's or the daughter's. From the first, Freud identified with the hysterics strongly enough that he could hear what they told him. Yet, although he could trace the etiology of hysteria to sexual abuse suffered in childhood, Freud could not bring himself to draw the conclusion that his evidence presented to him that the abuser was most often the father. The cases of Anna O., Lucy R., Katharina, Elizabeth von R., and Rosalia H. described in *Studies on Hysteria* all connect symptoms more or less closely with fathers or, in Lucy's case, with a father substitute. In two cases, however, Freud represented the father as an uncle, a misrepresentation that he corrected only in 1924; and his reluctance to implicate the father appears strikingly in a supplemental narrative of an unnamed patient whose physician-father accompanied her during her hypnotic sessions with Freud. When Freud challenged her to acknowledge that "something else had happened which she had not mentioned," she "gave way to the extent of letting fall a single significant phrase; but she had hardly said a word before she stopped, and her old father, who was sitting behind her, began to sob bitterly." Freud concludes: "Naturally I pressed my investigation no further; but I never saw the patient again." Here Freud's sympathies divide: had the father not intruded, Freud undoubtedly would have heard her out as he had Katharina; but, made aware of the father's anguish, he "naturally" cooperated with it even to the extent of repressing from his text the "single significant phrase" that may have held the key to her neurosis.

In larger terms, too, Freud's work on hysteria posed the dilemma of whether to elicit and credit the daughter's story, with which rested, as other cases had shown, his hope of curing her limping walk; or to honor the father's sob, which corroborated even as it silenced the girl's significant word. The list of reasons Freud gave Fliess for abandoning the seduction theory is, as Balmary points out, not very compelling; indeed, it contradicts the evidence of *Studies on Hysteria*. Freud complains that he cannot terminate the analyses, even though several cases (notably Anna O./Bertha Pappenheim, who was Breuer's patient) are there described as terminating in a lasting cure. He complains of not being able to distinguish between truth and "emotionally charged fiction" in his patients, even though he had linked the vanishing of symptoms with the recovery of traumatic experience through memory—whether narrated with apparent fidelity to literal fact, as in Katharina's case, or in dream imagery, as by Anna O., whom Breuer wrote that he always found "entirely truthful and trustworthy" (*Studies on Hysteria*, 43). And Freud claims to have been frustrated in his attempt to recover the buried trauma, despite his success in some instances. Only one item on the list is upheld by the earlier cases: "the astonishing thing that in every case *my own not excluded*, blame was laid on perverse acts by the father, and realization of the unexpected frequency of hysteria, in every case of which the same thing applied, though it was hardly credible that perverted acts against children were so general."

The problem was precisely that sexual abuse of children by fathers appeared "so general." In the years between conceiving and abandoning the seduction theory, Freud was engaged in his own self-analysis, in which he discovered, through dreams, his own incestuous wishes toward his daughter Mathilde and, through symptoms exhibited by his siblings, the possibility that his father Jakob had abused his children. Jakob himself died on October 23, 1896, initiating in Freud a complex process of mourning that ultimately strengthened his idealization of his father. Freud's dream of Irma's injection, which concerned a patient who shared his daughter Mathilde's name, superimposed a destructive father-daughter relationship upon one between physician and patient. Nor could the father's fault be contained within the bounds of the hysterics' individual histories. Recent research, for example Herman's, has traced many continuities between the problem of father-daughter incest and the dominance of male/paternal authority in society as a whole; Freud too faced implications that would have changed the focus of his work from individual therapy to social criticism. The "icy reception" with which the professional community of fin de siècle Vienna greeted his 1896 lecture, which did not explicitly implicate fathers in hysteria, was indication enough that Freud, if he credited the daughters, would risk sharing their fate of being silenced and ignored. The stakes for Freud were very high, for the fathers who paid him his (at that time meager) living also represented, as had Jakob, the privileged place that Freud, as a male, could himself hope to attain in the culture. Acceding, upon Jakob's death, to the place of the father, he acceded also to the father's text, which gave him small choice but to judge the daughters stories "hardly credible."

Yet Freud could not easily call in the credit that he had already invested in the daughters' stories. As Jane Gallop notes, he continued to speak of "actual seduction" long after he had supposedly repudiated it, with the difference that he now deflected guilt from the father to, variously, the nurse, the mother, and, by way of the oedipal complex, the child herself. Balmary argues persuasively that Freud's own hysterical symptoms grew more pronounced as he undertook to deny what he was the first to discover, that "the secret of hysteria is the father's hidden fault"; and that the texts documenting his turn to the oedipal complex betray that turn as a symptomatic effort to conceal the father's fault. Seduced by the father's sob story, Freud took upon himself the burden his patients bore of concealing the father's fault in mute symptomology. Hysterics, Freud wrote, suffer from reminiscence. As

Priam in his reply to Helen does not forget her words, so Freud in his later writings does not forget the daughter's story but rewrites it as the story of "femininity," attributing to mothers, nurses, and a female "Nature" the damage to female subjectivity and desire wrought by specific historical events. Yet when Freud concludes in "Femininity" that woman has an inferior sense of justice and suggests that the "one technique" she has contributred to culture, the invention of plaiting and weaving, is designed to conceal the shame of her genital lack, it is he who, like Priam, is weaving a cultural text whose obscured but still legible design is to protect the *father* (conceived broadly as general and cultural, that is, as male authority) from suspicion of an insufficiently developed sense of justice. Like Priam, Freud makes subtle war on woman's desire and on the credibility of her language in order to avert its perceived threat to the father's cultural preeminence. If, in doing so, he produces a theory that Krafft-Ebing could have approved, he also composes a genuine "scientific fairytale."

It appears, then, that Freud undertook not to believe the hysterics not because the weight of scientific evidence was on the father's side but because so much was at stake in maintaining the father's credit: the innocence not only of particular fathers—Freud's, Freud himself, the hysterics'—but also of the cultural structure that credits male authority at the expense of female authority, reproducing a social and political hierarchy of metaphorical fathers and daughters. The history of the seduction theory shows Freud's genius, but it also shows his seduction by the hysterical cultural script that protects the father's credit, and Freud's consequent inability, not unlike Helen's, the hysterics', or Woolf's fisherwoman's, to bring the story of sexual abuse and silencing to light. When Helen sublimely paints herself and Hektor as willing victims upon the altar of an art that serves the divine plan of Zeus, "father of gods and men," she speaks this cultural script; as Priam does in reminiscing about Amazons, as the hysterics with their bodily reminiscences and Freud with his theory of femininity did; and as Woolf's fisherwoman does, with her imagination gagged and petticoated in deference to the "conventions."

Women's literary history has important continuities with the actual and imaginative histories told by Homer, Freud, and Herman. Woman's cultural seduction is not merely analogous to the physical abuses that Freud's patients claimed to have suffered but *continuous* with them. Herman shows that the abusive or seductive father does serious harm to the daughter's mind as well as to her body, damaging her sense of her own identity and depriving her voice of authority and strength. For the literary daughter—the woman reader/writer as daughter of her culture—the metaphysical violence against women inscribed in the literary tradition, although more subtle and no less difficult to acknowledge and understand, has serious consequences. Metaphysically, the woman reader of a literary tradition that inscribes violence against women is an abused daughter. Like physical abuse, literary violence against women works to privilege the cultural father's voice and story over those of women, the cultural dauther's and indeed to silence women's voices. If Freud had difficulty telling the difference between his patients' histories and their fantasies, the power of such cultural fantasies as Homer's and Freud's to shape their audiences' sense of the world is self-evident.

But the Freud of 1892 understood the power of language to cure. Woolf, we remember, predicted a moment when women would break through the constraints of the cultural text. If the literary family history resembles the histories Freud elicited from his patients, we could expect the cultural daughter's telling of her story to work not only a "cure" of her silence in culture but, eventually, a more radical cure of the hysterical cultural text that entangles both women and men. To explore these possibilities, I will turn to a daughter's text that breaks even as it represents the daughter's hysterical silence, in doing so, crossing images of literal and literary sexual abuse: Maya Angelou's autobiographical *I Know Why the Caged Bird Sings*.

The Daughter's Story and the Father's Law

Early in her memoir, Angelou presents a brief but rich *biographia literaria* in the form of a childhood romance: "During these years in Stamps, I met and fell in love with William Shakespeare. He was my first white love. Although I enjoyed and respected Kipling, Poe, Butler, Thackeray and Henley, I saved my young and loyal passion for Paul Lawrence Dunbar, Langston Hughes, James Weldon Johnson and W. E. B. DuBois' 'Litany at Atlanta.' But it was Shakespeare who said, 'When in disgrace with fortune and men's eyes.' It was a state with which I felt myself most familiar. I pacified myself about his whiteness by saying that after all he had been dead so long that it couldn't matter to anyone any more." Maya and her brother Bailey reluctantly abandon their plan to memorize a scene from Shakespeare—"we realized that Momma would question us about the author and that we'd have to tell her that Shakespeare was white, and it wouldn't matter to her whether he was dead or not" (*I Know Why*, 11)—and choose Johnson's "The Creation" instead. This passage, depicting the trials attending those interracial affairs of the mind that Maya must keep hidden from her vigilant grandmother, raises the question of what it means for a female reader and fledgling writer to carry on a love affair with Shakespeare or with male authors in general. While the text overtly confronts and disarms the issue of race, the seduction issue is only glancingly acknowledged. But this literary father-daughter romance resonates quietly alongside Angelou's more disturbing account of the quasi-incestuous rape of the eight-year-old Maya by her mother's lover, Mr. Freeman—particularly by virtue of the line she finds so sympathetic in Shakespeare, "When in disgrace with fortune and men's eyes." Mr. Freeman's abuse of Maya occurs in two episodes. In the first, her mother rescues her from a nightmare by taking her into her own bed, and Maya then wakes to find her mother gone to work and Mr. Freeman grasping her tightly. The child feels, first, bewilderment and terror: "His right hand was moving so fast and his heart was beating so hard that I was afraid that he would die." When Mr. Freeman subsides, however, so does Maya's fright: "Finally he was quiet, and then came the nice part. He held me so softly that I wished he wouldn't ever let me go. . . . This was probably my real father and we had found each other at last" (*I Know Why*, 61). After the abuse comes the silencing: Mr. Freeman enlists the child's complicity by an act of metaphysical violence, informing her that he will kill her beloved brother Bailey if she tells anyone what "they" have done. For the child, this prohibition prevents not so much telling as asking, for confused as she is by her conflicting feelings, she has no idea what has happened. One day, however, Mr. Freeman stops her as she is setting out for the library, and it is then that he commits the actual rape on the terrified child, "a breaking and entering when even the senses are torn apart" (*I Know Why*, 65). Again threatened with violence if she tells, Maya retreats to her bed in a silent delirium, but the story emerges when her mother discovers her stained drawers, and Mr. Freeman is duly arrested and brought to trial.

At the trial, the defense lawyer as usual attempts to blame the victim for her own rape. When she cannot remember what Mr. Freeman was wearing, "he snickered as though I had raped Mr. Freeman" (*I Know Why*, 70). His next question, as to whether Mr. Freeman had ever touched her prior to that Saturday, reduces her to confusion because her memory of her own pleasure in being held by him seems to her to implicate her in his crime: "I couldn't say yes and tell them how he had loved me once for a few minutes and how he had held me close. . . . My uncles would kill me and Grandmother Baxter would stop speaking. . . . And all those people in the court would stone me as they had stoned the harlot in the Bible. And mother, who thought I was such a good girl, would be so disappointed" (*I Know Why*, 70–71). An adult can see that the daughter's need for a father's affection does not cancel his culpability for sexually abusing her. But the child cannot resolve the conflict between her desire to tell the truth, which means acknowledging the pleasure she felt when Mr. Freeman gently held her, and her awareness of the social condemnation that would greet this revelation. She knows the cultural script and its hermeneutic traditions, which hold all female pleasure guilty, all too well, and so she betrays her actual experience with a lie: "Everyone in the court knew that the answer had to be No. Everyone except Mr. Freeman and me. . . . I said No (*I Know Why*, 71). But she chokes on the lie and has to be taken down from the stand. Mr. Freeman is sentenced to a year and a day, but somehow manages to be released that very afternoon; and not long thereafter, he is killed by her Baxter uncles. Hearing of Mr. Freeman's death, Maya is overwhelmed with terror and remorse: "A man was dead because I lied" (*I Know Why*, 72). Taking his death as proof that her words have power to kill she descends into a silence that lasts for a year. Like Helen's sacrificial speech, Maya's silence speaks the hysterical cultural script: it expresses guilt and anguish at her own aggression against the father and voluntarily sacrifices the cure of truthful words.

Maya's self-silencing recalls the the link between sexual violation and silence in the archetypal rape myth of Philomela. Ovid's retelling of the Greek myth entwines rape with incest as Tereus, watching Philomela cajole her father into allowing her to visit her sister Procne, puts himself in her father's place: "He would like to be / Her father at that moment, and if he were / He would be as wicked a father as he is a husband." After the rape, in Ovid's story as in Angelou's, the victim's power of speech becomes a threat to the rapist and another victim of his violence: "Tereus did not kill her. He seized her tongue / With pincers, though it cried against the outrage, / Babbled and made a sound like *Father*, / Till the sword cut it off." The tongue's ambiguous cry connects rape/incest with the sanctioned ownership of daughters by fathers in the marriage structure and interprets Procne's symmetrical violation of killing her son Itys: she becomes a bad mother to her son as Tereus has been a bad father to the daughter entrusted to him. In the suspension wrought by metamorphosis, Tereus becomes a war bird and Procne and Philomela become nightingales whose unintelligible song resembles the hysterics' speech. In silencing herself, Maya—who knows why the caged bird sings—plays all the parts in this cultural drama. She suffers as victim, speaks the father's death, and cuts out her own tongue for fear of its crying "Father."

Maya breaks her silence when a woman befriends her by taking her home and reading aloud to her, then sending her off with a book of poems, one of which she is to recite on her next visit. We are not told which poem it was, but later we find that the pinnacle of her literary achievement at age twelve was to have learned by heart the whole of Shakespeare's *Rape of Lucrece*—nearly two thousand lines. Maya, it appears, emerges from her literal silence into a literary one. Fitting her voice to Shakespeare's words, she writes safe limits around the exclamations of her wounded tongue and in this way is able to reenter the cultural text that her words had formerly disrupted. But if Shakespeare's poem redeems Maya from her hysterical silence, it is also a lover that she embraces at her peril. In Angelou's text Shakespeare's Lucrece represents that violation of the spirit which Shakespeare's and all stories of sleeping beauties commit upon the female reader. Maya's feat of memory signals a double seduction: by the white culture that her grandmother wished her black child not to love and by the male culture which imposes upon the rape victim, epitomized in Lucrece, the double silence of a beauty that serves male fantasy and a death that serves male honor. The black child's identification with an exquisite rape fantasy of white male culture violates her reality. Wouldn't everyone be surprised, she muses, "when one day I woke out of my black ugly dream and my real hair, which was long and blond, would take the place of the kinky mass that Momma wouldn't let me straighten? My light-blue eyes were going to hypnotize them. . . . Because I was really white and because a cruel fairy stepmother, who was understandably jealous of my beauty, had turned me into a too-big Negro girl, with nappy black hair, broad feet, and a space between her teeth that would hold a number two pencil" (*I Know Why*, 2). Maya's fantasy bespeaks her cultural seduction but Angelou's powerful memoir, recovering the history that frames it, rescues the child's voice from this seduction by telling the prohibited story.

Re-creating the Universe

If Angelou presents one woman's emergence from the hysterical cultural text, Alice Walker's *The Color Purple* deepens and elaborates its themes to work a more powerful cure. Published in 1982 (right on schedule with respect to Woolf's prediction), Walker's novel not only portrays a cure of one daughter's hysterical silence but rewrites from the ground up the cultural text that sanctions her violation and dictates her silence. Whereas the memoir form holds Angelou's story within the limits of history, Walker stages her cure in the imaginary spaces of fiction. Yet Walker conceived *The Color Purple* as a historical novel, and her transformation of the daughter's story into a fiction that lays claim to historical truth challenges the foundation of the "conventions," social and cultural, that enforce women's silence. Walker retells the founding story of Western culture from a woman's point of view, and in an important sense, her historical novel—already celebrated as a landmark in the traditions of Black women's, Black, and women's writing—also stands in the tradition inaugurated by Homer and Genesis. Her hero Celie is a woman reborn to desire and language; and Walker, while not one with Celie as Angelou is with Maya, is a woman writer whom Woolf might well have considered a hero.

The Color Purple tells the story of a fourteen-year-old daughter's rape by her "Pa." It begins in its own prohibition: its first words, inscribed like an epigraph over Celie's letters, are her "Pa"'s warning, "*You better not never tell nobody but God. It'd kill your mammy*" (*Color*, 11). Thus is Celie robbed, in the name of her mother, of her story and her voice. Later, her pa further discredits her when he hands Celie over to Mr. ______ (ironically reduced to generic cultural father), a widower in need of a wife-housekeeper-caretaker of his children, with the warning: "She tell lies" (*Color*, 18). Isolated, ignorant, and confused, Celie follows her pa's prohibition literally, obediently silencing her speech but writing stumblingly of her bewilderment in letters to God: "Dear God, I am fourteen years old. ~~I am~~ I have always been a good girl. Maybe you can give me a sign letting me know what is happening to me" (*Color*, 11). Celie's rape leaves her with guilt that blocks her words. But through her letter writing she is able at once to follow the letter of the father's law and to tell her story, first to that imaginary listener, the God of her father's command, and later, to the friend who saves her from silence, Shug Avery.

These ends are all the more powerful in that they emerge from Celie's seemingly hopeless beginnings. With the first of Celie's two pregnancies by her pa, he forces her to leave school: "He never care that I love it (*Color*, 19). Celie keeps studying under her younger sister Nettie's tutelage, but the world recedes from her grasp. "Look like nothing she say can git in my brain and stay," Celie writes God. "She try to tell me something bout the ground not being flat. I just say, Yeah, like I know it. I never tell her how flat it look to me" (*Color*, 20). While this passage conveys the pathos of Celie's isolation, it also reveals what will eventually prove the source of her strength, for Celie's eventual emergence from silence, ignorance, and misery depends upon her fidelity to the way things look to her. One important instance is her feeling for her mother, who is too weak and ill to intervene in the incest and who dies soon after Celie's second child is born. "Maybe cause my mama cuss me you think I kept mad at her," Celie tells God. "But I ain't. I felt sorry for mama. Trying to believe his story kilt her" (*Color*, 15).

As Celie never loses her identification with her mother, so she is saved from her isolation by three other women who become her companions and examples and whose voices foil Celie's submissive silence. Sofia, who marries Mr. ______'s son Harpo, is at first a problem for Celie, who tells God: "I like Sofia, but she don't act like me at all. If she talking when Harpo and Mr. ______ come in the room, she keep right on. If they ast her where something at, she say she don't know. Keep talking" (*Color*, 42). When Harpo consults her about how to make Sofia mind, Celie advises: "Beat her" (*Color*, 43)—propounding the cultural script of violent male rule in marriage, the only one she knows. But when Sofia angrily confronts Celie, friendship forms, and Celie begins to abandon her numb allegiance to the father's law. Shug Avery, a brilliant blues singer and Mr. ______'s longtime lover, enters Celie's life when Mr. ______ brings her home ill for Celie to nurse. Like Sofia, Shug talks: "she say whatever come to mind, forgit about polite (*Color*, 73). Mary Agnes, Harpo's girl friend after Sofia's departure, begins, like Celie, as a relatively weak and silent woman. Yet when she is elected to go ask help from the white warden for Sofia in prison, she returns from her mission battered and bruised, and only after some urging—"Yeah, say Shug, if you can't tell us, who you gon tell, God?" (*Color*, 95)—is she able to tell the others that the warden has raped her. Telling the story, she becomes her own authority, symbolized in her self-naming: when Harpo says, "I love you, Squeak," she replies, "My name Mary Agnes" (*Color*, 95).

Mary Agnes's example is important for Celie, who, until now, has buried her story in her letters. One night soon afterward, when their husbands are away, Shug comes into bed with Celie for warmth and company, and Celie tells her everything: "I cry and cry and cry. Seem like it all come back to me, laying there in Shug arms. . . . Nobody ever love me, I say. She say, I love you, Miss Celie. And then she haul off and kiss me on the mouth. *Um*, she say, like she surprise. . . . Then I feels something real soft and wet on my breast, feel like one of my little lost babies mouth. Way after while, I act like a little lost baby too" (*Color*, 108–9). To know all alone, Balmary writes, is to know as if one did not know. To know with another is conscious knowledge, social knowledge, *con-science*. Celie's telling of her story is an act of knowing-with that breaks the father's law, his prohibition of conscience. Knowing her story with Shug begins to heal Celie's long-hidden wounds of body and voice.

The radical conscience of Walker's novel goes beyond restoring Celie's voice to break down the patriarchal marriage plot that sanctions violence against women. This dismantling begins with another wound when Shug and Celie find the letters from Nettie that Mr. ______ has spitefully hidden since the sisters' separation. From them, Celie learns her lost history: that their father had been lynched when they were babies for having a store that did too well; that their mother, then a wealthy widow had lost her reason and married a stranger, the man Celie knew as her " Pa"; that he had given Celie's two children to Samuel and Corrine, the missionaries to whom Nettie had also fled; and that, Corrine having died, Samuel, Nettie, and Celie's children are returning to the United States from their African mission. Celie's first response when she finds the intercepted letters is a murderous fury toward fathers both physical and metaphysical. Shug has to disarm her of the razor she is about to use to kill Mr. ______, and the scales fall from her eyes with respect to the God to whom she has been writing: "Dear God, . . . My daddy lynch. My mama crazy. All my little half-brothers and sisters no kin to me. My children not my sister and brother. Pa not pa. You must be sleep" (*Color*, 163).

With Shug's help, Celie is able to translate her murderous rage into powerful speech and to meet Mr. ______ on the battlefield of language. Patriarchal family rule and patriarchal metaphysics break down simultaneously as Shug and Celie leave Mr. ______'s house for Shug's Memphis estate. Celie's self-assertion is met with scorn by Mr. ______: "Shug got talent, he say. She can sing. She got spunk, he say. She can talk to anybody Shug got looks, he say. She can stand up and be notice. But what you got? You ugly. You skinny. You shape funny. You too scared to open your mouth to people" (*Color*, 186). But Celie's voice gains strength as she comes into possession of her history, and for the first time, she finds words to resist Mr. ______:

> I curse you, I say.
> What that mean? he say.
> I say, Until you do right by me, everything you touch will crumble.
> He laugh. Who you think you is? he say. . . .
> A dust devil flew up on the porch between us, fill my mouth with dirt. The dirt say, Anything you do to me, already done to you.
> Then I feel Shug shake me. Celie, she say. And I come to myself.
> I'm pore, I'm black, I may be ugly and can't cook, a voice say to everything listening. But I'm here.
> Amen, say Shug. Amen, amen. [*Color*, 187]

Celie's curse, which Walker enhances with epic machinery, is powerful. But unlike the razor which Shug takes out of her hand, it does not return Mr. ______'s violence in kind. Instead, the decline of the father's law in Walker's novel creates temporary separate spheres for women and men in which gender hierarchy breaks down in the absence of the "other," enabling women and men eventually to share the world again. Celie's authority is consolidated as she comes into economic independence Earlier, Shug had distracted Celie from her murderous rage toward Mr. _____ by suggesting that the two of them sew her a pair of pants. "What I need pants for?" Celie objects. "I ain't no man" (*Color*, 136). In Memphis, while trying to think what she wants to do for a living, Celie sits "making pants after pants" (*Color*, 190) and soon finds her vocation founding "Folkpants, Unlimited." In this comic reversal, the garment that Celie at first associates strictly with men becomes the means, symbolic and material, of her economic independence and her self-possession.

The magical ease with which Celie emerges from poverty and silence classes Walker's "historical novel" with epic and romance rather than with realist or socialist realist fiction. Walker's Shug has a power that is historically rare indeed, and Celie's and Nettie's inheritance of their father's house, in particular, indulges in narrative magic that well exceeds the requirements of the plot. But Celie's utopian history allegorizes not only women's need to be economically independent of men but the daughter's need to inherit the symbolic estate of culture and language that has always belonged to the father, a "place" in culture and language from which she, like Archimedes, can move her world. When Celie comes into the power of language, work, and love, her curse temporarily comes true. As the daughter learns to speak, Mr. ______ falls into a hysterical depression. Mr. ______'s crisis signals the death of the cultural father whom he had earlier embodied: "Harpo ast his daddy why he beat me. Mr. ______ say, Cause she my wife. Plus, she stubborn. All women good for—he don't finish. He just tuck his chin over the paper like he do. Remind me of Pa" (*Color*, 30). As cultural father, Mr. ______'s law was unspoken, his ways immutable, and his words so close to the patriarchal script that he didn't have to finish his sentences. By the end of the novel, however, Mr. ______ has abandoned that role to become Albert and to "enter into the Creation" (*Color*, 181). By the novel's last scenes, Albert's life is scarcely differentiable from Celie's, and he tells her, "Celie, I'm satisfied this the first time I ever lived on Earth as a natural man" (*Color*, 230).

An important effect of Albert's transition from patriarch to natural man is the abandonment of that strictly literal stake in paternity that the marriage structure serves. As a "natural man," Albert, like everyone else, spends a lot of time concocting devious recipes to hide the taste of yams from Henrietta—who, Celie explains, has to eat yams to control her chronic blood disease but "Just our luck she hate yams and she not too polite to let us know" (*Color*, 222). Henrietta, Sofia's youngest child whose "little face always look like stormy weather" (*Color*, 196), is a crucial figure in the novel. Though Harpo tries to claim her as his sixth child, she is nobody's baby; only Sofia (if anyone) knows who her father is. Nonetheless Harpo, Albert, and everyone else feel a special affection for "ole evil Henrietta" (*Color*, 247), and, as they knock themselves out making yam peanut butter and yam tuna casserole, it becomes apparent that, in Walker's recreated universe, the care of children by men and women without respect to proprietary biological parenthood is an important means of undoing the exploitative hierarchy of gender roles. If Celie's discovery that "Pa not pa" liberates her from the law of the father that makes women and children its spiritual and sexual subjects, Albert, in learning to "wonder" and to "ast" (*Color*, 247) and to care for Henrietta, escapes the confines of the patriarchal role. As the functions of father and mother merge, the formerly rigid boundaries of the family become fluid: Celie, Shug, and Albert feel "right" sitting on the porch together; love partners change with desire; and, most important, children circulate among many parents: Samuel, Corrine, and Nettie raise Celie's; Celie raises Mr. ______'s and Annie Julia's; Sofia, Odessa, and Mary Agnes exchange theirs and the whole community, including the white Eleanor Jane, becomes involved with yams and Henrietta. Whereas, in the patriarchal societies analyzed by Lévi-Strauss, the exchange of women forges bonds between men that support male culture, in Walker's creation story children are the miracle and mystery that bond all her characters to the world, each other, and the future.

Undoing the gender hierarchy necessitates a rewriting of the Creation myth and a dismantling of the hierarchical concepts of God and authority that underwrite them in Western tradition. The God to whom Celie writes her early letters loses credibility once she learns, through Nettie's letters, that nothing is as the law of the father proclaimed it. When Shug hears her venting her wrath, she is shocked: "Miss Celie, You better hush. God might hear you." "Let 'im hear me, I say. If he ever listened to poor colored women the world would be a different place, I can tell you." Shug deconstructs Celie's theology: "You have to git man off your eyeball, before you can see anything a 'tall," she explains. "He on your box of grits, in your head, and all over the radio. He try to make you think he everywhere. Soon as you think he everywhere, you think he God. But he ain't"; "God ain't a he or a she, but a It. . . . It ain't something you can look at apart from everything else, including yourself. I believe God is everything . . . that is or ever was or ever will be. And when you can feel that, and be happy to feel that, you've found It" (*Color*, 175–79). In Walker's cosmos, the monotheistic Western myth of origins gives way to one of multiple, indeed infinite, beginnings that the new myth of Celie's fall and self-redemption celebrates. Hers is not a Creation finished in the first seven days of the world but one in which all creators are celebrated, if at times reluctantly. When Sofia, with what Harpo calls her "amazon sisters," insists on bearing her mother's casket, Harpo asks,

> Why you like this, huh? Why you always think you have to do things your own way? I ast your mama bout it one time, while you was in jail.
>
> What she say? ast Sofia.
>
> She say you think your way as good as anybody else's. Plus, it yours. [*Color*, 196]

Walker echoes this moment in her epigraph, which translates Harpo's "here come the amazons" (*Color*, 198) into: "Show me how to do like you. Show me how to do it" (*Color*, i). She fills her historical novel with creators, authorities, beginnings, "others." Like all authors of epic, she collapses transcendence and history; but her history differs from that of earlier epics. Originating in a violation of the patriarchal law, it undoes the patriarchal cultural order and builds upon new ground. "Womanlike," Walker writes, "my 'history' starts not with the taking of lands, or the births, battles, and deaths of Great Men, but with one woman asking another for her underwear." The violation of "conventions" that this exchange of underwear stages breaks through the patriarchal sexual and spiritual economy, writing into history a story long suppressed and revising history by doing so. Celie's last letter—addressed to "Dear God. Dear stars, dear trees, dear sky, dear peoples. Dear Everything. Dear God"—records a conversation about history:

> Why us always have family reunion on July 4th, say Henrietta, mouth poke out, full of complaint. It so hot.
>
> White people busy celebrating they independence from England July 4th, say I Harpo, so most black folks don't have to work. Us can spend the day celebrating each other.
>
> Ah, Harpo, say Mary Agnes, sipping some lemonade. I didn't know you knowed history. [*Color*, 249–50]

Harpo's decentering history is a microcosm of Walker's, which ends with a beginning: "I feel a little peculiar round the children," Celie writes. "And I see they think [us] real old and don't know much what going on. But I don't think us feel old at all. . . . Matter of fact, I think this the youngest us ever felt" (*Color*, 251). As Celie's beginning could have been a silent end, so her ending continues the proliferating beginnings that the novel captures in its epistolary form, its characters' histories, and the daily revelations that Shug names "God."

Walker's telling of the daughter's long-repressed story marks an important beginning for literary history. In her hands, the forbidden story recreates the world by reclaiming female subjectivity. "What I love best about Shug," Celie tells Albert, "is what she been through. When you look at Shug's eyes, you know she been where she been, seen what she seen, and what she did. And now she know. . . . And if you don't git out the way, she'll tell you about it" (*Color*, 236). Walker's woman as hero, whose history is her identity and who recreates the universe by telling her story to the world, is not new in real life. But she is only now making her presence felt in the literary tradition, opening a powerfully transformative dialogue between herself and the world, between her story and his, and between ourselves and our cultural past. As she does so, we can look forward to that "most interesting, exciting, and important conversation" that Woolf predicted would begin once woman recovered her voice.

KENETH KINNAMON

Call and Response: Intertextuality in Two Autobiographical Works by Richard Wright and Maya Angelou

In his provocative account of Afro-American literary criticism from the 1940s to the present, Houston A. Baker, Jr., traces three stages of development: integrationism, the "Black Aesthetic," and the "Reconstruction of Instruction." As his major representative of the first stage, "the dominant critical perspective on Afro-American literature during the late 1950s and early 1960s," Baker makes a strange choice—Richard Wright, in the 1957 version of "The Literature of the Negro in the United States." According to Baker, Wright, sanguine because of the Supreme Court school desegregation decision of 1954, believed that the leveling of racial barriers in American society would lead to a homogenous American literature in which minority writers would be absorbed into the mainstream of cultural expression. Even the verbal and musical folk forms of the black masses would eventually disappear with the inevitable triumph of democratic pluralism in the social order. Actually, Wright's essay is not basically an optimistic statement of integrationist poetics. It is, rather, a document in the proletarian-protest stage of Afro-American literature and literary criticism that dominated the Thirties and Forties, constituting the stage immediately preceding Baker's first stage. The proletarian-protest stage anticipates elements of all three of Baker's stages. Like the integrationist stage it postulates a fundamental unity of human experience transcending racial and national (but not economic)

From *Studies in Black American Literature, Vol. II: Beliefs vs. Theory in Black American Literary Criticism*.

boundaries. Its commitment to an engaged literature is as fierce as that of the Black Aestheticians. And in "Blueprint for Negro Writing," at least, it advocates a sophisticated modern literary sensibility, as does the Stepto-Gates school. What it does not do is examine the special perspective of black women writers, a failing shared by the following three stages. This deficiency seems particularly conspicuous now that good women writers are so abundant and female critics are beginning to assess their achievement in relation to the total Afro-American literary tradition.

Despite its unfortunate effort at social disengagement, to my mind the most illuminating effort to provide a theoretical framework for the interpretation of Afro-American literature is Robert B. Stepto's *From Behind the Veil: A Study of Afro-American Narrative* (Urbana: University of Illinois Press, 1979). In this seminal work Stepto argues that the central myth of black culture in America is "the quest for freedom and literacy." Shaped by the historical circumstances of slavery and enforced illiteracy, this myth exists in the culture prior to any literary expression of it. Once this "pre-generic myth" is consciously articulated, it begins to take generic shape, especially as autobiography or fiction. The resulting narrative texts interact with each other in complex ways that constitute a specifically Afro-American literary tradition and history. In his book Stepto explores this intertextual tradition, dividing it into what he designates "The Call" and "The Response." In "The Call," he treats four slave narratives (by Bibb, Northup, Douglass, and Brown), *Up From Slavery*, and *The Souls of Black Folk*. To this call he discusses the twentieth century response of *The Autobiography of an Ex-Coloured Man*, *Black Boy*, and *Invisible Man*. All would agree that, of these nine works, those by Douglass, Washington, Du Bois, Johnson, Wright, and Ellison are classics of Afro-American literature, but notice that all of these authors are not only men, but race men, spokesmen, political activists. By way of complementing Stepto's somewhat narrow if sharp focus, I propose here to examine some intertextual elements in *Black Boy* and *I Know Why the Caged Bird Sings* to ascertain how gender may affect genre in these two autobiographical quests for freedom and literacy and, in Angelou's case, community as well.

In many ways these two accounts of mainly Southern childhoods are strikingly similar. Both narratives cover a period of fourteen years from earliest childhood memories to late adolescence: 1913 to 1927 (age four to eighteen) in Wright's case, 1931 to 1945 (age three to seventeen) in Angelou's case. Both Wright and Marguerite Johnson (Angelou's given name) are products of broken homes, children passed back and forth among parents and other relatives. Both have unpleasant confrontations with their fathers' mistresses. Both spend part of their childhoods in urban ghettoes (Memphis and St. Louis) as well as Southern small towns. Both suffer physical mistreatment by relatives. Both are humiliated by white employers. Lethal white violence comes close to both while they are living in Arkansas. Each child is subjected by a domineering grandmother to rigorous religious indoctrination, but each maintains a skeptical independence of spirit. From the trauma or tedium of their surroundings, both turn to reading as an escape. Both excel in school, Wright graduating as valedictorian from the eighth grade of Smith-Robinson School in Jackson, Mississippi, and Johnson as salutatorian of Lafayette County Training School in Stamps, Arkansas, fifteen years later.

In addition to these general similarities, some highly specific resemblances suggest more than mere coincidence or common cultural background. In *Black Boy Wright* recalls an incident in Memphis involving a preacher invited to Sunday dinner, the main course being "a huge platter of golden-brown fried chicken." Before the boy can finish his soup the preacher is picking out "choice pieces": "My growing hate of the preacher finally became more important than God or religion and I could no longer contain myself. I leaped up from the table, knowing that I should be ashamed of what I was doing, but unable to stop, and screamed, running blindly from the room. 'That preacher's going to eat all the chicken!' I bawled." The gluttonous preacher's counterpart in *I Know Why the Caged Bird Sings* is Reverend Howard Thomas, whose "crime that tipped the scale and made our hate not only just but imperative was his actions at the dinner table. He ate the biggest, brownest and best parts of the chicken at every Sunday meal." Wright's literary imagination was first kindled by the story of Bluebeard. As a child Angelou also learned of Bluebeard. A later common literary interest was Horatio Alger, who nurtured Wright's dreams of opportunities denied in the South. To Marguerite Johnson, however, Alger was a reminder that one of her dreams would be permanently deferred: "I read more than ever, and wished my soul that I had been born a boy. Horatio Alger was the greatest writer in the world. His heroes were always good, always won, and were always boys. I could have developed the first two virtues, but becoming a boy was sure to be difficult, if not impossible" (p. 74). One is tempted to think that Angelou had Wright specifically in mind in this passage, but even if she did not, her text provides an instructive gloss on Wright's, pointing out that sexism as well as racism circumscribes opportunity.

Other parallel passages provide additional intertextual clues to a basic difference in perspective on childhood experiences. One of the numerous relatives with whom young Richard could not get along was Aunt Addie, his teacher in a Seventh-Day Adventist school in Jackson. After a bitter confrontation in which the twelve-year-old boy threatens his aunt with a knife, she finds occasion for revenge:

> I continued at the church school, despite Aunt Addie's never calling upon me to recite or go to the blackboard. Consequently I stopped studying. I spent my time playing with the boys and found that the only games they knew were brutal ones. Baseball, marbles, boxing, running were tabooed recreations, the Devil's work: instead they played a wildcat game called popping-the-whip, a seemingly innocent diversion whose excitement came only in spurts, but spurts that could hurl one to the edge of death itself. Whenever we were discovered standing idle on the school grounds, Aunt Addie would suggest that we pop-the-whip. It would have been safer for our bodies and saner for our souls had she urged us to shoot craps.
>
> One day at noon Aunt Addie ordered us to pop-the-whip. I had never played the game before and I fell in with good faith. We formed a long line, each boy taking hold of another boy's hand until we were stretched out like a long string of human beads. Although I did not know it, I was on the tip end of the human whip. The leading boy, the handle of the whip, started off at a trot, weaving to the left and to the right, increasing speed until the whip of flesh was curving at breakneck gallop. I clutched the hand of the boy next to me with all the strength I had, sensing that if I did not hold on I would be tossed off. The whip grew taut as human flesh and bone could bear and I felt that my arm was being torn from its socket. Suddenly my breath left me. I was swung in a small, sharp arc. The whip was now being popped and I could hold on no more; the momentum of the whip flung me off my feet into the air, like a bit of leather being flicked off a horsewhip, and I hurtled headlong through space and landed in a ditch. I rolled over, stunned, head bruised and bleeding. Aunt Addie was laughing, the first and only time I ever saw her laugh on God's holy ground. (pp. 96–97)

In Stamps pop-the-whip was considerably less dangerous: "And when he [Maya's brother Bailey] was on the tail of the pop the whip, he would twirl off the end like a top, spinning, falling, laughing, finally stopping just before my heart beat its last, and then he was back in the game, still laughing" (p.

23). Now pop-the-whip is not among the gentlest of childhood activities, but surely it is less potentially deadly than Wright makes it out, surely it is closer to Angelou's exciting but essentially joyous pastime. With his unremittingly bleak view of black community in the South, Wright presents the game as sadistic punishment inflicted by a hateful aunt. In Angelou's corrective it becomes a ritual of ebullient youthful bravado by her "pretty Black brother" who was also her "unshakable God" and her "Kingdom Come" (p. 23).

Another pair of passages shows the same difference. Both Wright's Grandmother Wilson and Johnson's Grandmother Henderson ranked cleanliness close to godliness. On one occasion Wright remembers his grandmother bathing him:

> I went to her, walking sheepishly and nakedly across the floor. She snatched the towel from my hand and began to scrub my ears, my face, my neck.
>
> "Bend over," she ordered.
>
> I stooped and she scrubbed my anus. My mind was in a sort of daze, midway between daydreaming and thinking. Then, before I knew it, words—words whose meaning I did not fully know—had slipped out of my mouth.
>
> "When you get through, kiss back there," I said, the words rolling softly but unpremeditatedly. (p. 36)

Naturally the response to this call is a severe beating. Angelou treats a similar situation with humor:

> "Thou shall not be dirty" and "Thou shall not be impudent" were the two commandments of Grandmother Henderson upon which hung our total salvation.
>
> Each night in the bitterest winter we were forced to wash faces, arms, necks, legs and feet before going to bed. She used to add, with a smirk that unprofane people can't control when venturing into profanity, "and wash as far as possible, then wash possible." (p. 26)

No children like to scrub or be scrubbed, but Wright uses the occasion to dramatize hostility between himself and his family, while Angelou's purpose is to portray cleanliness as a bonding ritual in black culture: "Everyone I knew respected these customary laws, except for the powhitetrash children" (p. 27).

In *Black Boy* the autobiographical persona defines himself *against* his environment, as much against his family and the surrounding black culture as against the overt hostility of white racism. Like the fictional persona Bigger Thomas, the protagonist of *Black Boy* is all archetypal rebel who rejects all social norms. In the opening scene he sets his family's house on fire, eliciting a traumatically severe whipping from his mother. His father "was always a stranger to me, always alien and remote" (p. 9). Young Richard subverts his paternal authority by a disingenuous literalism in the cat-killing episode. At the end of the first chapter he recalls his last meeting with his father in 1940, providing an exaggerated geriatric description complete with toothless mouth, white hair, bent body, glazed eyes, gnarled hands. His father was a brutalized "black peasant," "a creature of the earth" without loyalty, sentiment, tradition, joy, or despair—all in contrast to his son, who lives "on a vastly different plane of reality," who speaks a different language, and who has traveled to "undreamed-of shores of knowing" (pp. 30, 31). Wright's symbolic effort to bury his father corresponds to a persistent attempt to come into his own by opposing or ignoring all members of his family, who consistently try to stifle his articulation of his individuality, to inhibit his quest for freedom. Shouting joyously at the sight of a free-flying bird outside his window, Richard is rebuked in the opening scene by his younger brother with the words "'You better hush.'" His mother immediately steps in to reinforce the message: "'You stop that yelling, you hear?'" (p. 3). These are the first words spoken to Richard in *Black Boy*, but they reverberate in other mouths throughout the work. His brother plays an exceedingly minor role before being sent to Detroit to live with an aunt. His mother is presented more sympathetically than are other members of the family, but even she functions as a harsh disciplinarian striving to suppress her son's dangerous individualism. His grandmother and other relatives join this effort leading often to violent arguments in which Richard threatens them with knife or razor blade.

Outside the family the boy's relations to other black children are marked by fights on the street and in the schoolyard described with the same hyperbolic violence employed in the pop-the-whip episode. In the classroom he has to struggle against a paralyzing shyness that renders him almost mute and unable to write his own name: "I sat with my ears and neck burning, hearing the pupils whisper about me, hating myself, hating them: I sat still as stone and a storm of emotion surged through me" (p. 67). In describing his contacts with the general black community Wright emphasizes brutalization and degradation, as in his account of saloons in Memphis or in this paragraph on life in West Helena:

> We rented one half of a double corner house in front of which ran a stagnant ditch carrying sewage. The neighborhood swarmed with rats, cats, dogs, fortunetellers, cripples, blind men, whores, salesmen, rent collectors, and children. In front of our flat was a huge roundhouse where locomotives were cleaned and repaired. There was an eternal hissing of steam, the deep grunting of steel engines, and the tolling of bells. Smoke obscured the vision and cinders drifted into the house, into our beds, into our kitchen, into our food; and a tarlike smell was always in the air. (p. 52)

Richard learns about sex voyeuristically by peeping at the whores at work in the other half of the duplex in the Arkansas town, as he had earlier watched the exposed rears of privies in Memphis. When he does manage to establish some degree of rapport with other boys, "the touchstone of fraternity was my feeling toward white people, how much hostility I held toward them, what degrees of value and honor I assigned to race" (p. 68). But as the reader of "Big Boy Leaves Home," *The Long Dream*, or biographies of Wright knows, in *Black Boy* the author minimizes the important role his friendship with peers actually played in his adolescent life. Religion is also rejected, whether the peripteral Seventh-Day Adventism of his grandmother or the mainstream black Methodism of his mother. So estranged and isolated from the nurturing matrices of black culture, an estrangement as much willed from within as imposed from without, Wright was able to utter this famous indictment:

> (After I had outlived the shocks of childhood, after the habit of reflection had been born in me, I used to mull over the strange absence of real kindness in Negroes, how unstable was our tenderness, how lacking in genuine passion we were, how void of great hope, how timid our joy, how bare our traditions, how hollow our memories, how lacking we were in those intangible sentiments that bind man to man, and how shallow was even our despair. After I had learned other ways of life I used to brood upon the unconscious irony of those who felt that Negroes led so passional an existence! I saw that what had been taken for our emotional strength was our negative confusions, our flights, our fears, our frenzy under pressure.
>
> (Whenever I thought of the essential bleakness of black life in America, I knew that Negroes had never been allowed to catch the full spirit of Western civilization, that they lived somehow in

> it but not of it. And when I brooded upon the cultural barrenness of black life, I wondered if clean, positive tenderness, love, honor, loyalty, and the capacity to remember were native with man. I asked myself if these human qualities were not fostered, won, struggled and suffered for, preserved in ritual form from one generation to another.) (p. 33)

In part this passage attempts to shame whites by showing them what their racism has wrought, but in a more crucial way it defines Wright's individualistic alienation from all sense of community, that permanent spiritual malaise that is both the key biographical fact and the idealogical center of his art.

With Maya Angelou the case is quite otherwise. If she never experienced the physical hunger that characterized much of Wright's childhood, he was not raped at the age of eight. Yet here youthful reponse to rejection and outrage is to embrace community, not to seek alienation. *I Know Why the Caged Bird Sings* is a celebration of black culture, by no means uncritical, but essentially a celebration. Toward her family, young Marguerite is depicted as loving, whether or not her love is merited. She idolizes her slightly older brother Bailey. Her Grandmother Henderson is presented not only as the matrifocal center of her family but as the leader of the black community in Stamps, strong, competent, religious, skilled in her ability to coexist with Jim Crow while maintaining her personal dignity. She is a repository of racial values, and her store is the secular center of her community. Crippled Uncle Willie could have been presented as a Sherwood Anderson grotesque, but Angelou recalls feeling close to him even if he was, like Grandmother Henderson, a stern disciplinarian. Angelou would seem to have every reason to share Wright's bitterness about parental neglect, but she does not. When her father shows up in Stamps she is impressed by his appearance, his proper speech, and his city ways. Her mother beggars description: "To describe my mother would be to write about a hurricane in its perfect power. Or the climbing, falling colors of a rainbow. . . . My mother's beauty literally assailed me" (p. 58). Absorbed in their own separate lives, her parents neglect or reject her repeatedly, but she is more awed by their persons and their personalities than she is resentful. Her maternal family in St. Louis is also impressive in its worldly way, so different in its emphasis on pleasure and politics from the religious rectitude of the paternal family in Stamps. Even Mr. Freeman, her mother's live-in boyfriend who first abuses and then rapes the child, is presented with more compassion than rancor.

Afflicted with guilt after Freeman is killed by her uncles, Marguerite lapses into an almost catatonic silence, providing an excuse to her mother to send her back to Stamps. Southern passivity provides a good therapeutic environment for the child, especially when she is taken under the wing of an elegant, intelligent black woman named Mrs. Bertha Flowers, who treats her to cookies, Dickens, and good advice. Better dressed and better read than anyone else in the community, she nevertheless maintains good relations with all and urges Marguerite not to neglect the wisdom of the folk as she pursues literary interests: "She said that I must always be intolerant of ignorance but understanding of illiteracy. That some people, unable to go to school, were more educated and even more intelligent than college professors. She encouraged me to listen carefully to what country people called mother wit. That in those homely sayings was couched the collective wisdom of generations" (p. 97). In contrast to Wright's grandmother, who banished from her house the schoolteacher Ella for telling the story of Bluebeard to Richard, Grandmother Henderson is quite friendly with "Sister" Flowers, both women secure in their sense of self and their mutual respect.

Angelou also recalls favorably the larger rituals of black community. Religious exercises, whether in a church or in a tent revival meeting, provide a festive atmosphere for Marguerite and Bailey. Racial euphoria pervades the black quarter of Stamps after a Joe Louis victory in a prizefight broadcast on Uncle Willie's radio to a crowd crammed into the store. A summer fish fry, the delicious feeling of terror while listening to ghost stories, the excitement of pregraduation activities—these are some of the pleasures of growing up black so amply present in *I Know Why the Caged Bird Sings* and so conspicuously absent in *Black Boy*.

A comparison of the graduation exercises in the two works is particularly instructive. Marguerite is showered with affectionate attention and gifts, and not only from her family and immediate circle of friends: "Uncle Willie and Momma [her Grandmother Henderson] had sent away for a Mickey Mouse watch like Bailey's. Louise gave me four embroidered handkerchiefs. (I gave her three crocheted doilies.) Mrs. Sneed, the minister's wife, made me an undershirt to wear for graduation, and nearly every customer gave me a nickel or maybe even a dime with the instruction 'Keep on moving to higher ground,' or some such encouragement" (p. 169). Richard feels more and more isolated as graduation nears: "My loneliness became organic. I felt walled in and I grew irritable. I associated less and less with my classmates" (p. 152). Refusing to use a speech prepared for him by the school principal, he resists peer and family pressure as well as the implicit promise of a teaching job, in order to maintain his sense of individual integrity. Giving his own speech, he rejects utterly the communal ceremony implicit in the occasion:

> On the night of graduation I was nervous and tense: I rose and faced the audience and my speech rolled out. When my voice stopped there was some applause. I did not care if they liked it or not: I was through. Immediately, even before I left the platform, I tried to shunt all memory of the event from me. A few of my classmates managed to shake my hand as I pushed toward the door, seeking the street. Somebody invited me to a party and I did not accept. I did not want to see any of them again. I walked home, saying to myself: The hell with it! With almost seventeen years of baffled living behind me, I faced the world in 1925. (p. 156)

The valedictorian of Marguerite's class accepts the help of a teacher in writing his speech, but before he mounts the podium a white politician delivers the Washingtonian message that "we were maids and farmers, handymen and washerwomen, and anything higher that we aspired to was farcical and presumptuous" (pp. 175–176). But this ritual of racial humiliation is immediately followed by a ritual of racial survival and solidarity. After giving his speech, the valedictorian improvises by singing "Lift Ev'ry Voice and Sing" with renewed meaning, joined by all present, the white man having left. From shame the collective emotion is transformed by the song of a black poet to pride: "We were on top again. As always, again. We survived. The depths had been icy and dark, but now a bright sun spoke to our souls. I was no longer simply a member of the proud graduating class of 1940; I was a proud member of the wonderful, beautiful Negro race" (p. 179). Unlike Wright, Angelou stresses the intimate relation of the black creator to the black audience. Gathering his material from the stuff of the black experience, with its suffering and its survival, James Weldon Johnson transmutes the experience into art, giving it back to the people to aid them to travel the stony road, to fortify their spirit by reminding them of their capacity to endure. The episode is a paradigm of Angelou's own artistic endeavor in *I Know Why the Caged Birds Sings.*

It is important to recognize that Angelou's Southern environment is as grievously afflicted by white racism as Wright's. Just as young Richard is tormented by whites, so is Marguerite by her employer Mrs. Cullinan who calls her out of her name, or by Dentist Lincoln, who owes Grandmother Henderson money but will not treat the child's toothache because ". . . my policy is I'd rather stick my hand in a dog's mouth than in a nigger's'" (p. 184). White violence comes dangerously close to both Uncle Willie and Bailey. Indeed, the town is quintessentially Southern in its racial attitudes, comparable to Wright's Elaine or West Helena or Jackson: "Stamps,

Arkansas, was Chitlin' Switch, Georgia: Hang 'Em High, Alabama; Don't Let the Sun Set on You Here, Nigger, Mississippi; or any other name just as descriptive. People in Stamps used to say that the whites in our town were so prejudiced that a Negro couldn't buy vanilla ice cream. Except on July Fourth. Other days he had to be satisfied with chocolate" (p. 47). It is not that Angelou de-emphasizes the racist assault on Black personality and community; it is just that she shows with respect if not always agreement the defensive and compensatory cultural patterns developed to survive in such an environment. This is Maya Angelou's response in *I Know Why the Caged Bird Sings* to the call of *Black Boy.*

One hesitates to generalize on the basis of a single book by one woman writer, but a quick recall of such writers as Linda Brent, Zora Neale Hurston, Gwendolyn Brooks, Margaret Walker, Paule Marshall, Sonia Sanchez, Toni Morrison, Sherley Anne Williams, Nikki Giovanni, Carolyn M. Rodgers, Ntozake Shange, Alice Walker, Gayl Jones, and numerous others suggests that, more than male writers, women are concerned with such themes as community, sexism (especially sexual exploitation), and relations with family and friends. They seem correspondingly less interested in individual rebellion, alienation, and success against the odds. A theory which can encompass both visions, adding community to the myth of freedom and literacy, accommodating *I Know Why the Caged Bird Sings* as easily as *Black Boy*, may follow the stages delineated by Houston Baker and become the primary contribution of the present decade to Afro-American literary criticism.

JOANNE M. BRAXTON

A Song of Transcendence: Maya Angelou

Maya Angelou's *I Know Why the Caged Bird Sings* (1970) and Ann Moody's *Coming of Age in Mississippi* (1968) appeared at the end of the civil rights movement of the 1960s, and they carry with them the bitter and hard-won fruit of this era. Angelou and Moody know the harsh realities of life in the Deep South in the mid-twentieth century—in Arkansas and Mississippi, respectively. As the critic Roger Rosenblatt has asserted, "No black American author has ever felt the need to invent a nightmare to make [her] point." As Maya Angelou writes of her childhood: "High spots in Stamps were usually negative: droughts, floods, lynchings and deaths." Touched by the powerful effects of these destructive forces, Maya Angelou and Ann Moody hold themselves together with dignity and self-respect. They move forward toward a goal of self-sufficiency, combining a consciousness of self, an awareness of the political realities of black life in the South, and an appreciation of the responsibility that such an awareness implies. For this chapter, I have selected *I Know Why the Caged Bird Sings* as representative of autobiographies written by black women in the post-civil rights era.

In the Arkansas South of Maya Angelou's childhood, recognized patterns of etiquette between the races asserted white superiority and black inferiority. This etiquette served as a form of social control that pervaded the daily experiences of blacks, who negotiated narrow paths of safety:

> Momma intended to teach Bailey and me to use the paths of life that she and her generation and all the Negroes gone before had

---

From *Black Women Writing Autobiography: A Tradition Within a Tradition*.

> found, and found to be safe ones. She didn't cotton to the idea that white folks could be talked to at all without risking one's life. And certainly they couldn't be spoken to insolently. In fact, even in their absence they could not be spoken of too harshly unless we used the sobriquet "They." If she had been asked to answer the question of whether she was cowardly or not, she would have said that she was realist. (*Caged Bird*, 39)

Throughout the course of *Caged Bird*, Maya Angelou moves toward this same realism, which is not only a practical political philosophy but also one of the dominant modes of the autobiography. *I Know Why the Caged Bird Sings* distills the essence of the autobiographical impulse into lyric imagery touched by poignant realism. Angelou once said, "I speak to the black experience, but I am always talking about the human condition—about what we can endure, dream, fail at, and still survive." In this spirit, she faithfully depicts her home ground as a version of the universal human experience.

This chapter undertakes the task of defining the characteristics that identify the text in terms of a tradition of black women's writing. George Kent has argued that *I Know Why the Caged Bird Sings* "creates a unique place within black autobiographical tradition . . . by its special stance toward the self, the community, and the universe, and by a form exploiting the full measure of imagination necessary both to beauty and absurdity." In *Caged Bird*, we witness the full outward extension of the outraged mother. Although, in some sense, this text seems yet too close to be explicated adequately, the availability of criticism outweighs the problem of dealing with a recent text, for as James Olney has noted, "Here we have an autobiography by a black woman, published in the last decade (1970), that already has its own critical literature." Not only does the preponderance of criticism herald "full literary enfranchisement" for "black writers, women writers, and autobiography itself," but it indicates the importance of the text to black autobiographical tradition.

Although I have selected *Caged Bird* because of the availability of criticism and because it covers a wider span of time than Angelou's subsequent autobiographies, one of the added advantages in considering this particular volume is that it can be read in relation to Angelou's other autobiographical works. In 1974, *Gather Together in My Name* followed *Caged Bird*, and *Singin' and Swingin' and Gettin' Merry Like Christmas* appeared in 1976, followed by The *Heart of a Woman in* 1981 and *All God's Children Need Traveling Shoes* in 1986. Additionally, Angelou has published several collections of poetry; almost all this poetry has some autobiographical content, and through much of it, Angelou celebrates her dark womanhood, as in "Woman Me":

Your smile, delicate
rumor of peace.
Deafening revolutions nestle in the
cleavage of
your breasts
Beggar-Kings and red-ringed Priests
seek glory at the meeting
of your thighs
A grasp of Lions, a Lap of Lambs.

Thus Angelou's autobiographical impulse manifests itself in lyrical forms as well as the prose narrative.

In *Black Autobiography*, Stephen Butterfield compares the dramatic structure, setting, and content of *I Know Why the Caged Bird Sings* with that of Richard Wright's *Black Boy* and concludes that "Maya Angelou's complex sense of humor and compassion for other people's defects . . . endow her work with a different quality of radiance." Elements of humor and compassion contribute greatly to the effect, but this "different quality of radiance" actually derives from *Caged Bird*'s special relationship to a tradition of black women writing autobiography. When Butterfield writes, "Ida Wells created the identity of mother and protectress: Maya Angelou in *I Know Why the Caged Bird Sings* inspires the urge to protect," he both demonstrates his respect for and betrays his ignorance of the black female autobiographical tradition. The identity of the mother and protectress is already firmly established in Harriet Brent Jacobs's *Incidents in the Life of a Slave Girl* of 1861. Angelou extends and enlarges that identity.

I Know Why the Caged Bird Sings treats themes that are traditional in autobiography by black American women. These include the importance of the family and the nurturing and rearing of one's children, as well as the quest for self-sufficiency, self-reliance, personal dignity, and self-definition. Like Ida B. Wells, Maya Angelou celebrates black motherhood and speaks out against racial injustice; but unlike Wells, she does so from a unified point of view and in a more coherent form. This derives, in part, from Wells's identity as a public figure and Angelou's identity as an artist. As a creative autobiographer, Angelou may focus entirely on the inner spaces of her emotional and personal life. In *I Know Why the Caged Bird Sings*, the mature woman looks back on her bittersweet childhood, and her authorial voice retains the power of the child's vision. The child's point of view governs Angelou's principle of selection. When the mature narrator steps in, her tone is purely personal, so it does not seem unusual that Angelou feels compelled to explore aspects of her coming of age that Ida B. Wells (and Zora Neale Hurston) chose to omit.

Here emerges the fully developed black female autobiographical form that began to mature in the 1940s and 1950s. Like Zora Neale Hurston and Era Bell Thompson, Maya Angelou employs rhythmic language, lyrically suspended moments of consciousness, and detailed portraiture. Her use of folklore and humor help to augment the effect she creates as tale-teller *par excellence.* Maya Angelou takes the genre of autobiography to the heights that Zora Neale Hurston took the novel in *Their Eyes Were Watching God.* If *I Know Why the Caged Bird Sings* reads like a novel, it carries the ring of truth. Speaking in terms of its literary merits, it is perhaps the most aesthetically satisfying autobiography written by a black woman in this period.

Necessarily, analysis begins with the title *I Know Why the Caged Bird Sings,* which originally appeared in the poem "Sympathy" by the great black poet, Paul Laurence Dunbar:

> I know why the caged bird beats his wings
> Till its blood is red on the cruel bars
> For he must fly back to his perch and cling
> When he would fain be on the bough aswing
> And a pain still throbs in the old, old scars
> And they pulse again with a keener sting—
> I know why he beats his wings!
>
> I know why the caged bird sings, ah me.
> When his wing is bruised and his bosom sore,—
> When he beats his bars and would be free
> It is not a carol of joy or glee,
> But a prayer that he sends from his heart's deep core,
> But a plea, that upward to Heaven he flings—
> I know why the caged bird sings!

The sentiment of this poem, one of Dunbar's best lyrics, presages the tone of Angelou's autobiography, and some of the feeling of her struggle to transcend the restrictions of a hostile environment. Clearly, Angelou is in "sympathy" with the "real" Dunbar, the bleeding bird behind the mask. And it seems likely that Dunbar would have been in "sympathy" with Angelou as well. For like the Dunbar poem and the spirituals sung by southern blacks, *I Know Why the Caged Bird Sings* displays a tremendous "lift" and an impulse toward transcendence. And like the song of the caged bird, the autobiography represents a prayer sent from the "heart's deep core," sent from the depth of emotion and feeling. The autobiographer prays that the bird be released from the cage of its oppression to fly free from the definitions and limitations imposed by a hostile world.

Development occurs on multiple levels in *I Know Why the Caged Bird Sings*. As in the autobiographies considered in the previous chapter, a maturation of consciousness parallels geographical movement (South to North and East to West). Sidonie Ann Smith argues that Angelou's narrative strategy in *Caged Bird* "itself is a function of the autobiographer's self-image at the moment of writing, for the nature of that self-image determines the pattern of self-actualization [she] discovers while attempting to shape [her] past experiences. Such a pattern must culminate in some sense of an ending, and it is this sense of an ending that informs certain earlier moments with significance and determines the choice of what [she] recreates, what she discards. . . . Ultimately, then, the opening material assumes the end, the end the opening movement."

In *Caged Bird*, Maya Angelou does not progress only from a state of semi-orphanhood to one of motherhood; she develops through various stages of self-awareness. At the beginning of the narrative, Angelou depicts her arrival in Stamps, Arkansas, as a "tagged orphan."

> When I was three and Bailey four, we had arrived in a musty little town, wearing tags on our wrists which instructed—"To Whom It May Concern"—that we were Marguerite and Bailey Johnson, Jr., from Long Beach, California, en route to Stamps, Arkansas, c/o Mrs. Annie Henderson. (*Caged Bird*, 3–4)

The autobiographer, receptive rather than active in her early childhood, absorbs the "hometraining" and humble teachings of her grandmother, Annie Henderson, a self-sufficient woman who provides for her two grandchildren and her crippled son, Marguerite's Uncle Willie. "Momma" owns a store that seems to cater to and survive on the support of poor blacks; Mrs. Henderson also owns some of the land rented by the "poor white trash." She is the only colored woman in Stamps whom the whites refer to as "Mrs."—a clear mark of respect. Throughout the autobiography, her mother and grandmother play an important role, both as protective and nurturing figures, and as models for Marguerite, who, at the end of the narrative, has become a mother herself and assumed a positive, if still somewhat problematic, identity.

For critic Myra K. McMurry, *Caged Bird* is "an affirmation . . . Maya

Angelou's answer to the question of how a Black girl can grow up in a repressive system without being maimed by it." As in the autobiographies of Era Bell Thompson, Zora Neale Hurston, and Laura Adams, *I Know Why the Caged Bird Sings* reveals the autobiographer's sense of geographic, cultural, and social displacement. "If growing up is painful for the Southern black girl," Angelou writes, "being aware of her displacement is the rust on the razor that threatens the throat. It is an unnecessary insult" (*Caged Bird*, 3). Once again, the quest is not only for survival but also for an authentic, self-defining black female identity, one that evinces care and concern for others. Angelou's treatment of the theme of limitation and restriction resembles Dunbar's treatment in the poem "Sympathy." Like the caged bird, the young Marguerite Johnson feels removed from the larger world. Marguerite is "big, elbowy and grating"; her playmates describe her as being "shit color." Her hair, she thinks, is like "black steel wool" (*Caged Bird*, 17). Still, Angelou finds "hope and a hope of wholeness" in the love and support received from Momma, Bailey, and Uncle Willie. Never considered attractive by the standards of her community, Marguerite develops her intellect:

> During these years in Stamps, I met and fell in love with William Shakespeare. He was my first white love. Although I enjoyed and respected Kipling, Poe, Butler, Thackeray and Henley, I saved my young and loyal passion for Paul Laurence Dunbar, Langston Hughes, James Weldon Johnson and W. E. B. Du Bois' "Litany in Atlanta." But it was Shakespeare who said, "When in disgrace with fortune and men's eyes." It was a state with which I found myself most familiar. (*Caged Bird*, 11)

Later she will become acquainted with Gorky, Dostoyevsky, Turgenev, and other writers who influence her choice of form and style, but during her childhood, Shakespeare and Dunbar speak directly to her dilemma—the problem of developing a positive self-image in a culture whose standards of beauty are uniformly white, and the problem of finding a place for herself in that culture.

The strongest portraits, the strongest images in *Caged Bird*, are the respected figures of Marguerite's mother and grandmother. She celebrates her grandmother's feminine heroism, wisdom, and unselfishness in much the same way that Harriet Brent Jacobs celebrates similar qualities in her own dear grandmother. George Kent argues that "Grandmother's religion gives her the power to order her being, that of the children, and usually the immediate space surrounding her. The spirit of the religion combined with simple, traditional maxims shapes the course of existence and rituals of facing up to something called decency." Mrs. Henderson nurtures Marguerite through her Stamps childhood and beyond, doing what she can to protect her son's young children from frequent intrusions of "white reality." Such painful confrontations can occur at any time, and can be instigated by whites from any age group or social class. Mrs. Henderson is even insulted by the poor white trash children whose parents rent land from her. The autobiographer writes of this as "the most painful experience I ever had with my grandmother":

> For an awful second I thought they were going to throw a rock at Momma, who seemed (except for the apron strings) to have turned into stone herself. But the big girl turned her back, bent down and put her hands flat on the ground she didn't pick up anything. She simply shifted her weight and did a hand stand.
>
> Her dirty bare feet and long legs went straight for the sky. Her dress fell down around her shoulders, and she had on no drawers. The slick pubic hair made a brown triangle where her legs came together. She hung in the vacuum of that lifeless morning for only a few seconds, then wavered and tumbled. The other girls clapped her on the back and slapped their hands.
>
> Momma changed her song to "Bread of Heaven, feed me till I want no more."
>
> I found that I was praying too. (*Caged Bird*, 25–26)

Through this depiction of her experience, Maya Angelou praises her grandmother's courage. It is from her grandmother and from people who raise and nurture her that Maya learns to use and develop this courage, which she views as the most important virtue of all. "Without courage," she had said, "you cannot practice any other virtue with consistency" (*ODU*).

There were ample opportunities for the development of courage in Maya Angelou's young life, and the fine edge of this virtue was honed in facing the commonplace dangers of life in Stamps, such as lynching. Lynching constituted a real danger and hence a legitimate fear in the minds of Arkansas blacks. The terror of lynching persists as a theme throughout the sections of the autobiography set in Arkansas. Early in the narrative, we are told how Mrs. Henderson hid a would-be lynch victim and provided him with supplies for a journey, even though she jeopardized her own security to do so. On another occasion, it is necessary to conceal Uncle Willie one night after an unknown black man is accused of "messing with" a white woman. Angelou forcefully conveys the emotional and psychological impact of the threat of lynching as she experienced it:

> Even after the slow drag of years, I remember the sense of fear which filled my mouth with hot, dry air, and made my body light. . . . We were told to take the potatoes and onions out of their bins and knock out the dividing walls that kept them apart. Then with a tedious and fearful slowness Uncle Willie gave me his rubber-tipped cane and bent down to get into the now enlarged empty bin. It took forever before he lay down flat, and then we covered him with potatoes and onions, layer upon layer, like a casserole. Grandmother knelt praying in the darkened store. (*Caged Bird*, 14–15)

Like Aunt Marthy in *Incidents in the Life of a Slave Girl*, Mrs. Henderson, "Momma," fulfills the archetypal role of the outraged mother by concealing her innocent child. Angelou succeeds in communicating a sense of the frustration and humiliation her family feels in these encounters. Without polemics, she shows the absurdity of lynching: Why should a crippled old man be forced to spend the night in a bin full of potatoes and onions in fear of his life because some unnamed black man has been accused of an unnamed crime?

Unlike Ida B. Wells, Maya Angelou speaks about lynching from a personal point of view, articulating her experience and her pain. On one occasion, Momma, Marguerite, and Uncle Willie wait for Bailey, who is late returning from the theater in town. Momma's apprehension, Angelou writes, "was evident in the hurried movements around the kitchen and in her lonely fearing eyes" (*Caged Bird*, 95). Later in the narrative (after the return from St. Louis and just before the permanent move to California), Bailey sees the body of a lynch victim whose "things had been cut off and put in his pocket and had been shot in the head, all because whitefolks said he 'did it' to a white woman" (*Caged Bird*, 30). These are harsh experiences for young children to endure, but Bailey and Marguerite survive, due in no small measure to the protection and sense of security they receive from their grandmother. Through Momma, Marguerite absorbs values and concepts that make it possible to maintain and replenish a sense of self-worth. Through Momma, Marguerite learns to pray.

An important theme throughout the autobiography, religion represents a sustaining force in the life of Mrs. Henderson, who derives spiritual sustenance and fortitude from the "Bread of Heaven." When threatened, Momma turns to her faith, which is clearly a source of her personal power. The early religious experiences of Maya Angelou resemble those of Zora Neale Hurston more nearly than those of any other autobiographer studied here; like Era Bell Thompson and Laura Adams, Maya Angelou displays the old "church of emotion," but unlike them, she is no stranger to it. Mrs. Henderson, a respected church elder, requires that Bailey and Marguerite participate fully in church activities and in the religious life of the community. Angelou's regard for black spirituality and black religion does not exempt the church from criticism. Like Wright, she finds comedy in the Sunday performances of "sisters" possessed by the spirit, and she ridicules the greedy minister when he eats more than his fair share of the fried chicken at Sunday dinner. But unlike Wright, she evokes this ridicule and paints this portrait without condescension—still recognizing the solvency of the basic spiritual trust.

Respecting her grandmother's homespun teaching, Maya became a part of the fabric of her culture, absorbing both literary and folk influences through observation, study, and loving imitation. Of the sermons and the spirituals, Angelou has said, "they run through my veins like blood." From her point of view, literature includes written as well as oral tradition, and she sees the spirituals as American classics; "to deny it [the spirituals as unwritten literature] is to spit upon your grandfather's grave. Like all art, it belongs to everyone who appreciates it" (*ODU*). *Caged Bird* shows the influence of myriad folk forms, including the sermon, the ghost story, the preacher tale, the tale of exaggeration, a children's rhyme, and secular and religious songs. The use of these oral forms, together with folk language, contributes to the unique tone, texture, and style of the autobiography. Their presence also helps identify the autobiographer in a relationship with her community and culture.

In *Caged Bird*, as in *American Daughter* and *Dust Tracks*, closeness to the land and continual involvement with nature are essential to the mood and imagery of the autobiography. Marguerite notes the passage of time by watching "the field across from the Store turn caterpillar green, then gradually frosty white. She knew exactly how long it would be before the big wagons would pull into the front yard and load on the cotton pickers at daybreak to carry them to the remains of slavery's plantations" (*Caged Bird*, 5). This mood is enhanced by the use of portraiture, rhythmic language, and the careful depiction of lyrically suspended moments of consciousness.

> In the dying sunlight the people dragged rather than their empty sacks. . . . The sounds of the new morning had been replaced

> with grumbles about cheating houses, weighted scales and dusty rows. . . . In cotton-picking time, the late afternoons revealed the harshness of Black Southern life, which in the early morning had been softened by nature's blessing of grogginess, forgetfulness and the soft lamplight. (*Caged Bird*, 7)

The entire "black community of Stamps," Sidonie Smith argues, is itself caged in the "social reality of racial subordination and impotence." Marguerite's "personal displacement is counterpointed by the ambiance of displacement within the larger black community."

Because she works in her grandmother's store, Marguerite has no direct experience of the intense labor of picking cotton, but she observes the workers as they go out into the fields and return. She has "seen the fingers cut by the mean little cotton bolls" and "witnessed the backs and arms and legs resisting any further demands" (*Caged Bird*, 7).

The use of portraiture and the feeling of being close to nature and the land contribute to the lyric sensibility of *Caged Bird*, but unlike the earlier autobiographies by Thompson and Hurston, *Caged Bird* admits harsh and painful aspects of the southern black experience before the civil rights era—the economic oppression and racial violence that Thompson and Hurston either knew little about or chose to ignore. This awareness lends Angelou's lyric imagery the knife-sharp edge of realism, something contributed to black female autobiographical tradition through the Richard Wright school of the 1940s and 1950s. Thematic and structural similarities between the autobiographies of Wright and Angelou result from their common descent from the slave narrative and from the influence of Russian writers, which both read. Another common denominator between Wright and Angelou concerns their view of the "Great Migration," of which both were a part. They depict themselves as participants in a vast historical drama—the movement of rural blacks from the Deep South to the urban centers of the North, hoping to improve their economic and social horizons by escaping the racism and exploitation of the South. Although Wright's tone seems more political than Angelou's, they respond to the same historic moment.

Afro-Americans who participated in the Great Migration can be compared with Europeans who emigrated to America only to find "identity problems in their mental baggage." As Erik Erikson has observed of the European-American group, "Emigration can be a hard and heartless matter, in terms of what is abandoned in the old country and what is usurped in the new one. Migration means cruel survival in identity terms, too, for the very cataclysms in which millions perish open up new forms of identity to the survivors." From her autobiography and her life work, Angelou has emerged as a survivor, a "whole" person, with her identity, her sense of humor, her dignity, and her style intact.

One of the important early turning points in the autobiography centers on Marguerite's move to St. Louis. Initially more of a change in geographic location than the beginning of a change of consciousness, the move precipitates profound problems of identity. After four years of living happily with Momma and Uncle Willie in Stamps, Marguerite and Bailey become aware of the impending move during Christmas. Having received presents from their mother and father, they conclude that their parents are about to come and get them. This occurrence raises strong emotions in the two young children, who have come to regard Stamps as their home:

> The gifts opened the door to questions neither of us wanted to ask. Why did they send us away? And what did we do so wrong? So Wrong? Why, at three and four, would we have tags put on our arms to be sent alone from Long Beach, California, to Stamps, Arkansas, with only the porter to look after us? (Besides, he got off in Arizona.) (*Caged Bird*, 43)

A year later, Bailey, Sr., arrives in Stamps without warning. And in a relatively short time the children are on their way west, headed for California or so they think. En route, their father tells them that they are actually going to St. Louis to visit their mother. In Pig Latin, Marguerite asks Bailey, Jr., "Ooday ooyay inkthay isthay is our atherfay, or ooday ooyay inkthay atthay eeway eeingbay idkay appednay?" Her father chuckles and responds, "Oohay oodway antway ootway idkay appnay ooyay? Ooday ooyay inkthay ooyay are indlay ergbay ildrenchay?" Angelou writes that hearing her father speak Pig Latin "didn't startle me so much as it angered. It was simply another case of the trickiness of adults where children were concerned. Another case in point of the Grownups' Betrayal" (*Caged Bird*, 49).

For the young Marguerite Johnson, fresh from Stamps, Arkansas, "St. Louis was a foreign country." "In my mind," writes Angelou, "I only stayed in St. Louis a few weeks" (*Caged Bird*, 58). In St. Louis, Marguerite endures the most shattering experience of her childhood when she is raped by her mother's boyfriend, Mr. Freeman. The experience is a brutal one and necessitates the child's hospitalization:

> Then there was the pain. A breaking and entering when even the senses are torn apart. The act of rape on an eight-year-old is a

> matter of the needle giving because the camel can't. The child gives, because the body can, and the mind of the violator cannot.
>
> I thought I had died. (*Caged Bird,* 65)

She feels physical and psychological pain as a result of the rape and guilt from exposing Freeman, who meets a violent death at the hands of "persons unknown," but presumably Marguerite's tough St. Louis uncles (*Caged Bird,* 71–72). The rape precipitates a period of intense identity crisis for Marguerite, who, after Freeman's death, stops speaking to everyone but her brother, Bailey: "Instinctively, or somehow, I knew that because I loved him so much I'd never hurt him, but if I talked to anyone else that person might die too" (*Caged Bird,* 73). As a result of Freeman's death, Marguerite becomes a voluntary mute. Although this temporary solution suits Marguerite, her St. Louis family grows weary of her muteness, which they interpret as insolent sullenness: "For a while I was punished for being so uppity that I wouldn't speak; and then came the thrashings by any relative who felt himself offended" (*Caged Bird,* 73). Marguerite loses much of her innocence during this "perilous passage," which cuts her childhood painfully short. She feels betrayed by adults in general, and she withdraws from their way of life into a world of silence. Although Marguerite longs to be free from her guilt, sadness, and the feeling that she is different from others, she cannot extricate herself from the burdens inflicted by her environment.

Soon Marguerite and Bailey find themselves on the train going back to Stamps, which provides the obscurity the eight-year-old craves "without will or consciousness." Not knowing the exact origin of Marguerite's unwillingness to talk, the blacks of Stamps sympathize with her, as she was known for being "tender-hearted." "Southern Negroes used that term to mean sensitive and tended to look upon a person with that affliction as being a little sick or in delicate health. So I was not so much forgiven as I was understood" (*Caged Bird,* 77). And because the sickness is acknowledged, the healing can begin. Marguerite Johnson returns to Stamps (the source of her strength) to begin rebuilding the identity shattered by her enforced migration and subsequent rape.

After a year of voluntary muteness, Marguerite "met, or rather got to know" Bertha Flowers, "the aristocrat of Black Stamps." This represents another important turning point in the development of the autobiographer's consciousness. Angelou writes of Flowers as "the lady who threw my first life line," and the portrait she paints shows her high regard for the woman (*Caged Bird,* 77).

> She had the grace of control to appear warm in the coldest

> weather, and on the Arkansas summer days it seemed she had a private breeze which swirled around. Her skin was rich black that would have peeled like a plum if snagged, but no one would have thought of getting close enough to Mrs. Flowers to ruffle her dress, let alone snag her skin. She didn't encourage familiarity. She wore gloves too.
>
> The action was so graceful and inclusively benign. (*Caged Bird*, 77–78)

From Flowers, Marguerite receives her "lessons in living."

> She said that I must always be intolerant of ignorance but understanding of illiteracy. That some people, unable to go to school, were more educated and even more intelligent than college professors. She encouraged me to listen carefully to what country people called motherwit. That in those homely sayings was couched the collective wisdom of generations. (*Caged Bird*, 83)

The value of Flowers's benign maternal influence should not be underestimated. Her model of black gentility takes root in the young girl's consciousness, and she remains for the mature narrator "the measure of what a human being can be" (*Caged Bird*, 78). Flowers makes tea cookies for Marguerite, reads aloud to her from *A Tale of Two Cities*, and teaches her to recite poetry. Flowers fulfills the role of teacher and healer, providing the traumatized youngster with a process through which to tap internal creative resources for self-healing: These "lessons in living" constitute part of the extensive preparation Marguerite receives for life as a mature black woman. Marguerite needs the values and beliefs these "lessons" contain in order to anchor her identity. The knowledge and wisdom passed down through generations supplement what she reads in books. She *needs* the strength that this knowledge imparts, and from this knowledge she gains power.

The patterns established in *Caged Bird* continue in Angelou's subsequent autobiographies, *Gather Together in My Name* (1974), *Singin' and Swingin' and Gettin' Merry Like Christmas* (1976), *The Heart of a Woman* (1980), and *All God's Children Need Traveling Shoes* (1986). The narrator adapts to her situation creatively, replenishing her sense of self in difficult circumstances, discovering her sexuality, and learning to play the role of nurturer-protector. Because of the loving protection, encouragement, and direction provided to Marguerite by her mother, her grandmother, and Flowers, she is better able to survive later confrontations with white society.

A specific encounter with racial violence motivates Momma to send her grandchildren to California. When whites force Marguerite's brother to help recover the sexually mutilated body of a lynching victim accused of "messing with" a white woman, Bailey begins to ask disturbing questions that his grandmother and uncle are not prepared to answer:

> His experience raised the question of worth and values, of aggressive inferiority and aggressive arrogance. Could Uncle Willie, a Black man, Southern, crippled moreover, hope to answer the questions, both asked and unuttered? Would Momma, who knew the ways of the whites and wiles of the Blacks, try to answer her grandson, whose very life depended on his not truly understanding the enigma? Most assuredly not. (*Caged Bird*, 168)

The enigma, of course, is the dialectical relationship between white hatred and black fear, which governed racial relationships in Stamps. Mrs. Henderson tried to protect Bailey and Marguerite by limiting their knowledge and by forbidding their discussion of certain topics (including "white people" and "doing it"), but the effectiveness of this method waned as her grandchildren approached young adulthood (*Caged Bird*, 30). Eventually, the two would unravel the enigma for themselves, based on observation and evidence.

Recognizing her inability to shelter her adolescent grandson and protect him from the routine racial violence that befell blacks in Stamps, Arkansas, Mrs. Henderson prays and begins making plans to relocate the children with their parents in California. Looking back on this experience in *Gather Together in My Name*, the autobiographer allows her grandmother to express a point of view she withholds in *I Know Why the Caged Bird Sings*. She says, "I never did want you children to go to California. Too fast that life up yonder. But then, you all's their children, and I didn't want nothing to happen to you, while you're in my care. Jew was getting a little too big for his britches." Mrs. Henderson views California as a land of opportunity for Bailey and Marguerite, "a place where lynchings were unheard of and a bright young Negro boy could go places. And even his sister might find a niche for herself."

Maya Angelou's celebration of self derives essentially from her celebration of the black women who nurtured her. She reveres not only the qualities of the individual women but also the tradition in which they participated and the way in which they prepared her, as best they could, to cope with the realities of being black and female. In *I Know Why the Caged Bird Sings*,

Momma conforms to the Jungian archetype of the Great Mother, protecting, nurturing, sheltering; Marguerite's own mother, Vivian Baxter, presents another representation of this same archetype. In "the transition from mother to grandmother," Jung wrote, "the archetype is elevated to higher rank." So it is with Marguerite's transition from childhood to motherhood; she is both initiated and reborn, becoming herself the carrier of the archetype.

In California, Marguerite comes under the primary care of her mother, a woman of great personal power, resourcefulness, and hypnotic beauty. "To describe my mother," writes Angelou, "would be to write about a hurricane in its perfect power. Or the climbing, falling colors of the rainbow. People she accepted paddled their own canoes, pulled their own weight, put their own shoulders to their own plows, and pushed like hell" (*Caged Bird*, 49). From her mother, Marguerite learns increased self-reliance; she grows out of the passive stage and begins to think for herself, asserting herself through action, and forging an identity and testing the perimeters of her cage through brief encounters with exploratory flight.

The motif of flight captures the spirit of Marguerite's adventurous attempts to transcend the limitations and restrictions imposed on her. Caught between her father's indifference and his jealous girlfriend when she goes to visit them in Southern California one summer, Marguerite runs away and lives for about a month in an abandoned junkyard with a financially independent and racially mixed group of youthful runaways. This experience has a positive effect in Marguerite's identity-building process:

> The unquestioning acceptance by my peers had dislodged the familiar insecurity. Odd that homeless children, the silt of war frenzy, could initiate me into the [brotherhood of man]. After hunting down unbroken bottles and selling them with a white girl from Missouri, a Mexican girl from Los Angeles, and a Black girl from Oklahoma, I was never again to sense myself so solidly outside the human race. (*Caged Bird*, 216)

Another positive identity-building experience occurs in the world of work. Marguerite is determined to become a "conductorette" on the San Francisco streetcars, even though no blacks have been hired previously. She visits the Market Street Railway Office with "the frequency of a person on salary" until she is hired, breaking the color barrier previously imposed against blacks and achieving a degree of independence (*Caged Bird*, 228).

The most significant area of challenge facing Marguerite is also the most intimate—that of self-image and sexuality. Considered less than attractive and not very well developed physically, Marguerite begins to harbor fears of being a lesbian after reading Radclyffe Hall's *Well of Loneliness.* Her heavy voice, large hands and feet, undeveloped breasts, and smooth armpits all seem clear indicators. A talk with her mother does nothing to alleviate her fear. Ironically, this irrational fear of lesbianism leads to Marguerite's pregnancy. What she needs, she decides, is "a boyfriend. A boyfriend would clarify my position to the world and, even more important, to myself. A boyfriend's acceptance would guide me into that strange and exotic land of frills and femininity." But in her social group, there are "no takers": "The boys of my age and social group were captivated by the yellow- or light-brown-skinned girls, with hairy legs and smooth little lips, whose hair 'hung down like horses' manes.' And even those sought-after girls were asked to 'give it up or tell where it is' " (*Caged Bird,* 238). Women deemed unattractive, Angelou writes, are "called upon to be generous" only if pretty girls are unavailable. Aware of this fact, Marguerite, like "Linda" in the Harriet Brent Jacobs narrative, plans the seduction of a handsome young man who lives in her neighborhood. Finding herself pregnant after the act (her first truly voluntary encounter with sex), she suffers feelings of "fear, guilt, self-revulsion" (*Caged Bird,* 241). She successfully conceals her pregnancy from her family for over eight months, managing to finish high school before revealing her secret to her mother.

The narrative itself ends, not with the birth of Guy, but with a poignant lesson taught by Marguerite's own mother. Though Marguerite could create a baby, she was herself still dependent on the protection and guidance of her mother. She lacked confidence in handling her child, her "total possession." "Mother handled him easily with the casual confidence of a baby nurse, but I dreaded being forced to change his diapers. Wasn't I famous for my awkwardness? Suppose I let him slip, or put my fingers on that throbbing pulse on top of his head?" (*Caged Bird,* 245).

One night, Marguerite's mother brings the three-week-old baby in to sleep with Marguerite, who protests vigorously, fearing that she will be "sure to roll over and crush out his life or break those fragile bones" (*Caged Bird,* 245). But her mother is insistent. In the night, she awakes to her mother's brisk but whispered command, ordering her to wake up but not to move. When she wakes up, she sees the infant sleeping peacefully by her side. "See," says her mother, "you don't have to think about doing the right thing. If you're for the right thing, then you do it without thinking" (*Caged Bird,* 246). Liliane Arensberg suggests that "Vivian Baxter, as a confident and compassionate mother lovingly bending over her daughter's bed . . . consummates Maya's growing sense of herself as an adult, life-giving woman."

As George Kent argues, *Caged Bird* "makes its public and political statements largely through generalizing statements which broaden individual characters into types: Grandmother Bailey into the Southern mother; Maya into the young black woman, etc."

Through her depiction of this nocturnal scene, Maya Angelou asserts her identity as both mother and daughter, as well as her relation to the maternal archetype. Her own mother, Vivian, still in the role of teacher-protector, is "elevated to a higher rank," becoming herself the grandmother or "Great Mother." Momma, of course, is elevated still higher. So having a baby was "the right thing to do" in that it opened new avenues of identity, not only for Marguerite, but for her mother and grandmother as well. Even though she was a young woman of only seventeen years who could not recognize the maternal instincts and imperatives that operated within her consciousness, she did, in fact, possess the necessary resources to raise and nurture her son. Through motherhood, she discovered new possibilities in her relationship with her mother and grandmother. In the words of Sidonie Smith, Marguerite "has succeeded in freeing herself from the natural and social bars imprisoning her in the cage of her own diminished self-image by assuming control of her life and fully accepting her black womanhood." And like her archetypal models, she would support her own child with ingenuity and inventiveness.

Maya Angelou has said that she is one of "a generation of women writers, writing in desperation to identify themselves and their times, to provide encouragement and direction" and to have a say in the definition of "what's really happening" (*ODU*). For her, the writing of autobiography is a conscious assertion of identity, as well as the presentation of an alternate version of reality seen from the point of view of the black female experience. Near the end of *I Know Why the Caged Bird Sings*, Angelou summarizes that point of view:

> The Black female is assaulted in her tender years by all those common forces of nature at the same time that she is caught in the tri-partite crossfire of masculine prejudice, white illogical hate and Black lack of power.
>
> The fact that the adult American Negro female emerges a formidable character is often met with amazement, distaste, and even belligerence. It is seldom accepted as an inevitable outcome of the struggle won by survivors and deserves respect if not enthusiastic acceptance. (*Caged Bird*, 231)

Like Era Bell Thompson, Maya Angelou speaks with the triple consciousness of the *American Daughter*. And she speaks, as do many other black autobiographers, both male and female, as a survivor. She knows why she has survived and what the source of her strength has been. She has chosen to honor that source even as she celebrates the emergence of her indeed "formidable character."

FRANÇOISE LIONNET

Con Artists and Storytellers: Maya Angelou's Problematic Sense of Audience

> The story, though allegorical, is also historical; . . . and it is as reasonable to represent one kind of imprisonment by another, as it is to represent anything that really exists by that which exists not.
>
> —Daniel Defoe, *Robinson Crusoe's Preface*

> My books. They had been my elevators out of the midden.
>
> —Maya Angelou; *Gather Together in My Name*

As a literary foremother, Zora Neale Hurston meant a great deal to Maya Angelou the autobiographer. Urged by her editor to start work on a multivolume project about her life, Hurston said that she really did not "*want*" to write an autobiography, admitting that "it is too hard to reveal one's inner self." Like Hurston, Angelou affirms that she "really got roped into writing *The Caged Bird*," challenged by an editor who dared her to succeed in the difficult task of writing "an autobiography as *literature*." That she wrote it as literature is the specific aspect of her work on which I shall focus in this chapter. Because the autobiographical project was a response to external pressures, it is in many ways directed to a white audience, but at the same time, it succeeds in gesturing toward the black community, which shares a long tradition among oppressed peoples of understanding duplicitous uses of language for survival. Thus a passage of *I Know Why the Caged Bird Sings* encapsulates the questions of "truth" and referentiality as well as Angelou's problematic sense of audience. In that passage, Angelou alludes to her grandmother's secretive and cautious ways with language:

> Knowing Momma, I knew that I never knew Momma. Her African-bush secretiveness and suspiciousness had been compounded by slavery and confirmed by centuries of promises made and promises broken. We have a saying among Black Americans which describes Momma's caution. "If you ask a Negro where he's been, he'll tell you where he's going." To understand this important information, it is necessary to know who uses this *tactic* and on whom it works. *If an unaware person* is told a part of the truth (it is imperative that the answer embody truth), he is satisfied that his query has been answered. *If an aware person* (*one who himself uses the stratagem*) is given an answer which is truthful but bears only slightly if at all on the question, he knows that the information he seeks is of a private nature and will not be handed to him willingly. Thus direct denial, lying and the revelation of personal affairs are avoided. [164–65; my italics]

For Momma, the "signifying" of truths and untruths varies according to the status of her interlocutors, and it is in this differentiation between the "unaware" interlocutor and the "aware" that we can begin to understand Angelou's conception of "autobiographical" narration and the double audience she addresses in her writings: an audience split along racial and gender lines but also—and this is the important point here—split between those interlocutors, on the one hand, who share with the narrator an unquestioned sense of community and those, on the other hand, who have a relationship of power over that narrator.

Clearly, for Angelou, writing an autobiography has little to do with "the revelation of personal affairs," and like Hurston, she does not "reveal [her] inner self." Indeed, the passage about Momma can be read as an important example of the "self-situating" power of literary texts. Momma's caution functions as an explicit warning to the reader, who is thus challenged to take note of the double-voiced nature of Angelou's text. Her narrator alternates between a constative and a performative use of language, simultaneously addressing a white and a black audience, "image making" (CT 1) and instructing, using allegory to talk about history and myths to refer to reality, thus undermining the institutions that generate this alienated form of consciousness. Here, Angelou provides us with a model for reading and interpreting her narratives, just as Hurston had in her discussions of form and content, truth and hyperbole.

But unlike Hurston, whom we could see as strongly connected to other women in a network of friendly relationships, as well as to rich and solid folk traditions she helps to reclaim—that of "conjure women," for example—Angelou's narrator is a much more picaresque heroine, a modern-day Moll Flanders, who learns to survive by her wits. In that respect, she too is related to a black folk tradition, but one that is perhaps perceived as more "male": the shiftless trickster or con man, who relies on his ability to tell a good "story" to get out of sticky situations (Brer Rabbit, for instance). The narrator's mother also fits into this tradition. She is a consummate "business woman," runs her rooming house with a fist of steel, has "a roster of conquests" (*IK* 186) that testify to her independent nature. She is a Jill-of-all-trades who, by the fourth volume of the narrative, is said to have been "a surgical nurse, a realtor, had a barber's license and owned a hotel" (*HW* 28). The relationship between Maya and her mother has puzzled critics who have tried to approach the "autobiography" from the perspective of a "metaphysics of matrilinearism." I prefer to see in the descriptions of Vivian Baxter's life and character the model of a streetwise, self-confident, "finger-snapping" woman (cf. *IK* 54). It is against this maternal persona and role model that Maya the narrator keeps measuring her accomplishments, only to find herself lacking. Her mother is so competent that she can only feel inadequate when she tries to emulate Vivian's indomitable individualism.

An example of Maya's imitative strategy is her attempt at running a whorehouse on the outskirts of San Diego. (*GT* chaps. 13–15). This episode ends, after her efforts at outsmarting the tough lesbian whores who "work" for her prove unsuccessful, in her bewildered flight back to her grandmother's store in Arkansas. As the narrative develops, Maya gradually acquires her own survival techniques. These are, in a metaphoric way, closely linked to the development of her skills as "singer," "dancer," and "storyteller." In one of her San Francisco nightclub acts, for instance, she adopts the stage role of Scheherazade and succeeds, she says, because "I convinced myself that I was dancing to save my life" (*SS* 60). Her stated frame of reference is fiction and literature, and her style parodies that of such fictional autobiographies as *Moll Flanders*.

In this chapter, while focusing on Angelou's double-voiced technique of storytelling, I would like to emphasize three points. The chapter's first section shows how the narrator's love of books, always and everywhere, manages to pull her "out of the midden" (*GT* 90). As Tzvetan Todorov has said, "The desire to write does not come from life but from other writings." Books are Angelou's "first life line" after the traumatic events of her childhood (*IK* 77) and will continue to inspire her throughout her career. During her travels, for example, it is often through the prism of literature that she discovers and appreciates the peoples and places she visits: Verona through Shakespeare, Paris through Maupassant, London through Dickens. It thus seems appropriate, when analyzing her text, to use the literary paradigms she so cleverly manipulates. My second point concerns her use of the religious tradition: she inverts its messages, creating in the process nothing less than a feminist response to Augustine's *Confessions*. Finally, the third section shows how her problematic sense of audience is translated textually by an astute use of various embedded instances of alienated and nonalienated forms of human communication deriving from her folk traditions.

The Picaresque Heroine

Angelou's style owes as much to eighteenth- and nineteenth-century English narratives—those of Swift, Defoe, and Dickens in particular—as it does to the black vernacular. It is truly a crossroads of influences and, at its best, weaves all these strands into a pattern in which, though they have become indistinguishable from one another, they give depth and detail to the narrative. George E. Kent has shown that "two areas of black life" subtend the development of Angelou's narrative, "the religious and the blues traditions." Her grandmother represents the religious influence: black fundamentalism, the Christian Methodist Episcopal church. Her mother, on the other hand, stands for the "blues-street" tradition, the fast life. I agree with Kent's analysis but also believe there is a third term to add to this comparison: the literary tradition, all the fictional works the narrator reads avidly. This third tradition is represented figuratively in the text by two other strong women, Bertha Flowers and Martha Flowers (*IK* 77; *SS* 115). The text constructs these characters as fictional, boldly giving them almost identical names and stating that *flowers* is a recognizable slang word for "monthlies," or menstruation, in the black prostitutes' subculture (*GT* 39). When the narrator learns this "special" meaning of *flowers* from the two lesbian whores, she shows embarrassment and immediately resorts to "words" to conceal her feelings, to cope with her discomfort: "I knew that words, despite the old saying, never fail. And *my reading had given me words to spare*. I could and often did to myself or my baby, recite whole passages of Shakespeare, Paul Lawrence Dunbar poems, Kipling's 'If,' Countee Cullen, Langston Hughes, Longfellows's [*sic*] *Hiawatha*, Arna Bontemps. *Surely I had enough words to cover a moment's discomfort.* I had enough for hours if need be" (*GT* 40; my italics).

The flow of words is meant to cover a momentary discomfort, a discomfort due to an allusion to "flowers," which thus connotes an implicit comparison between women's creative and procreative powers. The juxtaposition between the slang word and "literary" words points back to the narrator's rediscovery of human language after her deflowering at the age of eight. It is thanks to the help of "Bertha Flowers," who teaches her to recite poetry, that she begins to talk again after a year of sensory numbness and dumbness, following the rape trial. This juxtaposition also points forward to her friendship with "Martha Flowers," "a great soprano" and a member of the *Porgy and Bess* touring company, who will share her European experiences. Language and menstruation are thus brought into implicit parallel as flow, voice, words, songs all connote by association the fluid movements of music or text. There is a creative tension between Angelou's Nietzschean need to be free to "write with blood" and the narrative control she exerts on plot development. What this tension denotes is her attempt to come to terms with the paradoxes and contradictions inherent in the concept of female creativity.

Indeed, the comparison between intellectual production and pregnancy, creativity and procreation, has been a commonplace of Western discourse since Socrates, who practiced intellectual *maieusis* on his students. What seems to be implied in Angelou's text is that menstruation is a far better paradigm for creativity, a paradigm Marie Cardinal will use with considerable effect in *The Words to Say It.* Are we to infer that Angelou is implying a conflict between writing and mothering? I would suggest not, in view of the role assigned to her mother, Vivian Baxter. Full of energy and self-confidence, she represents creativity in the "rhythm and blues" tradition, and Angelou uses images of liquids to describe her: "As I scrambled around the foot of the success ladder, Mother's life flowed radiant. Fluorescent-tipped waves on incoming tides" (*GT* 104).

The mother's energy flows unchecked and unselfconsciously. She has raw power, and her style is improvised like the ebb and flow of jazz. If this flow of creative rhythms is in counterpoint to the actual mothering of a real child, it is interesting to note again that Angelou the author dedicates her first volume to her son. Perhaps this is a perfect example of the ambivalence that occupies the center of all feminist problematics about writing: to produce the book, the woman must follow rhythms of creativity which may be in conflict with the mothering/nurturing role. To be sure, one can see Vivian Baxter as a nonnurturing, highly competitive, and goal-oriented mother. Yet she is the one who teaches Maya to trust her body, to follow her maternal instincts when her son Guy is born. *I Know Why the Caged Bird Sings* ends in the physical experience of giving birth to Guy. "Famous for [her] awkwardness," the narrator "was afraid to touch him." But Vivian coaxes her into sleeping with the baby, although at first she "lay on the edge of the bed, stiff with fear, and vowed not to sleep all night long" (245). Eventually she relaxes and sleeps with her arm curled and the baby touching her side. This experience teaches Maya the same lesson that Milkman, the hero of Toni Morrison's *Song of Solomon*, learns facing death, that "if you surrendered to the air, you could *ride* it."

Vivian puts it in a less poetic, more pragmatic way, teaching Maya that her body is a friend she can trust: "See, you don't have to think about doing the right thing. If you're for the right thing, then you do it without thinking" (246). What this remark implies is that the conflict between productive and reproductive roles is a false problem, a myth created by false anxieties; nonetheless it is a myth internalized by women writers, perhaps because there are as yet so few "creative mothers," like Vivian Baxter, who can show us how to "surrender to the air" *not* just in order to face death but so as to do "the right thing . . . without thinking," without being petrified by fear and guilt in the face of life, which is always change, flux, flow, tide, rhythm—like the music Vivian Baxter loves.

To the extent that Angelou feels strongly that a mother can never be fully independent—psychologically detached, that is—she constantly wrestles with this conflict. Her text embodies these tensions in its structure. During her year in Europe, she keeps having pangs of anxiety about her son, although she enjoys "every minute" of freedom: "Uncomfortable thoughts kept me awake. I had left my son to go gallivanting in strange countries and had enjoyed every minute except the times when I had thought about him" (*SS* 230). Hysterical from guilt and anxiety after her son becomes sick, she pays a useless visit to a psychiatrist, for whom, she imagines, she is only "another case of Negro paranoia" (235). Finally, she follows the advice of a friend and *writes* down her blessings: " I can hear / I can speak . . . I can dance / I can sing . . . I can write" (236). She regains her self-confidence, and her son simultaneously recovers: "Before my eyes a physical and mental metamorphosis began, as gradually and as inexorably as a seasonal change" (237). To write is to give herself the permission not to feel guilty. To write is to love her son in a life-affirming way. The third volume ends on this image of rebirth for both mother and son: she writes and he "names" himself, as we shall see presently. There is no real conflict: it was only a societal myth about maternal neglect, an internalization of false dichotomies between mothering and smothering or mothering and working.

Angelou attempts to solve the conflict textually by creating metaphors that point to a reality beyond this form of deadly dualism. She creates a mythology of the "creative mother" so that other mothers writing do not have to "feel like a motherless child" (as the spiritual says) when attempting to be creative. For Nikki Giovanni, another contemporary black autobiographer, to "feel like a motherless child" is to be without a mythology of our own because we have "underestimated our strength." The power to create mythology is a characteristic of the "honkies" that Black women should imitate, she says. "the honkie is the best mythologist in creation. He's had practice because his whole wrap [*sic*] is to protect himself from his environment." Clearly stated here is the quintessential Western dichotomy between nature and culture. Learning to "ride the air," however, would mean learning to be nurtured by nature—as Colette knew well—learning to take pleasure in the materiality of the world (our children), as well as the materiality of the word (our writing), as Angelou discovers. We are not very far from Roland Barthes's statements in *The Pleasure of the Text*:

> If it were possible to imagine an aesthetic of textual pleasure, it would have to include *writing aloud* [*l'écriture à haute voix*]. . . . its aim is not the clarity of messages, the theater of emotions; what it searches for (in a perspective of bliss [jouissance]) are the pulsional incidents, the language lined with flesh, a text where we can hear the grain of the throat, the patina of consonants, the voluptuousness of vowels, a whole carnal stereophony: the articulation of the body, of the tongue, not that of meaning, of language. A certain art of singing can give an idea of this vocal writing.

This "vocal writing" is familiar to Vivian who "sang the heavy blues . . . [and] talked with her whole body" (*IK* 54), and to Bertha Flowers, who advises Maya: "Words mean more than what is set down on paper. It takes the human voice to infuse them with the shades of deeper meaning" (*IK* 82). It is also familiar to anyone who has ever told stories to a small child, stories that infuse words with meaning and let the child hear "the grain of the voice," as Barthes would say. Children who are learning to use language enjoy the density of words in precisely that playful way.

Angelou's own playfulness with words is evident in her choice of names for the characters. The names of the narrator, her brother, her mother, her son, and her lovers all bear interesting indications of a fictional and metaphoric use of language, closely resembling Defoe's in *Moll Flanders*. Maya Angelou, as she explains, is the stage name of Marguerite Johnson (*marguerite* being the French word for a flower, the daisy). Maya, she writes, is a name created for her in childhood when her brother started calling her first "my sister," then "my," "mya," and finally "Maya" (*IK* 57). Angelou is a corruption of her first husband's name, Angelos. Tosh Angelos is a Greek who shares her love of jazz (i.e., black) music and English (i.e., white) literature, but their marriage fails because "he wrapped us in a cocoon of safety" (*SS* 27), which was like another cage, a shield, a veil against reality. After her divorce, she finds a job as a dancer in a bar: "If men wanted to buy my drinks, I would accept and tell them [the truth]. . . . That, along with imaginative dancing, would erase the taint of criminality. *Art* would be my *shield* and honesty my spear" (*SS* 58; italics mine).

The narrator abandons one kind of shield—marriage—but adopts a new one—art and dance. Now, in the Hindustani language, *māyā* is the word for "veil," and in Vedantic philosophy it is synonymous with the power to produce illusions and appearances. The Goddess Mahāmāyā personifies the world of illusion, and she is the power that creates phenomena. Might the author want to imply that the narrative is fiction and illusion, creations of Angelou, the author? That, like God, she has the power to (re)create the life story of the narrator, to show that she is an "angel," but in appearance only? That she "sings" like an angel, perhaps? And dances, like Salome, a "Dance of the Seven Veils" (*SS* 45), creating a multilayered artistic illusion? The text clearly allows for all these interpretations. Furthermore, if "Maya" is a creator and a goddess, she is invested with powers comparable to those of the "conjure women" of black tradition, and we would thus be justified in reinscribing this text within that tradition. I do not intend to do this here, but I do want to point out that this possibility exists, especially when we consider that the Greek word *angelos, -ou* means "messenger." Maya thus figures as the creator, Angelou as her messenger, the one who brings her forth while remaining veiled (*maya angelou* means the veil of the messenger: an interesting combination of Indo-European roots).

Ironically, Vivian Baxter's name points to an eighteenth-century figure with whose writings Defoe was familiar, the Reverend Richard Baxter, whose preaching style and "technique of persuasion," writes Ian Watt, "depended almost entirely on the simplest of rhetorical devices, repetition." Defoe and Angelou both rely heavily on the same device. In her texts repetition is most striking in the short summaries or recapitulations of past events that stud the narrative and serve as reminders to the reader before the onset of new developments. These are more and more frequent in the third and fourth volumes, becoming a leitmotiv, like the choral responses of church prayer and music, which are meant to create familiarity and audience participation. This style of conscious repetition harks back to the advice Baxter gives as a preacher. Discussing Baxter and the influence he has had on Defoe, Ian Watt quotes the eighteenth century preacher: "If we speak anything briefly, they feel not what we say. Nay, I find if we do not purposely dress out the matter into such a length of words, and use some repetition of it, that they may hear it inculcated on them again, we do but overrun their understandings, and they presently lose us."

All preachers, and those in the black church especially, use this technique. Angelou follows Baxter's advice on a purely textual level: her narrative mimics and parodies this style. On metaphoric and symbolic levels, however, she constructs an interesting inversion of this paradigm: Vivian Baxter, fast living, impatient, with no interest in details and repetitions ("Vivian Baxter could and would deal with grand schemes and large plots, but please, pray God, spare her the details." [*SS*, 101]), is the female character she most admires and openly tries to emulate, as daughters emulate mothers. Vivian Baxter is a figurative inversion of her eighteenth century namesake—the preacher—as her "blues-street" life makes clear. So, on the one hand, we have a religious style that allows us to insert Angelou's work back into the black *religious* context. On the other hand, we have a textual figure, Vivian, who is a model for the narrator and who embodies the free style of improvisation (with variation on and repetition of a single basic pattern) in black *music*: jazz and the blues. The link between these two poles is the literary tradition, which relays Richard Baxter, by means of Defoe's *Moll Flanders*, to the twentieth-century black female writer. The biological mother, Vivian Baxter, has a fictional counterpart in Moll, whose "autobiography" could be seen as the matrix that allows Angelou to produce and reproduce her own narrative discourse. As a central and polysemic narrative figure, Vivian embodies all the traditions whose combined influences are evident in Angelou's textual production.

Furthermore, the anxieties Maya feels before her mother seem to metaphorize the author's relation to the British narrative tradition: meeting her mother in St. Louis, Maya is stunned by Vivian's beauty and presence. Her light skin, straight hair, and talented dancing make her unreal to her children. "I could never put my finger on her realness" (*IK* 57), and she is "like a pretty kite that floated just above my head," (54) says Maya. She is an unattainable ideal, distant and out of reach for her "ugly" daughter. I would suggest that we can read in the descriptions of this too beautiful, almost white mother, the same "anxiety of authorship" that Angelou the writer may feel before her literary precursors, such as Daniel Defoe, for example, whose *Moll Flanders* she nonetheless tries to emulate. This eighteenth century narrative, closer in language to many southern idioms than those are to contemporary standard English, offers a sympathetic yet inescapably alienating reading of an individualistic "heroine." Vivian Baxter is such an individualist, and in *Gather Together in My Name*, the narrator does attempt to adopt her mother's life-style. But in sharing ideals of beauty and independence which are beyond reach, the daughter only alienates herself. Similarly, the English literary tradition has a beauty and a power that attract Angelou the writer, yet must leave her feeling inadequate before her precursor's discursive models of staunch individualism.

Angelou gives other clues to help the reader understand her naming technique: her son's name in the second volume is Guy. Then in the third volume, he becomes "Clyde," without explanation. We could see this as one example of the kind of "casual attitude to . . . writing," as Ian Watt puts it, which goes far toward explaining the "inconsistencies in matters of detail which are very common in all [Defoe's] works." Except that in Angelou's case, the matter of her son's name is hardly a "detail." At the end of the third volume, we are given the explanation that he himself has just decided to change his name to Guy. Clyde, he says, is "an O.K. name for a river, but my name is Guy" (238). At no point does the narrative explain or suggest why he was Guy throughout the second volume. What we can infer from the name Clyde however (the Clyde River of Scotland), is the idea of flowing waters, metaphoric female creation and procreation. Changing his name to Guy, this fatherless son appropriates the absent father's prerogative of naming and chooses a first name that is unmistakably "masculine": he thus sets himself apart from the female creative principle. As Janheinz Jahn says in his study of African culture: "The new-born child becomes a muntu only when the father or the 'sorcerer' gives him a *name* and *pronounces* it. Before this the little body is a kintu, a thing; if it dies it is not even mourned. . . . A creature . . . which has its place in the community of men is produced, not by act of birth, but by the word-seed: it is designated." Thus Clyde becomes a true member of the community after he has assumed the responsibility of naming himself. It marks the beginning of his separation and emancipation from the maternal realm. He is nine years old, and his show of independence connotes another separation, as in the act of birth, after a nine-month gestation. The child of her "immaculate pregnancy" (*IK* 245), he has now become a true "muntu" and designated himself as such: Guy, a guy, a man who rejects the erasure of his African past in much the same way that Malcolm X did by changing his name.

The names given to Maya's lovers and husbands suggest a duplicitous use of language and a conscious effort of fictional narration. *Tosh* in Scottish, means trim (and in black slang, to get or give "some trim" means to get laid [cf. *IK* 240]), as well as neat and proper. Tosh Angelos is a very proper and protective husband until marriage turns him into a louse. On the cruise ship that takes the opera company from Italy to Egypt, Maya meets the ship's doctor whose "eyes smoldered wonderful promises" (*SS* 201). He too is Greek: Geracimos Vlachos. But he says, "l am called Maki." He wants to marry her in order to emigrate to the United States, where he will be able to "make money" (214) practicing medicine. She flatly refuses. In the next volume, she marries a black South African freedom fighter. "His name was Vusumzi Make (pronounced Mahkay)" (*HW* 104). He turns out to be pretentious and overbearing. In Cairo she soon becomes disillusioned with this fake "African King," who furnishes their apartment in "Louis XVI brocaded sofa and chairs . . . French antique furniture . . . Oriental rugs," (*HW* 214). Instead of experiencing the "African" way of life, she is burdened with all the external signs of European monarchy. The words *make* (Old English) and *maki* (Old Norse) are cognates: they both mean mate, consort, spouse. It is quite clear that these three characters are facets of the same type and that Angelou is playfully suggesting ironic similarities among them.

The theme of similarity within difference in their names seems to point to a philosophy of life at once similar and different from Moll's (and Vivian Baxter's): the economic individualism of Moll would have dictated that she marry Maki, the doctor, since his M.D. degree could be turned into real currency, real wealth. Also, Moll would have taken advantage of Make's lavish life-style, but Maya only finds it distasteful and alienating. Defoe is "not ashamed to make economic self-interest his major premise about human life," says Watt. Angelou's premise is more *engagé* and more modern. Like Defoe, she uses what Watt calls "an episodic but life-like plot sequence," but her aim is always to return to the familiar and nurturing domain of books and literature. Like Moll, Angelou's narrator has definite ambitions, but whereas Moll wants to become a gentlewoman, Maya wants immortality and fame. She wants to join the "elite group of published writers" (*HW* 85): "I decided that one day I would be included in the family legend. . . . my name would be among the most illustrious. . . . I had written a juicy melodrama in which I was to be the star" (*GT* 28). Defoe writes with great sympathy for women's restricted roles in society, and Moll is a good example of a woman "smart enough" not to allow herself to be involuntarily restricted by a feminine role. Angelou's narrator struggles against similar social codes, and eventually finds the courage to stand her ground and define her territory, but it is the territory of a "too smart" woman (*GT* 166): libraries, books, and writing. In Cairo, she becomes a journalist (as Defoe was), and takes refuge in the newsroom of the *Arab Observer* and in its "library with hundreds of books in English" (HW 231). She achieves a measure of emancipation thanks to her intellectual talents and her love of books. It is quite an accomplishment for the little girl from Stamps, who grew up in the red dirt of the American South, "where children become bald from malnutrition" (*SS* 110). Her checkered existence finally comes to a resting point in Accra, where she lands a job as administrative assistant at the University of Ghana.

Language and Silence

The title of Maya Angelou's first volume, *I Know Why the Caged Bird Sings*, introduces the major metaphors that will run through all four of her books: imprisonment and singing. *In Black Autobiography in America*, Stephen Butterfield compares this work with those of Richard Wright and Frederick Douglass. The male writers, he says, tend to portray their lives of struggle against the white oppressor and their efforts to destroy the "cage" of racism and slavery, "But, unlike *Black Boy* and *The Life and Times*, the subject of *I Know Why the Caged Bird Sings* is not really the struggle of the bird; it is the exploration of the cage, the gradual discovery of its boundaries, the loosening of certain bars that she can slip through when the keepers' backs are turned.

Indeed Maya's "struggle" is of a different nature from that of the males: more personal and less public or social. There are no direct or violent confrontations with intense racial overtones. Her sense of humor is in sharp contrast to the seriousness of a Richard Wright. But I would suggest that, as the title of the volume implies, her subject is much more than the "exploration" or representation of this circumscribed domain. It is, rather, the investigation of the process through which the "bird" learns how to sing and the reasons why she does so in the face of adversity. To discuss the how and the why of the song, however, requires us to do a careful analysis of the textual layers and of their structuring moments.

For example, the store where Maya and her brother live, "her favorite place to be" (13), the center of activity in Stamps and the source of food and surprises, is an important structuring image, whereas the rape trial is a central and structuring moment of the first volume. The store full of treasures is like a book that contains unexpected pleasures for the reader ("Alone and empty in the mornings, it looked like an unopened present from a stranger. Opening the front doors was pulling the ribbon off the unexpected gift"

[13]). The only place she calls "home" (*GT* 63), the store is a metaphor for the storehouse of memory, which can be opened—as the "cage" will be opened—by the ribbon of language. It is a refuge like the libraries and the books she loves (and indeed she will seek refuge in a library after her rape). For Marie-Therese Humbert too the village store will function as a protective matrix, as a safe and enclosed space where the narrator can feel restored and reborn.

The way in which Angelou's text presents the events leading both to her rape and to the trial provides an interesting context to the whole notion of familial rape vs. social violation. The trial scene is the subject of chapter 13, but it is already symbolically implied in the opening scene of the book, where the experience of being on display—in church—is powerfully rendered. This opening scene is a classic example of the theme of woman-as-spectacle, woman unwillingly displaying herself. Here, it is a little girl thrust before a community of people gathered to worship God the Father. She had been looking forward to this day, dreaming that she was going to "look like a movie star" when she recited her poem in church: "What you looking at me for? / I didn't come to stay . . ." But on that Easter morning, she does not metamorphose into "one of the sweet little white girls who were everybody's dream of what was right with the world" (1). Instead, she is painfully aware of the gap between that dream and her actual physical appearance: she is wearing a dress that is "a plain ugly cut-down from a white woman's once-was-purple throwaway" (2); her "skinny legs" and skin that "look[s] dirty like mud" seem to be the focus of everyone's gaze. Not surprisingly, she loses all her aplomb, forgets her lines, hears only the "wiggling and giggling" (1) of the other children, runs out of church: "I stumbled and started to say something, or maybe to scream, but a green persimmon, or it could have been a lemon caught me between the legs and squeezed. I tasted the sour on my tongue and felt it in the back of my mouth. Then before I reached the door, the sting was burning down my legs and into my Sunday socks" (3). As she runs back home "peeing and crying," all she can think about is that (as the popular superstition goes) she must *not* hold back the flow of urine or "it would probably run right back up to my head and my poor head would burst like dropped watermelon, and all the brains and spit and tongue and eyes would roll all over the place" (3). The problem is that she will surely "get a whipping" for losing mental and physical control and be mercilessly teased by the "nasty children" of the congregation. Her performance anxiety leads to complete failure, and failure results in harsh punishment imposed by family (the whipping) and society (the laughter of her peers).

This scene encapsulates all the elements that have become identified with the ambiguities of female performance: having to live up to an idealized image; feeling imprisoned in a body that does not correspond to the idealized image; dreaming of escaping from that "cage"; dealing with the problematics of public speech when "other things [are] more important," (1) such as the feeling of giving-oneself-away-as-spectacle (an "ugly" spectacle at that) and the literal numbness and dumbness that ensues. The flow of involuntary excretions is perceived as both releasing and threatening: if she holds it back, she may "die from a busted head"'; (3) if she lets it flow, she will surely be punished. To write or not to write is another facet of the same predicament. Until abolition de jure, but until much later de facto, it was a punishable crime to teach a black to read or write; yet we also believe that a talented person may be "driven to a numb and bleeding madness" if creativity is constantly stifled and finds no outlet. The bottom line remains painful: whatever her choices, the consequences are going to be difficult. In this case, she runs away from the public eye, choking back tears and laughter, her lines unspoken, her pride wounded. Her body has had the upper hand, its physical release from tension manifested in this uncontrolled urge to urinate.

This opening scene squarely pits the mind against the body, the mind biting the red dust of Arkansas because the body is such a great liability. It is particularly significant that this episode, chronologically out of sequence in the narrative, should set the tone for the story. For this is clearly the tale of a woman who learns to "let the words flow," to perform in public and sing "gloriously," and to find the positive links between body and mind that will allow her to break free of the cage of prejudice and self-hatred. As discussed before, the book ends on another physical experience, the birth of her son, which teaches her to trust her body's language and knowledge, to make it the source and the model of her creativity. This trajectory is a familiar one in many women writers' autobiographies. The positive links that Angelou finds are literature and music.

Initially, however, she is literally brainwashed into silence by religion, family, and society. Grandmother Henderson is the primary agent—and model—of this silence. During cotton-picking season, she would get up everyday at four o'clock and "creak down to her knees, and chant in a sleep-filled voice: 'Our Father, thank you for letting me see this New Day. . . . Guide my feet this day along the straight and narrow, and help me *put a bridle on my tongue*,'"(5; my italics). Saying too much or saying the wrong thing is akin to being impudent, and "the impudent child was detested by God" (22). The consistent self-control that Momma can exert in stressful encounters (cf. 24–27) is in sharp contrast to Maya's frequent loss of control in church. There is another instance of hysterical laughter and uncontrolled urinating in chapter 6, and these episodes are severely punished. The hysteria, however, comes right after the narrator has been commenting on her increasing capacity for tuning out the world and wrapping herself in a cocoon of silence and private daydreams: "Turning off or tuning out people was my highly developed art. The custom of letting obedient children be seen but not heard was so agreeable to me that I went one step further: Obedient children should not see or hear if they chose not to do so" (34).

This is the first ominous hint we have of the state of catatonic indifference she will fall into after the rape trial. Raped by her mother's neglected lover, she identifies with her rapist, whose densely physical presence had released in the lonely child a sense of belonging, of affiliation and security. Yet her trust is betrayed by the man she wanted to love as a father. Her body has suffered excruciating pain, but that in itself is nothing new for a child used to repeated corporal punishment. Her imaginary world of language and literature is stolen by the intrusion of phallic power. Her family, as a whole, fails her. Yet the "rape" is not over. She also has to confront society in the courtroom, and that encounter reduces her to total silence. It is during the trial that she finally internalizes the religious teachings of her childhood completely and consequently begins to perceive herself as evil: "I had sold myself to the Devil and there could be no escape" (73). The defendant's lawyer attempts to put the blame on her, and the child becomes convinced that she is responsible for the rape: "I didn't want to lie, but the lawyer wouldn't let me think, so *I used silence as a retreat* " (70; my italics). The child quickly learns how to decode the social system in order not to be victimized any further. She has no choice but to lie for survival's sake. On the familial and social level, the rapist has been punished, justice has been done. On a personal level, however, Maya's ordeal is just beginning: having sworn on the Bible to say the truth, she is now much more traumatized by the memory of the lie and by the belief that she is responsible for the man's death.

She begins to see herself, through society's eyes, as an ambiguous victim. She gets the message that she must, on some level, have done something wrong. Since the rapist is responsible for making her lie, he must be evil. Because of him, evil invades her too, she is hopelessly contaminated by those troublesome bodily fluids, which are polluting and taboo: "Obviously I had forfeited my place in heaven forever, and I was as gutless as the doll I had ripped to pieces ages ago. . . . *I could feel the evilness flowing through my body and waiting, pent up, to rush off my tongue if I tried to open my mouth*. I clamped my teeth shut, I'd hold it in. If it escaped, wouldn't it flood the world and all the innocent people?" (72; my italics). Language is a form of "evilness," waiting to escape from her inner self like those fluids and involuntary excretions that can be hard to control (urine or semen) or simply embarrassing ("flowers," or menstruation). Language is evil, polluting, uncontrollable, and most of all the source of undeserved and incomprehensible punishments. The little girl is thus in possession of another deadly secret: that every word she utters may allow her inner and evil reality to escape and to hurt or kill others. She has no choice but to remove herself from the community by refusing language:

> Just my breath, carrying my words out, might poison people and they'd curl up and die like the black fat slugs that only pretended.
>
> I had to stop talking.
>
> I discovered that to achieve perfect personal silence all I had to do was to attach myself leechlike to sound. . . . I simply stood still—*in the midst of the riot of sound. After a minute or two, silence would rush into the room from its hiding place because I had eaten all the sounds* (73; my italics).

Her isolation and alienation are complete. She achieves control over yet other bodily functions, her tongue, her breath. She closes off all her orifices, paradoxically, by letting the outside world of sounds rush in, so that the inner reality of evil is prevented from rushing out. She achieves "perfect personal silence" by being totally open, or *disponible*, to the external world while keeping her inner world repressed or suppressed.

The sequence of textual events Angelou establishes draws a close parallel between the experience of rape and the child's internalization of societal and religious standards. First, her body is appropriated by the father figure precisely on Saturday, the day she would normally have exercised her freedom to read, to "breath[e] in the world" of literature (64). Then, in the courtroom, she is given a reflection of herself as evil, just as in the opening scene of the book she saw herself mirrored in the eyes of the church community as a shameful and "black ugly dream" (2) who was "sucking in air to breath out shame" (1). Now she sees herself as a sinful and dirty vessel. Her secret and imaginary world has been violated, contaminated, and she can no longer escape there. Performance anxiety made her speechless in church. Now she discovers that language can perform, create reality, that language *is* powerful performance because it can kill. Mr. Freeman dies, and Maya metaphorically cuts off her own tongue.

In the Greek legend of Philomela, Tereus, and Procne, it is Tereus the rapist who, after violating Philomela, rips out her tongue in order to prevent her from telling the truth to her sister Procne, Tereus's wife. Philomela then sends to her sister a piece of embroidery on which she has woven her story. Maya's self-inflicted punishment is similar to Philomela's. But it is as a result of her own absorption of patriarchal, social, and religious discourses that she stifles herself. She has become a docile and benumbed element of the oppressive system that controls her life, until the discovery of literature allows her to weave her own story. It is clear from her own remarks that Angelou the author identifies with Philomela: when she first becomes a showgirl and a dancer in San Francisco, she is attracted to a drummer who befriends her but loves only his wife Philomena, about whom he says: "—pretty name, ain't it? She can tell a story that would break your heart. Or else she can make you split your sides" (*SS* 58). Angelou's own narrative is a tragicomic tale of growing up black and female in America. She creates an allegory of the feminine condition which cuts across historical, social, and racial lines, using laughter and compassion to defuse the implicit violence of her subject matter.

We may recall that in the *Confessions*, Augustine discusses his access to human language. ("I ceased to be an infant unable to talk, and was now a boy with the power of speech [non enim eram infans. . . . sed iam puer loquens eram]" as a function of his initiation into the "stormy or tempestuous life of human society [procellosam societatem]." His acquisition of the power of speech as well as his schooling in rhetoric are paralleled with the "fornications" he began to engage in, meaning "lying and cheating," as well as other "perversions." Ultimately, his progress to God must include a gradual silencing of his tongue, a quieting of the "storm" of language. It is the example of Bishop Ambrose which teaches him a nondiscursive spirituality of silence ("his voice was silent and his tongue was still"). That is why his "autobiography" ends with an exegetic reading of Genesis, a reading that puts the narrative chapters under erasure and eliminates all further "personal" or "literary" use of language by the author. Augustine becomes filled with the otherness of God and transcends his corporeality as he reaches a spiritual resting point in the Word of God, and in the text of Genesis. From then on, his use of language is confined to its ontological purposes: words are signifiers used to convey the transcendental signified, God.

Angelou's narrator also wants "to achieve perfect personal silence" as a means of redemption from the "evilness flowing through [her] body." That is why she quiets her tongue and thus removes herself from human society. But she cannot find peace in God because she had already "sworn on the Bible that everything [she] said would be the truth, the whole truth, so help [her] God" (*IK* 71). And the God she knows is not a warm, loving black father; rather she imagines him looking like the policeman who announces to her family the death of Mr. Freeman: "Had they found out about the lie?

. . . The man in our living room was taller than the sky and whiter than my image of God. He just didn't have the beard" (71). So she creeps into a cocoon of numbness and becomes almost catatonic, all her senses dulled: she hears people's voices as though muffled, cannot perceive colors very well, and forgets names. Meanwhile, her brother Bailey is becoming adept at using his "silver tongue" to shape words and "two-pronged sentences" (76) of sarcasm and jokes that enchant the rural community of Stamps, where they have both returned after the trial. Bailey is becoming the consumate con artist while the girl is sinking deeper into silence.

It is after a year in Stamps that she meets Mrs. Bertha Flowers, a very dark-skinned woman, whose color "was a rich black" (78). She is a maternal and nurturing figure like Momma, but her aristocratic demeanor and formal education make her an instant role model for Maya, the imaginative reader of English novels. This woman has a positive self-image and makes Maya "proud to be a Negro, just by being herself" (79). As a narrative figure, she is the opposite of the tall white godlike policeman, and she becomes Maya's savior, a sort of tribal deity who helps her reevaluate her position within the community as well as the community's virtues. Maya begins to compare the "uneducated" speech patterns of her grandmother unfavorably to Mrs. Flowers's perfect diction and elocution. The child begins to notice the "texture" of the human voice and simultaneously opens up to human language as Mrs. Flowers encourages her to read aloud and to try "to make a sentence sound in as many different ways as possible" (82). But she also teaches Maya that illiteracy is not ignorance and that in the "mother wit" of country people is "couched the collective wisdom of generations" (83). Thus, from the start, Maya is forestalled from a destructive temptation to hierarchize different cultural models or to devalue the "primitive" folk attitudes of her rural background—an insight which Angelou the writer surely owes to her familiarity with Hurston's work.

Mrs. Flowers recites *A Tale of Two Cities* and Maya hears poetry "for the first time" (84) in her life:

> "It was the best of times and the worst of times. . . ." Her voice slid in and curved down through and over the words. She was nearly singing. I wanted to look at the pages. Were they the same that I had read? Or were there notes, music, lined on the pages, as in a hymn book? Her sounds began cascading gently. I knew from listening to a thousand preachers that she was nearing the end of her reading, *and I hadn't really heard, heard to understand, a single word.* [84; my italics]

In contrast to the noise and "riot of sound" that make her deaf to the world and to herself, the narrator now discovers "vocal writing": the materiality of language, the self-referential nature of the poetic word, "the patina of consonants, the voluptuousness of vowels" as Barthes would suggest. She hears the sounds but does not understand their meaning, because meaning is not important. Language becomes an arbitrary system of signs not grounded in external reality, especially not in the transcendent meaningful reality of God but rather in the pure, playful immanence of sounds. The sensual joy of literature favors a process of ecstasis and self-dispossession as Maya escapes through imagination:

> I have tried often to search behind the sophistication of years for the enchantment I so easily found in those gifts. The essence escapes but its aura remains. To be allowed, no, invited, into the private lives of strangers, and to share their joys and fears, was a chance to exchange the Southern bitter wormwood for a cup of mead with Beowulf or a hot cup of tea and milk with Oliver Twist. When I said aloud, "It is a far, far better thing that I do, than I have ever done . . ." tears of love filled my eyes at my *selflessness*. [84; my italics]

Augustine too finds "selflessness" in reading: it is the process of reading which allows him to absorb in his human, historical, linear dimension the timelessness of eternal substance, the plenitude of intercourse and communion with God, and thus to return to his transcendent origins. His narrative and decentered use of language makes way for a selfless and silent disappearance into God's otherness which becomes his ideal self. And we may also recall here Nietzsche's warnings about "selflessness," which reading can favor, although it is also the source of great happiness: "Come to me pleasant, brilliant, clever books." For Augustine, "selflessness" is deference to God; for Nietzsche, it is the alienation by our cultural selves of our creatural, animal, and biocentric drives.

Reading, for Maya, is also depersonalizing, but this depersonalization returns her instead to the *collectively human* dimensions she had forsaken, with language, in her attempt to shield herself from the wrath of God the Father. Reading enables her to enter into a human dialogue with Mrs. Flowers, to discover a loving and nurturing intellectual relationship. She loses her *self* but merges with a community of *others*. Bertha Flowers is an ideal other but *not* a mirroring presence: she mediates and guides Maya's entry into a multiplicity of "private lives," which can only enlarge and enrich the girl's point of view, as they become her frames of reference, her lifelines to adulthood. It is worth noting that the literary texts Maya actually mentions correspond to the two secular poles discussed in this chapter, the folk tradition and literary discourse. Some critics read *Beowulf* as a medieval folktale, and *Oliver Twist* is a fictional autobiographical narrative. In this and many other such instances of situational self-reflexivity, the narrative signals to us the frame of reference within which it attempts to situate itself. It thus encodes models of reading appropriate to its messages and intrinsic to its structure, offering to the attentive reader the key paradigms needed for interpretative analysis.

Another such instance of situational self-reflexivity, this one within the religious mode, occurs when Maya starts having "secret crawl[s] through neighborhood churches" (*SS*, 28), in search of a way to get back in touch with a heritage and a territory that are gradually eroding under Tosh's white influence. She visits a black fundamentalist Baptist church and the text for the sermon is from the Old Testament: "Dry Bones in the Valley." The preacher is a master of his craft: "He told the story simply at first, weaving a quiet web around us all, binding us into the wonder of faith and the power of God" (31). Hypnotized by his style, she joins in the dancing and singing trances and is "reborn" as she surrenders to the power of the community. The teaching of this particular sermon, as she describes it, is a metaphor for the process of autobiography and anamnesis: "I knew of no teaching more positive than the legend which said that will and faith caused a *dismembered skeleton*, dry on the desert floor, to knit back together and walk" (*SS* 31; my italics). To re-member and piece together the past in the hope of achieving a degree of self-integration within language which will miraculously redeem her, save her from death and emptiness, indeed give her immortality, is the acknowledged project of writing for Maya. This "legend" of the Old Testament is a powerful way for her to get back in touch with her vernacular tradition after her more "cerebral" excursus into "high" art and literature.

If, living with Tosh, she begins to miss her "religious" tradition, with Make and in his political milieu she will miss "literature." This movement back and forth between religion and literature is dialectical only in appearance, for in both traditions she manages to extract the means of communication, the techniques of storytelling, which help her learn and refine her craft as a writer. She rejects the "white God" of religion but retrieves the cultural heritage of the black church, the sermons and the music, the gospel songs and spirituals, which are so close to the secular blues. When she starts going to church secretly, it is the music that attracts her at first: "The spirituals and gospel songs were sweeter than sugar" (28). This contact with the culture of her slave ancestors keeps her firmly anchored in the reality of her past, putting into perspective the "cerebral exercises and intellectual exchange" (*SS* 29) that were the basis of her relationship to Tosh. This episode is another allegorical representation within the "autobiographical" text of the history of black people in America. Religious gatherings were forbidden to slaves. Here, Tosh is violently opposed to religion. The slaves would still gather secretly to sing and chant and pray for "freedom" (usually in an afterlife) and to ritualistically glorify death as a release from the ills of this world. The narrator's and Tosh's relationship thus takes on mythic dimensions as it symbolizes an aspect of race (or master-slave) relations during preabolition days. Religion, like literacy, was considered a potentially subversive instrument in the hands of the slaves, and the masters needed to prevent, or severely repress, any hint of resistance or disobedience. Hence the "secret meetings in the woods to praise God ('For where two or three are gathered together in my name, there am I in the midst of them')" as the narrator recalls her great-grandmother, the former slave, teaching her (*SS* 28). Her secret church visits echo and connote that historical past.

Revival services and sermons are a *locus classicus* of black autobiographical narratives, and the treatment they receive varies according to the degree of alienation the narrator feels toward the evangelism of the black church. Not all black writers share Angelou's belief in the positive elements of black religion. Richard Wright is bitterly opposed to religious rhetoric, believing that it generates hypocrisy, sadism, cruelty, and hatred. Langston Hughes and James Weldon Johnson do not share her emotional response to revivalism. Johnson, for example, has a patronizing and humorous attitude toward the simple faith of southern blacks. Participating in a revival service, he falls asleep, and when someone shakes him, he pretends to be in a trance, and wakes up fully only to recount a "vision" and thus avoid blame. His distance and detachment are in contrast to Maya's surrender to the electrifying atmosphere of the Baptist church. As narrator, she handles the scene with irony and humor; but it is a wry commentary, after the fact, on her capacity for losing herself in the folk process of religious revival, for undergoing an emotional "rebirth."

Structurally, this episode of "rebirth" in the third volume, is a counterpoint to the narrative segment dealing with poetry and Mrs. Flowers in the first volume. Initially, Maya is reborn when she reenters the community of speaking humans via the medium of literature. Here, by contrast, we have a "religious" rebirth in the traditional revival mode: it is in fact a return to her black folk background. She succeeds in avoiding conflict between the various traditions as she adopts from each one the elements that are truly a part of "popular" or "vernacular" culture, be it folk tales or folk poems, (fictional) personal narratives, gospels, spirituals, or blues. The experience of rebirth could thus be seen as an exorcism from the self of those "polluting" thoughts and beliefs that lead to the devaluing of the collective wisdom and "mother wit" of her black heritage. With Tosh, the white atheist, it is the dryness of her overly refined life-style which begins to weigh on her: "After watching the multicolored people in church dressed in their gay Sunday finery and praising their Maker with loud voices and sensual movements, Tosh and my house looked very pale. Van Gogh and Klee posters which would please me a day later seemed irrelevant. The scatter rugs, placed so artfully the day before, appeared pretentious" (*SS* 29). Clearly, "the multicolored people" are so not just because of their "Sunday finery" but because the skin color of "black" people runs the gamut from the "fresh-butter color" of her mother (*IK* 49) to the "rich black . . . plum" of Mrs. Flowers (78), with all the intermediate variations: the "brown moon" of Momma's face (26), the "dark-chocolate" skin of her best friend, Louise (118): "Butter-colored, honey-brown, lemon- and olive-skinned. Chocolate and plum-blue, peaches-and-cream. Cream. Nutmeg. Cinnamon. I wondered why my people described our colors in terms of *something good to eat* " (*GT* 14; my italics). In variety and heterogeneity there is a sensual pleasure upon which her talent feeds (much as Augustine tells of "feeding" on God ["fruens te" 4:1]). Marriage to Tosh is a lonely and marginalizing experience, like her year of silence. By contrast, whenever she is integrated in a group of heterogeneous—though marginal—individuals, she feels truly comfortable. It is thus clear that the search for community and audience informs the whole process of narration for Angelou.

The month she spends hiding in a junkyard at the age of sixteen provides the first such experience of real community: a "collage of Negro, Mexican and white" (*IK* 214) homeless, outcast children become her "family." Liliane K. Arenberg has pointed out that "of signal importance is that these children disprove the racial prejudice—and its concurrent death fantasies—of her earlier experiences." She sleeps in a wrecked car, spends the day scavenging, and learns to survive against the odds. Instead of being acted upon, she increasingly gains control by acquiring useful skills: "During the month that I spent in the yard, I learned to drive . . . to curse and to dance" (215). Her brief stay in this small utopia—ironically referred to as Brobdingnag—gives her the self-confidence to accept the perniciousness of the real world while learning to shield herself from it and to use it to her advantage: "Odd that the homeless children, the silt of war frenzy, could initiate me into the brotherhood of man. After hunting down unbroken bottles and selling them with a white girl from Missouri, a Mexican girl from Los Angeles and a Black girl from Oklahoma, I was never again to sense myself so solidly outside the pale of the human race. The lack of criticism evidenced by our ad hoc community influenced me, and set a tone of tolerance for my life" (*IK* 216). This "ad hoc community" of multicolored children teaches her peace. Meanwhile the bulk of the adults are literally and figuratively engaged in war (World War II). Her experience of being unquestioningly accepted changes her completely, "dislodge[s] the familiar insecurity" (216) of displacement and dis-ease which had reached its apex when she was stabbed by Dolores, her father's girlfriend. Textually, she manages to encode a similar variety and diversity because she draws on so many traditions and weaves them into a narrative that integrates as many styles and influences as the "multicolored people" of the church gathering and the junkyard do. We are truly in the realm of *bricolage* here: biological miscegenation, social "junk" or "silt," and textual braiding, or *métissage*, of traditions.

Con Artists and Storytellers

In his discussion of Homer's *Odyssey*, Tzvetan Todorov distinguishes among three properties of speech: speech-as-action, or *parole-action*, speech-as-narrative, or pa*role-récit*, and feigned speech, or *parole feinte*. The last, he says, belongs simultaneously to both of the first two categories because it frees the sign from the referent (as in a *récit* or tale) with the express purpose of performing an act conveying information that can affect reality (as in speech-as-action). Feigned speech, then, is always performative.

In talking about the "tactics" and "stratagems" black narrators use to avoid dealing directly with "truth," Angelou stresses the performative aspect of Momma's cautious means of communication. We have seen how she signifies upon this tradition in her use of fictional narrative devices and in her naming, but Angelou also makes use of vernacular traditions that represent a purely constative case of "speech-as-narrative." This is a mode of oral narrative that can be divided into three categories: "poetic" speech (toasts and jokes), ghost stories, and fantasy.

First, the poetry of Maya's maternal uncles. They represent the urban traditions; they like to gossip, tell jokes, and roughhouse. Theirs, however, is a totally gratuitous and playful love of words: "Uncle Tommy . . . strung ordinary sentences together and they came out sounding either like the most profane curses or like comical poetry" (*IK* 56). The hearer is completely free to adduce his own meaning from Uncle Tommy's droll statements. He is a deft and natural comedian, whose purpose is only to entertain and thereby to reinforce an existing sense of community. The Baxter clan is a tightly knit, highly competitive group in which each individual must pull his own weight and do so with ease and aplomb. They have a high tolerance for variety and difference, so long as this difference does not reflect negatively on their strong sense of family. Here *parole-récit* is a humorous art and discourse, playful pleasure.

Second, the popular oral tradition of ghost stories, which help pass the time on long winter nights. The storytellers usually try "to best each other in telling lurid tales of ghosts and hants, banshees and juju, voodoo and other anti-life stories" (*IK* 133). Audience and performers share a common fascination for evoking the unknown, for conjuring the eerie. Again, the sense of community is intact. The purpose of these ghost stories is commonly understood: to frighten and entertain, to reinforce rural superstitions or old African beliefs, while the whole group shares sweet potatoes and peanuts slowly roasted under coals or ashes. In an episode of chapter 22 the visitor who comes to spend the stormy evening with them shares their dinner and impersonates his dead wife as he tells a ghoulish tale of her apparitions in the night. Like the parasite who entertains his hosts, he gets nourishment and pays it back with words. Of special interest in the staging of that episode is the intermingling of literature and folklore. Maya and Bailey are keeping warm by the potbellied stove while reading: he is immersed in *Huckleberry Finn* and she is rereading *Jane Eyre*. The arrival of the visitor interrupts that activity but the children remain suspended out of time as the ghost story inserts itself into their consciousness, becoming superimposed on the fantasy worlds of Twain and Brontë, worlds that happen to appeal to the same emotions: fascination with the unknown and escapism.

Third, fantasy, which is Maya's forte. When Momma takes her to a bigoted dentist, Maya imagines a triumphant confrontation between them, her toothache abating as she dreams of her grandmother obliterating the evil Dr. Lincoln. In the embedded story that she recounts to herself to alleviate the pain, the most significant distortion of reality is in the speech patterns of Momma: "Her tongue had thinned and the words rolled off well enunciated. Enunciated and sharp like little claps of thunder" (*IK* 161). She fantasizes that the dentist, on the other hand, stutters, drools, and has a very humble voice. Momma is larger than life and can even "afford to *slip into the vernacular* because she ha[s] such eloquent command of English" (161; my italics). In other words, to use the vernacular is a conscious choice the writer can allow herself after she has shown her ability to articulate her point of view in the "King's English."

In this instance of alienated, imaginary discourse (wishful thinking and feelings of impotence before an all too powerful and degrading social system), the fundamental dis-ease of this marginal character reveals itself. The narrator's conscious remarks about levels of language indicates that mastery of the master's English is the sine qua non of any subversive intent in a fictive utterance. Her fantasy, a counterpoint to the later episode in the dead car junkyard, is like a science fiction tale. It does not claim to have a direct bearing on daily reality, yet it satirizes the social structures that generate this alienated discourse, thus providing a powerful comment on reality. Its message is directed to Maya's initial, original community, the one that is powerless, and peripheral to the larger social sphere where Dr. Lincolns gravitate: yet, she implies, her community could wield mythic force (like Momma) if only it cared to appropriate (the master's) language.

As is becoming clear, the narrator learns many different styles of human communication from her extended family's tale telling, escapist tales that are antilife (like ghost stories) or triumphant (like her fantasy world in which villains are dispatched). But escapist tales involve no risks, and the story is a pleasurable (if sometimes scary) experience for both narrator and narratee(s). The didactic intent, if it exists, is of secondary importance. The primary consideration is the art of entertaining an audience whose presence and feedback are unproblematic.

But what happens when the storyteller becomes alienated from this initial community? Language then becomes a means of obtaining what is not willingly given, that is, attention, justice, reparation, and so on. And indeed it would seem that for Angelou, the process of writing is a way of articulating those particular alienations and the demands that ensue. To judge by her use of standard English (rather than dialectal speech patterns), it would seem that she aims her book at a primarily "white" audience of urbanized and educated readers. She does use some slang and colloquialisms, but her grammar is almost always standard, as is her spelling. Discussing her schooling in San Francisco, she says: "In the classroom we all learned past participles, but in the streets and in our homes the Blacks learned to drop *s*'s from plurals and suffixes from past-tense verbs. We were alert to the gap separating the written word from the colloquial. *We learned to slide out of one language and into another without being conscious of the effort*" (*IK* 191; my italics).

The "written word" is directed toward an audience that may not have the patience to decode the vernacular. Angelou, the "messenger," thus acts as translator. More important, however, Angelou self-consciously makes a distinction between written and oral which implies that mastery of the written language is the prerequisite to mastery over one's fate. Just as she had realized, with Mrs. Flowers, that "language is man's way of communicating with his fellow man and it is language alone which separates him from the lower animals" (*IK* 82), she now asserts that education and the ability to write correctly are tools in the hands of the oppressed, tools that must be honed and sharpened, the better to serve their purpose of communication. Since her stance, as indicated before, is clearly one of *engagement*, she thus assumes a responsibilty which can be fulfilled only if the "written word" is an instrument of social change. It is clear that she sees language as a tool that helps shape destiny. She is interested in its performative as well as its purely sensual aspects. Thus when her brother Bailey becomes estranged from his family and gets into drugs, gangs, and pimping, she notes: "His language had changed. He was forever dropping slangy terms into his sentences like dumplings in a pot" (*IK* 217), whereas he had been apt at manipulating speech patterns: "The double entendres, the two-pronged sentences, slid over his tongue to dart rapier-like into anything that happened to be in the way" (*IK* 76). He could still, when arguing with his mother, be a master of sharp wit: "Bailey looped his language around his tongue and issued it out to Mother in alum drops" (*IK* 219). But when trying to articulate, under stress, his love/hate relationship to ruthless Vivian, who pushes her children out of the nest, Bailey exerts control over his feelings by resorting to careful, almost painful efforts of language: "he chose his words with the precision of a Sunday school teacher" (*IK* 223).

Maya too makes great efforts to please her mother. She drops her southern euphemisms (cf. *IK* 234). She tries to become self-sufficient and worldly and acquires the difficult art of "dexterous lying" (229) in order to obtain what she wants. In one case, she wants a job as streetcar conductor; she wants to be the first black San Francisco "conductorette." As she goes to apply for the job, she must write a resume: "Sitting at a side table my mind and I wove a cat's ladder of near truths and total lies. I kept my face blank (an old art) and wrote quickly the fable of Marguerite Johnson, aged nineteen, former companion and driver for Mrs. Annie Henderson (a White Lady) in Stamps, Arkansas" (*IK* 229). She does get the job and acquires new status in her mother's eyes. It is hard-earned status, for between Bailey and Vivian, the expert verbal duelists, she is either a neutral third and excluded middle or a mediating confidante in their dialogue of deaf ears. Her normal tendency being to avoid confrontation, she prefers to give up territory and remain silent. As she explains, she does not dare compete with, or interfere in, Vivian's vast capacity to enjoy life and to fly into legendary rages: "Her tongue was sharper than the creases in zoot pants and I knew better than to try to best her. I said nothing" (*GT* 83).

In order to handle her own family, the narrator learns from a position of weakness how to swerve and to survive. This knowledge prepares her for life in white society, where the safest strategy is to wear masks: "Never let white folks know what you really think. If you're sad, laugh. If you're bleeding inside, dance" (*GT* 86). This training in adaptive behavior is an apprenticeship in dissimulation, a lesson in how to become a trickster, a manipulator of signs, a con artist and a writer. The trickster is like the fool, the one who draws attention to the king's nakedness and satirizes the accepted norms of a social order. In a pragmatic sense, though, for the satire or social critique to be effective it must be disguised, guileful, or artful, but not so deceitful as to be completely misunderstood, not so deceptive as to make us miss its "point." Of paramount importance, then, is the sense of an audience whose attention must be captured and retained. As a liminal figure, caught between her mother and brother, who are "entangled in the Oedipal skein" (*IK* 218), the narrator finds her ability to make herself heard severely curtailed. Her newfound sense of self-certainty and community after the junkyard experience collapses on itself as she reenters family life. She cannot share that experience, tell that tale, because her primary audience is indifferent and impatient. Busy Vivian has no time for details and increasingly slick Bailey is orbiting a different planet, no longer the brother she knew: "He may have been glad to see me, but he didn't act much like it. When I tried to tell him of my adventures and misadventures, he responded with a casual indifference which *stilled the tale on my lips*" (*IK* 217). Having a story to tell and the confidence to do so is not enough. Interaction with a real or virtual hearer is an integral part of the storytelling situation. At the end of the first volume, the narrator has found her voice, literally (with Mrs. Flowers) and figuratively (she now has a message to transmit). But she has no audience, or more precisely, her audience's indifference forces her into self-imposed silence. This is the familiar position of the spokesperson who feels that s/he is preaching to those who don't want to (can't) hear and who, consequently, either gives up, tries to find alternate means of reaching an audience, or resorts to various violent and confrontational tactics.

Of these alternatives, however, the only one possible for the artist is to seek means of expression which will convey her point of view without provoking blinding fear, disbelief, utter revulsion, and the concurrent tuning out of the audience. Perhaps it was Billie Holiday, the blues singer, who best exemplified that dilemma when she recalled her first rehearsals of the song "Strange Fruit," from Lewis Allan's story of a lynching: "I worked like the devil on it because I was never sure . . . I could get across to a plush nightclub audience the things that it meant to me." When there is no shared experience between singer and audience, the impact of the song can only be weighed hypothetically. Translation of the content into a form of expression that appeals to the subjective desires of the audience and facilitates their entry into the world of the other is hard work for the performer and becomes inseparable from her message.

As singer, dancer, and performer, Maya Angelou has an acute sense of audience interaction. She thus stages her own alienated relationship to her hypothetical reader, knowing full well that the reader must be "conned" into believing that she has a privileged relation to an autobiographical "truth," which the rhetorical features of her style explicitly problematize. This double bind determines her narrative choices of events and metaphors. In the narrative segment that describes her initial attempts at tale telling within the confines of her own indifferent family, we clearly see her giving up. At the other extreme, when she and Bailey come back south to live in the store after the St. Louis episode, the sense of community is unquestioned. All of Stamps would come to the store to be entertained with stories of their trip north, enabling Bailey to sharpen his "silver tongue" at the expense of the naive country folk. His audience is clearly defined and eager to lend its ears, even if he is shown to be considerably alienated from the rural people toward whom he directs his sarcasms. His experience of the urban North has estranged him from this initial community. Congruence between teller and listener need not be perfect if the teller has sufficient firsthand knowledge of the listener's general frame of reference and can tailor his discourse to (partially) fit that frame.

These linguistic skills differ only in degree from those of the successful and affluent gamblers (or numbers men), the real con men, their mother's friends. Foremost among them is Daddy Clidell, who introduces Maya to the colorful characters of the black underground and teaches her the fine art of swindling to keep her from ever becoming "anybody's mark" (*IK* 187). From Clidell's tales emerges a single pattern: the more stupid the con man acts, the more likely he is to win over his arrogant white "mark." This kind of ingenuity gives the con man hero status in the ghetto, where the ability to turn "the crumbs from his country's table. . . [into] a Lucullan feast" (190) is the most admired of skills. This skill rests on the culture-hero's ability to take control of a situation and assume certain risks while appearing to relinquish all authority. In other words, it involves a carefully planned strategem of deception, feigning, and role playing. We have already seen that the outcome of the rape trial had depended on Maya's ability to do just that: to decode the social system and respond to it in a deceitful way that put her in control. Her lie, or *parole feinte*, brought her to her mother's arms, "her desired destination" (71), while putting her at risk in the eyes of God. For the con artist, the aim is to spin a tale—*parole feinte*—with the express purpose of swindling the mark and profiting by it. The risk involved is in the eyes of the law: the punishment may be prison if the swindler is caught. In both cases, control puts the protagonist at risk with respect to the symbolic (religious or social) order and hence bears tragic or heroic dimensions. To have lied was deeply disturbing for Maya, the child raised in a fundamentalist milieu, and that was the religious tragedy of her success in the courtroom. What she now learns from these smart tricksters is the poetic justice of fighting back with tall tales and becoming wealthy in the bargain. Only then does she see the possibility of becoming the heroine of such triumphant tales.

At the end of her fourth volume, Angelou recounts a tale of Brer Rabbit: how he succeeded in winning his freedom from the angry farmer by pretending to be more afraid of the thorny briar patch than of the farmer's cooking pot. She identifies completely with Brer Rabbit, feeling just as free, standing in the library of the newsroom where she has earned the right to work and write for a living, despite Vusumzi Make's pompous initial objections. She has safeguarded his sense of honor by a ritualistic and complex appeal to his desire for power, control, and authority. In this instance, Maya is the fool and Make, the mark: all previous and implicit racial connotations in the tale of Brer Rabbit undergo a radical transformation. On the level of signifiers, the only remaining element of the tale is that power and control are best defined by an authoritative use of language. Power resides in the narrative figure, Maya, who can best reach out to the other, Make, and articulate his desires in terms of *her* needs. This is a technique that the narrative text shows Maya learning from many sources: her oral tradition as well as her newly acquired skills as a dancer and performer. What this suggests in terms of audience interaction is that Angelou's narrator, like Brer Rabbit, often seems to be telling us just what we want to hear, as "unaware persons" deserving only "a part of the truth." Once we understand her "tactics" and "stratagems," however, it becomes clear that for her, writing is a way of claiming her territory from forces that refuse to grant it, a way of telling us "not where she has been, but where she is going." Her technique, then would correspond exactly to what Michel de Certeau has termed "the practice of everyday life": an art of storytelling like the one Homer and the Greeks practiced and the con artists of today continue to perfect. It is a way of operating within a system of power which allows the "weak" to seize victories over the "strong" by employing "tactics" known to the Greeks under the name of *mētis*. It is a form of intelligence and savoir faire, a resourcefulness and an opportunism that is the hallmark of those who will never be the masters of the terrain on which their daily struggles are fought but who develop in practice multiple and polyvalent means of survival that allow them to elude that power system successfully. The double-voiced nature of Angelou's text allows her to oppose an oppressive social system without risk of becoming a term within that system, since a part of her message—because it relies on indirect "signifying" practices—will always elude any direct attempt to inscribe it within the general frame of that dominant discourse. This elusiveness bespeaks a form of alienation differing only in degree from Momma's "secretiveness and suspiciousness" and inherent in all survival strategies.

Indeed, in the briar patch Brer Rabbit is free to claim his space in the communal warren, whereas in the library, Angelou relentlessly explores the constantly changing boundaries of alienated human communication. We have the distinct feeling that she would like (us) to believe that her tale is a triumphant one but cannot quite convince herself of it. Hers is a *parole feinte* that mourns the loss of the illusory possibility of pure *parole-recit*, of direct and unmediated communication with interlocutors who share the same referential and mythic world as she does. In other words, she mourns the disappearance of a mirage, the mirage that is Africa for the children of the colonialist diaspora.

MARY JANE LUPTON

Singing the Black Mother: Maya Angelou and Autobiographical Continuity

> Now my problem I have is I love life, I love living life and I love the art of living, so I try to live my life as a poetic adventure, everything I do from the way I keep my house, cook, make my husband happy, or welcome my friends, raise my son; everything is part of a large canvas I am creating, I am living beneath.
>
> (Chrisman interview 46)

This energetic statement from a 1977 interview with Maya Angelou merely hints at the variety of roles and experiences which sweep through what is presently her five-volume autobiographical series: *I Know Why the Caged Bird Sings* (1970), *Gather Together in My Name* (1974), *Singin' and Swingin' and Gettin' Merry Like Christmas* (1976), *The Heart of a Woman* (1981), and *All God's Children Need Traveling Shoes* (1986). It is fitting that Angelou, so adept at metaphor, should compare her "poetic adventure" to the act of painting: ". . . everything is part of a large canvas I am creating, I am living beneath." Like an unfinished painting, the autobiographical series is an ongoing creation, in a form that rejects the finality of a restricting frame. Its continuity is achieved through characters who enter the picture, leave, and reappear, and through certain interlaced themes—self-acceptance, race, men, work, separation, sexuality, motherhood. All the while Angelou lives "beneath," recording the minutest of details in a constantly shifting environment and giving attention to the "mundane,

---

From *Black American Literature Forum* 24:2.

though essential, ordinary moments of life" (O'Neale 34).

I Know Why the Caged Bird Sings is the first and most highly praised volume in the series. It begins with the humiliations of childhood and ends with the birth of a child. At its publication, critics, not anticipating a series, readily appreciated the clearly developed narrative form. In 1973, for example, Sidonie Smith discussed the "sense of an ending" in *Caged Bird* as it relates to Angelou's acceptance of Black womanhood: "With the birth of her child Maya is herself born into a mature engagement with the forces of life" (374). But with the introduction in 1974 of Angelou's second autobiographical volume, *Gather Together in My Name*, the tight structure appeared to crumble; childhood experiences were replaced by episodes which a number of critics consider disjointed or bizarre. Selwyn Cudjoe, for instance, noted the shift from the "intense solidity and moral center" in *Caged Bird* to the "conditions of *alienation* and *fragmenta*tion" in *Gather Together*, conditions which affect its organization and its quality, making it "conspicuously weak" (17, 20). Lynn Z. Bloom found the sequel "less satisfactory" because the narrator "abandons or jeopardizes the maturity, honesty, and intuitive good judgment toward which she had been moving in *Caged Bird*" (5). Crucial to Bloom's judgment is her concept of movement *toward*, which insinuates the achievement of an ending.

The narrator, as authentic recorder of the life, indeed changes during the second volume, as does the book's structure; the later volumes abandon the tighter form of *Caged Bird* for an episodic series of adventures whose so-called "fragments" are reflections of the kind of chaos found in actual living. In altering the narrative structure, Angelou shifts the emphasis from herself as an isolated consciousness to herself as a Black woman participating in diverse experiences among a diverse class of peoples. As the world of experience widens, so does the canvas.

What distinguishes, then, Angelou's autobiographical method from more conventional autobiographical forms is her very denial of closure. The reader of autobiography expects a beginning, a middle, and an end—as occurs in *Caged Bird.* She or he also expects a central experience, as we indeed are given in the extraordinary rape sequence of *Caged Bird.* But Angelou, by continuing her narrative, denies the form and its history, creating from each ending a new beginning, relocating the center to some luminous place in a volume yet to be. Stretching the autobiographical canvas, she moves forward: from being a child, to being a mother; to leaving the child; to having the child, in the fifth volume, achieve his independence. Nor would I be so unwise as to call the fifth volume the end. For Maya Angelou, now a grandmother, has already published a moving, first-person account in *Woman's Day* of the four years of anguish surrounding the maternal kidnapping of her grandson Colin.

Throughout the more episodic volumes, the theme of motherhood remains a unifying element, with Momma Henderson being Angelou's link with the Black folk tradition—as George Kent, Elizabeth Schultz, and other critics have mentioned. Since traditional solidity of development is absent, one must sometimes search through three or four books to trace Vivian Baxter's changing lovers, Maya Angelou's ambivalence towards motherhood, or her son Guy's various reactions to his non-traditional upbringing. Nonetheless, the volumes are intricately related through a number of essential elements: the ambivalent autobiographical voice, the flexibility of structure to echo the life process, the intertextual commentary on character and theme, and the use of certain recurring patterns to establish both continuity and continuation. I have isolated the mother-child pattern as a way of approaching the complexity of Angelou's methods. One could as well select other kinds of interconnected themes: the absent and/or substitute father, the use of food as a psycho-sexual symbol, the dramatic/symbolic use of images of staring or gazing, and other motifs which establish continuity within and among the volumes.

Stephen Butterfield says of *Caged Bird*: "Continuity is achieved by the contact of mother and child, the sense of life begetting life that happens automatically in spite of all confusion—perhaps also because of it" (213). The consistent yet changing connection for Maya Angelou through the four subsequent narratives is that same contact of mother and child—with herself and her son Guy; with herself and her own mother, Vivian Baxter; with herself and her paternal grandmother; and, finally, with the child-mother in herself.

Moreover, in extending the traditional one-volume form, Angelou has metaphorically mothered another book. The "sense of life begetting life" at the end of *Caged Bird* can no longer signal the conclusion of the narrative. The autobiographical moment has been reopened and expanded; Guy's birth can now be seen symbolically as the birth of another text. In a 1975 interview with Carol Benson, Angelou uses such a birthing metaphor in describing the writing of *Gather Together*: "If you have a child, it takes nine months. It took me three-and-a-half years to write *Gather Together*, so I couldn't just drop it" (19). This statement makes emphatic what in the autobiographies are much more elusive comparisons between creative work and motherhood; after a three-and-a-half-year pregnancy she gives birth to *Gather Together*, indicating that she must have planned the conception of the second volume shortly after the 1970 delivery of *Caged Bird*.

Each of the five volumes explores, both literally and metaphorically, the significance of motherhood. I will examine this theme from two specific perspectives: first, Angelou's relationship to her mother and to mother substitutes, especially to Momma Henderson; second, Angelou's relationship to her son as she struggles to define her own role as mother/artist. Throughout the volumes Angelou moves backwards and forwards, from connection to conflict. This dialectic of Black mother-daughterhood, introduced in the childhood narrative, enlarges and contracts during the series, finding its fullest expression in *Singin' and Swingin' and Gettin' Merry Like Christmas.*

In flux, in defiance of chronological time, the mother-child configuration forms the basic pattern against which other relationships are measured and around which episodes and volumes begin or end. Motherhood also provides the series with a literary unity, as Angelou shifts positions—from mother to granddaughter to child—in a non-ending text that, through its repetitions of maternal motifs, provides an ironic comment on her own sense of identity. For Angelou, despite her insistence on mother love, is trapped in the conflicts between working and mothering, independence and nurturing—conflicts that echo her ambivalence towards her mother, Vivian Baxter, and her apparent sanctification of Grandmother Henderson, the major adult figure in *Caged Bird.*

Annie Henderson is a solid, God-fearing, economically independent woman whose general store in Stamps, Arkansas, is the "lay center of activities in town" (*Caged Bird* 5), much as Annie is the moral center of the family. According to Mildred A. Hill-Lubin, the grandmother, both in Africa and in America, "has been a significant force in the stability and the continuity of the Black family and the community" (257). Hill-Lubin selects Annie Henderson as her primary example of the strong grandmother in African-American literature—the traditional preserver of the family, the source of folk wisdom, and the instiller of values within the Black community. Throughout *Caged Bird* Maya has ambivalent feelings for this awesome woman, whose values of self-determination and personal dignity gradually chip away at Maya's dreadful sense of being "shit color" (17). As a self-made woman, Annie Henderson has the economic power to lend money to whites; as a practical Black woman, however, she is convinced that whites cannot be directly confronted: "If she had been asked and had chosen to answer the question of whether she was cowardly or not, she would have said that she was a realist" (39). To survive in a racist society, Momma Henderson has had to develop a realistic strategy of submission that Maya finds unacceptable. Maya, in her need to re-image her grandmother, creates a metaphor that places Momma's power above any apparent submissiveness: Momma "did an excellent job of sagging from her waist down, but from the waist up she seemed to be pulling for the top of the oak tree across the road" (24).

There are numerous episodes, both in *Caged Bird* and *Gather Together*, which involve the conflict between Maya and her grandmother over how to deal with racism. When taunted by three "powhitetrash" girls, Momma quietly sings a hymn; Maya, enraged, would like to have a rifle (*Caged Bird* 23–27). Or, when humiliated by a white dentist who'd rather put his "hand in a dog's mouth than in a nigger's" (160), Annie is passive; Maya subsequently invents a fantasy in which Momma runs the dentist out of town. In the italicized dream text (161-62), Maya endows her grandmother with superhuman powers; Momma magically changes the dentist's nurse into a bag of chicken seed. In reality the grandmother has been defeated and humiliated, her only reward a mere ten dollars in interest for a loan she had made to the dentist (164). In Maya's fantasy Momma's "*eyes were blazing like live coals and her arms had doubled themselves in length*"; in actuality she "looked tired" (162).

This richly textured passage is rendered from the perspective of an imaginative child who re-creates her grandmother—but in a language that ironically transforms Annie Henderson from a Southern Black storekeeper into an eloquent heroine from a romantic novel: "*Her tongue had thinned and the words rolled off well enunciated.*" Instead of the silent "nigra" (159) of the actual experience, Momma Henderson is now the articulate defender of her granddaughter against the stuttering dentist. Momma Henderson orders the "*contemptuous scoundrel*" to leave Stamps "now and herewith." The narrator eventually lets Momma speak normally, then comments: "(*She could afford to slip into the vernacular because she had such eloquent command of English.*)"

This fantasy is the narrator's way of dealing with her ambivalence towards Momma Henderson—a woman who throughout *Caged Bird* represents to Maya both strength and weakness, both generosity and punishment, both affection and the denial of affection. Here her defender is "*ten feet tall with eight-foot arms*," quite capable, to recall the former tree image, of reaching the top of an oak from across the road. Momma's physical transformation in the dream text also recalls an earlier description: "I saw only her power and strength. She was taller than any woman in my personal world, and her hands were so large they could span my head from ear to ear" (38). In the dentist fantasy, Maya eliminates all of Momma Henderson's "negative" traits—submissiveness, severity, religiosity, sternness, down-home speech. It would seem that Maya is so shattered by her grandmother's reaction to Dentist Lincoln, so destroyed by her illusions of Annie Henderson's power in relationship to white people, that she compensates by reversing the true situation and having the salivating dentist be the target of Momma's wrath. Significantly, this transformation occurs immediately before Momma Henderson tells Maya and Bailey that they are going to California. Its position in the text gives it the impression of finality. Any negative attitudes become submerged only to surface later, in *Gather Together*, as aspects of Angelou's own ambiguity towards race, power, and identity.

In *Caged Bird* Momma Henderson had hit Maya with a switch for unknowingly taking the Lord's name in vain, "like whitefolks do" (87). Similarly, in *Gather Together* Annie slaps her granddaughter after Maya, on a visit to Stamps, verbally assaults two white saleswomen. In a clash with Momma Henderson that is both painful and final, Maya argues for "the principle of the thing," and Momma slaps her. Surely, Momma's slap is well intended; she wishes to protect Maya from "lunatic cracker boys" and men in white sheets, from all of the insanity of racial prejudice (78–79). The "new" Maya, who has been to the city and found a sense of independence, is caught in the clash between her recently acquired "principles" and Momma's fixed ideology. Thus the slap—but also the intention behind it—will remain in Maya's memory long after the mature Angelou has been separated from Annie Henderson's supervision. Momma makes Maya and the baby leave Stamps, again as a precaution: "Momma's intent to protect me had caused her to hit me in the face, a thing she had never done, and to send me away to where she thought I'd be safe" (79). Maya departs on the train, never to see her grandmother again.

In the third volume Angelou, her marriage falling apart, is recuperating from a difficult appendectomy. When she tells her husband Tosh that she wants to go to Stamps until she is well, he breaks the news that Annie Henderson died the day after Angelou's operation. In recording her reaction to her grandmother's death Angelou's style shifts from its generally more conversational tone and becomes intense, religious, emotional:

> Ah, Momma. I had never looked at death before, peered into its yawning chasm for the face of the beloved. For days my mind staggered out of balance. I reeled on a precipice of knowledge that even if I were rich enough to travel all over the world, I would never find Momma. If I were as good as God's angels and as pure as the Mother of Christ, I could never have Momma's rough slow hands pat my cheek or braid my hair.
>
> Death to the young is more than that undiscovered country; despite its inevitability, it is a place having reality only in song or in other people's grief. (*Singin' and Swingin'* 41)

This moving farewell, so atypical of Angelou's more worldly autobiographical style, emerges directly from a suppressed religious experience which Angelou narrates earlier in the same text—a "secret crawl through neighborhood churches" (28). These visits, done without her white husband's knowledge, culminate in Angelou's being saved at the Evening Star Baptist Church. During her purification, Angelou cries for her family: "For my fatherless son, who was growing up with a man who would never, could never, understand his need for manhood; for my mother, whom I admired but didn't understand; for my brother, whose disappointment with life was drawing him relentlessly into the clutches of death; and, finally, I cried for myself, long and loudly" (33). Annie Henderson is strangely absent from this list of family for whom Angelou cries during the short-lived conversion. But only a few pages later, Angelou remembers her grandmother's profound importance, in the elegiac passage on Momma's death.

In this passage Angelou creates a funeral song which relies on the Black gospel tradition, on the language of Bible stories, and on certain formative literary texts. Words like *chasm*, *precipice*, *angels*, and *beloved* have Sunday School overtones, a kind of vocabulary Angelou more typically employs for humorous effects, as in the well-known portrait of Sister Monroe (*Caged Bird* 32–37). The gospel motif, so dominant in the passage, seems directly related to Angelou's rediscovery of the Black spiritual: "The spirituals and gospel songs were sweeter than sugar. I wanted to keep my mouth full of them and the sounds of my people singing fell like sweet oil in my ears" (*Singing' and Swingin'* 28). During her conversion experience Angelou lies on the floor while four women march round her singing, "Soon one morning when death comes walking in my room" (33); in another spiritual the singers prepare for the "walk to Jerusalem" (31). These and similar hymns about death had been significant elements of the "folk religious tradition" of Momma Henderson (Kent 76). Now, for a brief time, they become part of the mature Angelou's experience. That their revival is almost immediately followed by the death of Momma Henderson accounts, to a large extent, for Angelou's intensely religious narrative.

Angelou's singing of the Black grandmother in this passage contains other refrains from the past, most notably her desire to have "Momma's rough slow hands pat my cheek." These are the same hands that slapped Maya for having talked back to the white saleswomen—an event that was physically to separate grandmother and granddaughter (*Gather Together* 86–88). That final slap, softened here, becomes a loving pat on the cheek akin to a moment in *Caged Bird* in which Maya describes her grandmother's love as a touch of the hand: "Just the gentle pressure of her rough hand conveyed her own concern and assurance to me" (96). Angelou's tone throughout the elegy is an attempt, through religion, to reconcile her ambivalence towards Momma Henderson by sharing her traditions. Angelou wishes to be "as good as God's angels" and as "pure as the Mother of Christ," metaphors which seem to represent Angelou's effort to close off the chasm between herself and Momma Henderson through the use of a common language, the language of the church-going grandmother.

As Momma Henderson, the revered grandmother recedes from the narrative, Angelou's natural mother gains prominence. By the third volume Maya Angelou and Vivian Baxter have established a closeness that somewhat compensates for Maya's having been sent off to Stamps as a child, a situation so painful that Maya had imagined her mother dead:

> I could cry anytime I wanted by picturing my mother (I didn't quite know what she looked like) lying in her coffin. . . . The face was brown, like a big O, and since I couldn't fill in the features I printed M O T H E R across the O, and tears would fall down my cheeks like warm milk. (*Caged Bird* 42–43)

Like Maya's fantasy of her grandmother and Dentist Lincoln, the above passage is an imaginative revision of reality, Maya's way to control the frustrations produced by Vivian's rejection. The images of the dream text invoke romance fiction and Amazonian strength. Here the images concern, first, the artist who fills in the empty canvas (the O) with print; second, the motherlike child who cries tears of "warm milk" in sympathy for her imagined dead mother. These interlaced metaphors of writing and nurturance appear frequently in the continuing text, as Angelou explores her relationships with mothers and children.

When Maya is eight years old, she and Bailey visit their mother in St. Louis, where Maya discovers her exquisite beauty. "To describe my mother would be to write about a hurricane in its perfect power. Or the climbing, falling colors of a rainbow. . . . She was too beautiful to have children" (*Caged Bird* 49–50). Ironically, this mother "too beautiful to have children" is to a large degree responsible for her own child's brutal rape. Vivian's beauty attracts a lover, Mr. Freeman, who is constantly in the house waiting for a woman who is not there, and he "uses Angelou as an extension of her mother" to satisfy his sexual urges (Demetrakopoulos 198). It could also be suggested that Vivian uses Maya, somehow knowing that in her own absence Maya will keep her lover amused. When Maya becomes ill, Vivian responds in a motherly manner: making broth, cooking Cream of Wheat, taking Maya's temperature, calling a doctor. After she discovers the rape, Vivian sends Maya to a hospital, bringing her flowers and candy (*Caged Bird* 69).

It is Grandmother Baxter, however, who sees to it that the rapist is punished; after the trial a policeman comes to the house and informs an unsurprised Mrs. Baxter that Freeman has been kicked to death. Mrs. Baxter is a political figure in St. Louis, a precinct captain and gambler whose light skin and "six mean children" bring her both power and respect (51). Like Momma Henderson, Grandmother Baxter is a source of strength for Maya. Both grandmothers are "strong, independent[,] skillful women who are able to manage their families and to insure their survival in a segregated and hostile society" (Hill-Lubin 260).

Despite their positive influence, however, Maya has ambivalent feelings towards her powerful grandmothers. Maya feels guilty for having lied at the trial, a guilt compounded when she learns of Grandmother Baxter's part in Freeman's murder. To stop the "poison" in her breath, Maya retreats into a "perfect personal silence" which neither of the Baxter women can penetrate, and which Maya breaks only for Bailey (73). The disastrous St. Louis sequence stops abruptly, without transition: "We were on the train going back to Stamps . . ." (74). Thus, the end of the visit to Grandmother Baxter parallels chapter one of *Caged Bird;* a train moves from an urban center to rural Arkansas and to the protection of Annie Henderson.

Back at her grandmother's general store, Maya meets Mrs. Bertha Flowers, "the aristocrat of Black Stamps" (77). This unambivalently positive mother figure helps Maya to recover her oral language through the written text—reading *A Tale of Two Cities*. In a series of sharp contrasts, the narrator conveys Maya's divided feelings between the sophisticated mother figure, Mrs. Flowers, and her more provincial grandmother. Mrs. Flowers wears gloves, whereas Mrs. Henderson has rough hands. Mrs. Flowers admires white male writers, whereas Annie Henderson will not tolerate them. And in a set of contrasts that occurs almost simultaneously in the text, the literary Mrs. Flowers rewards Maya's language with sweets, whereas the religious grandmother punishes Maya's spoken words ("by the way") without making any effort to explain her anger. In an earlier passage, however, the narrator merges these basic oppositions into a dynamic interaction between two Black women: "I heard the soft-voiced Mrs. Flowers and the textured voice of my grandmother merging and melting. They were interrupted from time to time by giggles that must have come from Mrs. Flowers (Momma never giggled in her life). Then she was gone" (79). These contrasts appear following Maya's failed relationship with Vivian Baxter. They are indications of the split mother—the absent natural mother, the gentle Mrs. Flowers, the forceful Annie Henderson—whose divisions Angelou must articulate if she is to find her own autobiographical voice.

Although most critics have seen a wholeness in Maya's personality at the conclusion of *Caged Bird*, a few have observed this division of self, which Demetrakopoulos relates to Maya's conflicts about the mother: She "splits the feminine archetype of her mother's cold Venus and her grandmother's primal warm sheltering Demeter aspects" (198). The Jungian metaphors may jar in this African-American context, but I agree with Demetrakopoulos that at the end of *Caged Bird* the narrator is split. She is a mother who is herself a child; a daughter torn by her notions of mother love; an uncertain Black teenager hardly capable of the heavy burden of closure placed on her by Sidonie Smith, Stephen Butterfield, Selwyn Cudjoe, and other critics.

Nor is this split mended when Angelou gives birth to *Gather Together*. Here she introduces herself by way of contradictions: "I was seventeen, very old, embarrassingly young, with a son of two months, and I still lived with my mother and stepfather" (3). Vivian Baxter intermittently takes care of Guy while his young mother works as a cook or shopkeeper. When Momma Henderson forces Maya and her son to leave Stamps, they go immediately to the security of Vivian's fourteen-room house in San Francisco. One gets a strong sense throughout *Gather Together* of Maya's dependence on her mother. Angelou admires her mother for her self-reliance, her encouragement, and her casual approach to sexuality. She also continues to be captivated by Vivian's beauty by her "snappy-fingered, headtossing elegance" (*Singin' and Swingin'* 70). On the other hand, she recognizes Vivian Baxter's flaws: "Her own mind was misted by the knowledge of a failing marriage, and the slipping away of the huge sums of money which she had enjoyed and thought her due" (*Gather Together* 24).

As for her son, Angelou reveals similar contradictory feelings. After quitting a job to be with Guy, Angelou writes: "A baby's love for his mother is probably the sweetest emotion we can savor" (*Gather Together* 90). In a more depressed mood, however, she comments that her child's disposition had "lost its magic to make me happy" (174). What Angelou does in these instances is to articulate her feelings as they convey the reality of her experiences, even though some of these negative emotions might not represent her best side.

The most dramatic mother-child episode in *Gather Together* occurs while Angelou is working as a prostitute. She leaves Guy with her sitter, Big Mary. Returning for Guy after several days, she learns that her son has been kidnapped. Angelou finally recovers her child, unharmed; at that moment she realizes that they are both separate individuals and that Guy is not merely a "beautiful appendage of myself" (163). Angelou's awareness of the inevitable separation of mother and child, expressed here for the first time, is a theme that she will continue to explore through the remaining autobiographical volumes.

Gather Together closes with Angelou's and Guy's returning to the protection of Vivian Baxter, following Angelou's glimpse at the horrors of heroin addiction: "I had no idea what I was going to make of my life, but I had given a promise and found my innocence. I swore I'd never lose it again" (181). In its tableau of mother, child, and grandmother, this concluding paragraph directly parallels the ending of *Caged Bird.*

In the next volume, *Singin' and Swingin'*, the closeness between mother and daughter continues. As she matures, Angelou becomes more in control of her feelings and more objective in her assessment of Vivian Baxter's personality. Additionally, the separation of egos that Angelou perceived after locating her kidnapped son would extend to the mother-daughter and grandmother-granddaughter relationships as well. But *Singin' and Swingin' and Gettin' Merry Like Christmas* is, despite its joyful title, a mesh of conflicts—many of them existing within the autobiographical self; many of them involving separations which, although consciously chosen, become unbearable. A number of ambiguities appear throughout the book, especially as they concern the mother-child pattern which is to dominate this and the subsequent texts.

The underlying drama in *Singin' and Swingin'* is played out between Angelou, the single parent of a young son, and Angelou, the actress who chooses to leave that son with Vivian Baxter in order to tour Europe with the company of *Porgy and Bess.* Angelou is keenly aware that putting Guy in the care of his grandmother is an echo of her own child-mother experience:

> The past revisited. My mother had left me with my grandmother for years and I knew the pain of parting. My mother, like me, had had her motivations, her needs. I did not relish visiting the same anguish on my son, and she, years later, told me how painful our separation was to her. But I had to work and I had to be good. I would make it up to my son and one day would take him to all the places I was going to see. (129)

Angelou's feelings are compounded by the fact that, as a young, Black, single mother, she alone is finally responsible for giving her child a sense of stability. In identifying the conflict between working and mothering, Angelou offers a universalized representation of the turmoil which may arise when a woman attempts to fulfill both roles.

Angelou suffers considerably on the European tour. In some instances her longings for Guy make her sleep fitfully (147) or make her distracted—

as when she sees some young Italian boys with "pale-gold complexions" who remind her of her son (148). When she is paged at a Paris train station, Angelou fears that something dreadful has happened to Guy, and she blames herself: "I knew I shouldn't have left my son. There was a telegram waiting for me to say he had been hurt somehow. Or had run away from home. Or had caught an awful disease" (151–52). On other occasions she speaks quite directly of her guilt: "I sent my dollars home to pay for Clyde's [Guy's] keep and to assuage my guilt at being away from him" (153).

Of the many examples in *Singin' and Swingin'* which address this conflict, I have selected one particular passage to illustrate the ways in which Angelou articulates her ambivalence about mothering. While she is in Paris, Angelou earns extra money by singing in a nightclub and decides to send the money home rather than spend it on a room with a private bath: "Mom could buy something wonderful for Clyde every other week and tell him I'd sent it. Then perhaps he would forgive my absence" (157). The narrator shows no qualms about lying to her son; Vivian could "tell him I'd sent it.' Additionally, she makes no connection between her efforts to buy forgiveness and the anger she felt as a child when her absent mother, the same "Mom" of the above passage, sent Maya a tea set and a doll with yellow hair for Christmas: "Bailey and I tore the stuffing out of the doll the day after Christmas, but he warned me that I had to keep the tea set in good condition because any day or night she might come riding up" (*Caged Bird* 43). Liliane K. Arensberg interprets the tea cups as "symbols of a white world beyond Maya's reach of everyday experience," whereas the torn doll "serves as an effigy of her mother by virtue of being female and a gift" (281). Although I agree with Arensberg's interpretation, I tend to read the gifts as metaphors for Maya's divided self. The preserved tea set, the torn doll—what better signifiers could there be for the split feelings of the abandoned child, who destroys one gift to show anger but saves the other in anticipation of the mother's return? I would also suggest that the seemingly inappropriate title *Singin' and Swingin' and Gettin' Merry Like Christmas* may be intended to signal the reader back to the very unmerry Christmas of *Caged Bird*.

In the Paris sequence the narrator seems to have suppressed, in her role as mother, some of the anguish she had experienced during childhood—although in the passage previously cited (*Singin' and Swingin'* 129), she recognizes the similarities between her own "pains of parting" and her son's. Angelou refers to this separation from her son so frequently in the text that he becomes a substantial part of the narrative, the source of Angelou's guilt but also the major factor in the development of dramatic tension. Angelou, in this most complex of the autobiographies, is richly and honestly rendering the split in her own psyche between being a "good" mother (being at home) and being a "bad" mother (selfishly staying in Europe). The narrator pretends to herself that her son wants a gift, thus prolonging the admission that he really wants his mother—as Maya had wanted hers.

To arrive at this interpretation the reader must move back and forth among the texts, perceiving parallels in order to decipher the narrator's motivations. The frequent references in *Singin' and Swingin'* to separation and to guilt give one considerable access to the narrator's complex personality; at the same time, these references demand to be read against and with the entire series—intertextuality in its strictest sense.

Angelou returns from Europe to find her son suffering from a skin disease that is an overt expression of his loneliness. In a promise that recalls the last lines of *Gather Together* (never again to lose her innocence), Angelou vows to Guy: "I swear to you, I'll never leave you again. If I go, you'll go with me or I won't go" (*Singin' and Swingin'* 232). She takes Guy with her to Hawaii, where she has a singing engagement. *Singin' and Swingin'* closes in a sentence which highlights, through its three nouns, the underlying tensions of the book: "Although I was not a great *singer* I was his *mother*, and he was my wonderful, dependently independent *son*" (242, emphasis added). Dialectical in phrasing, this statement not only functions to close the first three books but also opens itself to the mother-son patterns of the future volumes: fluctuations between dependence and independence.

In *The Heart of a Woman* the tension between mothering and working continues, but to a lesser extent. Guy is now living with his mother and not with Vivian Baxter. But Angelou, despite her earlier vow, does occasionally leave her son. During a night club engagement in Chicago, Angelou trusts Guy to the care of her friend John Killens. One night Killens phones from Brooklyn and informs her that "there's been some trouble" (75). In a moment of panic that recalls her fears at the Paris train station (*Gather Together* 151–52), Angelou again imagines that Guy has been injured, stolen, "struck by an errant bus, hit by a car out of control" (75).

Angelou confronts these fears in the Brooklyn adventure, the most dramatic episode of *The Heart of a Woman*. Unlike the internal conflicts of *Gather Together*, this one operates outside of the narrator, showing Maya Angelou as a strong, aggressive Black mother rather than a mother torn by self-doubt. While Angelou was in Chicago, Guy had gotten in trouble with a Brooklyn street gang. In order to protect her son, she confronts Jerry, the gang leader, and threatens to shoot his entire family if Guy is harmed. Jerry's response is an ironic comment on the motherhood theme of the autobiographies: "O.K., I understand. But for a mother, I must say you're a mean motherfucker" (84).

Powerful, protective of her son, Angelou has become in this episode a reincarnation of Momma Henderson.

Unfortunately, no mother or grandmother or guardian angel, no matter how strong, can keep children forever from danger. Near the end of *The Heart of a Woman,* Guy is seriously injured in a car accident. In a condensed, tormented autobiographical passage, Angelou gazes at the face of her unconscious son and summarizes their life together:

> He was born to me when I was seventeen. I had taken him away from my mother's house when he was two years old, and except for a year I spent in Europe without him, and a month when he was stolen by a deranged woman, we had spent our lives together. My grown life lay stretched before me, stiff as a pine board, in a strange country, blood caked on his face and clotted on his clothes. (263)

Guy gradually recovers, moving, during the process of physical healing, toward a position of greater independence from his mother.

But Angelou, too, moves towards a separateness, much as she had predicted in *Gather Together* (163). In *The Heart of a Woman* the texture of Angelou's life changes significantly. She travels a lot, seeing far less of Vivian—although she does write to her mother from Ghana asking for financial help after Guy's accident (268). She strengthens her public identity, becoming a coordinator in the Civil Rights Movement and a professionally recognized dancer and actress. She also, for the first time in the autobiographies, begins her account of self as writer. Angelou attends a writer's workshop; publishes a short story; becomes friends with John Killens, Rosa Guy, Paule Marshall, and other Black novelists. Most important, writing forces her into a conscious maturity: "If I wanted to write, I had to be willing to develop a kind of concentration found mostly in people awaiting execution. I had to learn technique and surrender my ignorance" (41). By extension, the rich ambivalence of *Singin' and Swingin'* could only have been achieved by a writer who had abandoned "ignorance" for a conscious self-exploration.

Paradoxically, the independent writer/mother establishes this "kind of concentration" in maternal solitude. *Singin' and Swingin'* had ended with mother and son reunited, both dependent and independent. *The Heart of a Woman* ends in separation. Guy, now a student at the University of Ghana, is moving to a dormitory. In the last two paragraphs we find Angelou alone:

> I closed the door and held my breath. Waiting for the wave of

> emotion to surge over me, knock me down, take my breath away. Nothing happened. I didn't feel bereft or desolate. I didn't feel lonely or abandoned.
>
> I sat down, still waiting. The first thought that came to me, perfectly formed and promising, was "At last, I'll be able to eat the whole breast of a roast chicken by myself." (272)

Angelou's reaction to having "closed the door" on her son is, like so many of her feelings in this complicated relationship, ambivalent. The language of the passage is initially charged with negativity: "Nothing happened. I didn't feel . . . . I didn't feel . . . ." The son she had loved through all of "our lives together" (263) is gone. Angelou sits waiting for something dreadful to happen to herself—as she had earlier imagined Guy's being stolen or being hit by a bus. But the narrator counters this negative attitude with a note of irony in which she reverses the biological assumption of the mother as she-who-nourishes: She can now have the "whole breast" to herself.

The family chicken dinner is a recurring motif in the autobiographical series. Recall the marvelous scene from *Caged Bird* in which Maya and Bailey watch Reverend Howard Thomas gobble down Momma Henderson's chicken dinner: "He ate the biggest, brownest and best parts of the chicken at every Sunday meal" (28). Now there is no competition. Angelou has the best part, the breast, to herself. On the negative side, Angelou is left, at the end of the fourth volume, in isolation; the last word of *The Heart of a Woman* is "myself." But the negativity is outweighed by the more "promising" aspects of being alone, the word *promising* an echo of the resolutions of *Gather Together* and *Singin' and Swingin'*, which end in vows of innocence and of commitment. The "perfectly formed" thought at the end of *The Heart of a Woman* is Angelou's realization of a new "myself," of a woman no longer primarily defined as granddaughter or daughter or mother—a woman free to choose herself.

All God's Children Need Traveling Shoes opens by going back in time to Angelou the mother, who anxiously waits at the hospital following Guy's car accident. In an image that parodies the well-fed mother of *The Heart of a Woman*, Angelou compares her anxiety over Guy to being eaten up:

> July and August of 1962 stretched out like fat men yawning after a sumptuous dinner. They had every right to gloat, for they had eaten me up. Gobbled me down. Consumed my spirit, not in a wild rush, but slowly, with the obscene patience of certain victors. I became a shadow walking in the white hot streets, and a dark spectre in the hospital. (4)

The months of helplessly waiting for Guy to heal are like fat, stuffed men, a description that evokes memories of Reverend Thomas, who ate Momma Henderson's chicken, and of Mr. Freeman, who ate in Vivian Baxter's kitchen and raped her daughter. Guy's accident has an effect similar to the rape; Angelou retreats into silence. She is a "shadow," a "dark spectre," a Black mother silenced by the fear of her son's possible death.

Guy does recover. Their relationship, which like the autobiographical form itself is constantly in flux, moves once again from dependence to independence, climaxing in a scene in which Angelou learns that her son is having an affair with an American woman a year older than herself. Angelou at first threatens to strike him, but Guy merely pats her head and says: "Yes, little mother. I'm sure you will" (149). Shortly afterwards Angelou travels to Germany to perform in Genet's *The Blacks*. Guy meets her return flight and takes her home to a dinner of fried chicken he has cooked for her. Then, asserting his independence, he announces that he has "plans for dinner" (186).

Reading between the texts, we see Angelou alone again before a plate of chicken, as she was at the conclusion of *The Heart of a Woman*. In the *Traveling Shoes* episode, however, the conflicting feelings of love and resentment are more directly stated:

> He's gone. My lovely little boy is gone and will never return. That big confident strange man has done away with my little boy, and he has the gall to say he loves me. How can he love me? He doesn't know me, and I sure as hell don't know him. (186)

In this passage Angelou authentically faces and records the confusions of seeing one's child achieve selfhood, universalizing the pain a mother experiences when her "boy" is transformed into a "big confident strange man" who refuses to be his mother's "beautiful appendage" (*Gather Together* 162).

Yet through much of the fifth volume, Angelou continues to separate herself from Guy and to form new relationships. She shares experiences with other women, including her two roommates; she befriends an African boy named Koko; she enjoys her contacts with the colony of Black American writers and artists living in Ghana; and she continues her sexual involvements with men. The love affair which seems most vital in *Traveling Shoes*, however, is with Africa herself. In her travels through West Africa Angelou discovers certain connections between her own traditions and those of her African ancestors. She takes great satisfaction in her heritage when she is mistaken for a Bambara woman. Among African women she discovers strong mother figures, most notably Patience Aduah, whose custom of giving away food by the campfire evokes memories of Momma Henderson's having shared her table with Black American travelers denied rooms in hotels or seats in restaurants during the era of segregation in much of America (*Traveling Shoes* 102). Through her identification with Africa, Angelou reaffirms the meaning of motherhood.

Although captivated by the oral traditions of Mother Africa, Angelou chooses to leave, at the conclusion of *Traveling Shoes,* in order to return to the rhythms of Southern Black churches, the rhythms of her grandmother. In so doing, however, she must also leave her son. The final scene in the book is at the Accra airport. Angelou is saying farewell to her friends and, most specifically, to Guy, who "stood, looking like a young lord of summer, straight, sure among his Ghanaian companions" (208). Through this suggestion of Guy as an African prince, Angelou roots him in the culture of West Africa.

If we look at the closure of *Traveling Shoes* on a literal level, then Angelou's son is a college student, staying on to complete his degree. But if we accept a grander interpretation, Guy has become, through his interaction with the Ghanaians, a "young lord" of Africa, given back to the Mother Continent freely, not lost, like so many other children, in mid-passage or in slavery. Angelou lovingly accepts the separation, knowing that "someone like me and certainly related to me" will be forming new bonds between himself and Mother Africa (209). Guy is making an essentially free choice that centuries of Black creativity in America have helped make possible: "Through the centuries of despair and dislocation we had been creative, because we faced down death by daring to hope" (208).

As in the four earlier autobiographies, this one closes with the mother-son configuration. But in the final, puzzling line of *Traveling Shoes* Angelou swings the focus away from Guy and towards the edge of the canvas: "I could nearly hear the old ones chuckling" (209). In this spiritual call to her ancestors Angelou imaginatively connects herself to the Ketans and the Ghanaians, to the people placed in chains, to all of God's children who had "never completely left Africa" (209). Ironically, the narrator herself has not completely left Africa either. The rhythmic prose that concludes the fifth volume is an anticipated departure to a new world, with the narrator still at the airport. As in the other volumes, the closure is thus another opening into the next narrative journey.

CAROL E. NEUBAUER

Maya Angelou: Self and a Song of Freedom in the Southern Tradition

Within the last fifteen years, Maya Angelou has become one of the best-known black writers in the United States. Her reputation rests firmly on her prolific career as an autobiographer, poet, dancer-singer, actress, producer, director, scriptwriter, political activist, and editor. Throughout her life, she has identified with the South, and she calls Stamps, Arkansas, where she spent ten years of her childhood, her home.

Maya Angelou was born Marguerite Annie Johnson on 4 April 1928 in St. Louis to Vivian Baxter and Bailey Johnson, a civilian dietitian for the U.S. Navy. At age three, when her parents' marriage ended in divorce, she was sent, along with her brother, Bailey, from Long Beach to Stamps to be cared for by their paternal grandmother, Mrs. Annie Henderson. During the next ten years, a time of severe economic depression and intense racial bigotry in the South, she spent nearly all of her time either in school, at the daily meetings of the Colored Methodist Episcopal Church, or at her grandmother's general merchandise store. In 1940, she graduated with top honors from the Lafayette County Training School and soon thereafter returned to her mother, who lived in the San Francisco–Oakland area at that time. There she continued her education at George Washington High School under the direction of her beloved Miss Kirwin. At the same time, she attended evening classes at the California Labor School, where she received a scholarship to

From *Southern Women Writers: The New Generation.*

study drama and dance. A few weeks after she received her high school diploma, she gave birth to her son, Guy Bailey Johnson.

Her career as a professional entertainer began on the West Coast, where she performed as a dancer-singer at the Purple Onion in the early 1950s. While working in this popular cabaret, she was spotted by members of the *Porgy and Bess* cast and invited to audition for the chorus. Upon her return from the play's 1954–55 tour of Europe and Africa, she continued to perform at nightclubs throughout the United States, acquiring valuable experience that would eventually lead her into new avenues of professional work.

In 1959, Angelou and her son moved to New York, where she soon joined the Harlem Writers Guild at the invitation of John Killens. Together with Godfrey Cambridge, she produced, directed, and starred in *Cabaret for Freedom* to raise funds for the Southern Christian Leadership Conference. Following the close of the highly successful show, she accepted the position of Northern coordinator for the SCLC at the request of Dr. Martin Luther King, Jr.

Her work in theater landed her the role of the White Queen in Genet's *The Blacks*, directed by Gene Frankel at St. Mark's Playhouse. For this production, she joined a cast of stars—Roscoe Lee Brown, Godfrey Cambridge, James Earl Jones, and Cicely Tyson. In 1974, she adapted Sophocles' *Ajax* for its premiere at the Mark Taper Forum in Los Angeles. Original screenplays to her credit include the film version of *Georgia, Georgia* and the television production of *I Know Why the Caged Bird Sings* and *The Sisters.* She also authored and produced a television series on African traditions inherent in American culture and played the role of Kunte Kinte's grandmother in *Roots.* For PBS programing, she served as a guest interviewer on *Assignment America* and most recently appeared in a special series on creativity hosted by Bill Moyers, which featured a return visit to Stamps.

Among her other honors, Maya Angelou was appointed to the Commission of International Women's Year by former President Carter. In 1975, *Ladies' Home Journal* named her Woman of the Year in communications. A trustee of the American Film Institute, she is also one of the few women members of the Directors Guild. In recent years, she has received more than a dozen honorary degrees, including one from the University of Arkansas located near her childhood home. Fluent in seven languages, she has worked as the editor of the *Arab Observer* in Cairo and the *African Review* in Ghana. In December 1981, Angelou accepted a lifetime appointment as the first Reynolds Professor of American Studies at Wake Forest University in Winston-Salem, where she lectures on literature and popular culture. In 1983, Women in Communications presented her with the Matrix Award in the field of books.

Her personal life has been anything but smooth. As a young mother, Angelou had to endure painful periods of separation from her son while she worked at more than one job to support them. Often her ventures into show business would take her far from home, and she would put Guy in the care of her mother or baby-sitters. When she was twenty-one years old, she married Tosh Angelos, a sailor of Greek-American ancestry, but their marriage ended after three years. While working in New York, she met and later married Vusumzi Make, a black South African activist who traveled extensively raising money to end apartheid. They divided their time between New York and Cairo, but after a few years their marriage deteriorated. In 1973, Angelou married Paul du Feu, a carpenter and construction worker she had met in London. They lived together on the West Coast during most of their seven-year marriage.

Southern Roots and Literary Reputation

Although she is rarely called a regional writer, Maya Angelou is frequently identified with the new generation of Southern writers. She has always called the South her home, and recently, after much deliberation, she settled in North Carolina, ending an absence of more than thirty years. Her autobiographies and poetry are rich with references to her childhood home in Arkansas and to the South in general. For Angelou, as for many black American writers, the South has become a powerfully evocative metaphor for the history of racial bigotry and social inequality, for brutal inhumanity and final failure. Yet the South also represents a life-affirming force energized by a somewhat spiritual bond to the land itself. It is a region where generations of black families have sacrificed their brightest dreams for a better future; yet it is here that ties to forebears whose very blood has nourished the soil are most vibrant and resilient. Stamps, Arkansas, in the 1930s was not a place where a black child could grow up freely or reach her full intellectual and social potential, but the town was nevertheless the home of Angelou's grandmother, who came to stand for all the courage and stability she ever knew as a child.

Her literary reputation is based on the publication of five volumes of autobiography (*I Know Why the Caged Bird Sings*, *Gather Together in My Name*, *Singin' and Swingin' and Gettin' Merry Like Christmas*, *The Heart of a Woman*, and *All God's Children Need Traveling Shoes*) and five volumes of poetry (*Just Give Me a Cool Drink of Water 'fore I Diiie*, *Oh Pray My Wings Are gonna Fit Me Well*, *And Still I Rise*, *Shaker, Why Don't You Sing?* and *Now Sheba*

Sings the Song). In the twenty years of her publishing history, she has developed a rapport with her audiences who await each new work as a continuation of an ongoing dialogue with the author. Beginning with *Caged Bird* in 1970, her works have received wide critical acclaim and have been praised for reaching universal truths while examining the complicated life of one individual. The broad appeal of her autobiographies and poetry is evidenced in the numerous college anthologies that include portions of her work and in the popularity of the television adaptation of *Caged Bird*. In years to come, Angelou's voice, already recognized as one of the most original and versatile, will be measured by the standards of great American writers of our time.

Autobiography

In her first volume of autobiography, *I Know Why the Caged Bird Sings* (1970), Maya Angelou calls displacement the most important loss in her childhood, because she is separated from her mother and father at age three and never fully regains a sense of security and belonging. Her displacement from her family is not only an emotional handicap but is compounded by the equally unsettling sense of racial and geographic displacement. Her parents frequently move Angelou and her brother, Bailey, from St. Louis to Arkansas to the West Coast. As young children in Stamps in the 1930s, racial prejudice severely limits their lives. Within the first pages, she sums up this demoralizing period of alienation: "If growing up is painful for the Southern Black girl, being aware of her displacement is the rust on the razor that threatens the throat." The pain of her continual rejection comes not only from the displacement itself, but even more poignantly, from the child's acute understanding of prejudice. A smooth, clean razor would be enough of a threat, but a rusty, jagged one leaves no doubt in the victim's mind.

In *Caged Bird*, Angelou recounts many explosive incidents of the racial discrimination she experienced as a child. In the 1930s, Stamps was a fully segregated town. Marguerite and Baily, however, are welcomed by a grandmother who is not only devoted to them but as owner of the Wm. Johnson General Merchandise Store, is highly successful and independent. Momma is their most constant source of love and strength. "I saw only her power and strength. She was taller than any woman in my personal world, and her hands were so large they could span my head from ear to ear" (*CB*, 38). As powerful as her grandmother's presence seems to Marguerite, Momma uses her strength solely to guide and protect her family but not to confront the white community directly. Momma's resilient power usually reassures Marguerite, but one of the child's most difficult lessons teaches her that racial prejudice in Stamps can effectively circumscribe and even defeat her grandmother's protective influence.

In fact, it is only in the autobiographical narrative that Momma's personality begins to loom larger than life and provides Angelou's memories of childhood with a sense of personal dignity and meaning. On one occasion, for example, Momma takes Marguerite to the local dentist to be treated for a severe toothache. The dentist, who is ironically called Lincoln, refuses to treat the child, even though he is indebted to Momma for a loan she extended to him during the depression: "'Annie, my policy is I'd rather stick my hand in a dog's mouth than in a nigger's.'" As a silent witness to this scene, Marguerite suffers not only from the pain of her two decayed teeth, which have ben reduced to tiny enamel bits by the avenging "Angel of the candy counter," but also from the utter humiliation of the dentist's bigotry as well: "It seemed terribly unfair to have a toothache and a headache and have to bear at the same time the heavy burden on Blackness" (*CB*, 159–60).

In an alternative version of the confrontation, which Angelou deliberately fantasizes and then italicizes to emphasize its invention, Momma asks Marguerite to wait for her outside the dentist's office. As the door closes, the frightened child imagines her grandmother becoming "ten feet tall will eight-foot arms." Without mincing words, Momma instructs Lincoln to "'leave Stamps by sundown'" and "'never again practice dentistry'": "'When you get settled in your next place, you will be a vegetarian caring for dogs with the mange, cats with the cholera and cows with the epizootic. Is that clear?'" (*CB*, 162). The poetic justice in Momma's superhuman power is perfect; the racist dentist who refused to treat her ailing granddaughter will in the future be restricted to treating the dogs he prefers to "niggers." After a trip to the black dentist in Texarkana, Momma and Marguerite return to Stamps, where we learn the "real" version of the story by overhearing a conversation between Momma and Uncle Willie. In spite of her prodigious powers, all that Momma accomplishes in Dr. Lincoln's office is to demand ten dollars as unpaid interest on the loan to pay for their bus trip to Texarkana.

In the child's imagined version, fantasy comes into play as the recounted scene ventures into the unreal or the impossible. Momma becomes a sort of superwoman of enormous proportions ("ten feel tall with eight-foot arms") and comes to the helpless child's rescue. In this alternate vision, Angelou switches to fantasy to suggest the depth of the child's humiliation and the residue of pain even after her two bad teeth have been pulled. Fantasy, finally, is used to demonstrate the undiminished strength of the character of

Momma. Summarizing the complete anecdote, Angelou attests, "I preferred, much preferred, my version." Carefully selected elements of fiction and fantasy in the scene involving Dr. Lincoln and her childhood hero, Momma, partially compensate for the racial displacement that she experiences as a child.

When Angelou is thirteen, she and Bailey leave the repressive atmosphere of Stamps to join their mother. During these years, she continues to look for a place in life that will dissolve her sense of displacement. By the time she and Bailey are in their early teens, they have criss-crossed the western half of the country traveling between their parents' separate homes and their grandmother's in Stamps. Her sense of geographic displacement alone would be enough to upset any child's security, since the life-styles of her father in southern California and her mother in St. Louis and later in San Francisco represent worlds completely different and even foreign to the pace of life in the rural South. Each time the children move, a different set of relatives or another of their parents' lovers greets them, and they never feel a part of a stable family group, except when they are in Stamps at the general store with Momma and Uncle Willie.

Once settled in San Francisco in the early 1940s, Angelou enrolls at George Washington High School and the California Labor School, where she studies dance and drama in evening classes. She excels in both schools, and her teachers quickly recognize her intelligence and talent. Later she breaks the color barrier by becoming the first black female conductor on the San Francisco streetcars. Just months before her high school graduation, she engages in a onetime sexual encounter to prove her sexuality to herself and becomes pregnant. *Caged Bird*, however, ends on a note of awakening with the birth of her son and the beginning of a significant measure of strength and confidence in her ability to succeed and find her place in life. As autobiographer, Angelou uses the theme of displacement to unify the first volume of her life story as well as to suggest her long-term determination to create security and permanency in her life.

Between the conclusion of *Caged Bird* and the beginning of Angelou's second volume of autobiography, *Gather Together in My Name (1974*), there is virtually no break in the narrative. As the first ends with the birth of her son, the second starts when Guy is only a few months old. As a whole, *Gather Together* tells the story of his first three years and focuses on a young single mother's struggle to achieve respect, love, and a sense of self-worth. Her battle to win financial independence and the devotion of a faithful man could hardly have been easy in the years immediately following World War

II, when racial discrimination, unemployment, and McCarthyism were all on the rise. In spite of her initial optimism, which is, incidentally, shared by many members of the postwar black community who fervently believed that "race prejudice was dead. A mistake made by a young country. Something to be forgiven as an unpleasant act committed by an intoxicated friend" (*GT*, 2), Angelou soon realizes that her dreams for a better America are still too fragile to survive. But worst of all is the burden of guilt that rests on the shoulders of the seventeen-year-old mother who desperately believes that she must assume full adult responsibility. Fortunately, her mother encourages her to set high goals, to maintain her sense of dignity and self-worth, and to work hard to succeed. Her mother's words come back to her through her life: "Anything worth doing is worth doing well," and "be the best of anything you get into" (*GT*, 24).

Like many young women who came of age in the postwar era, Angelou easily imagines herself moving into a life modeled on *Good Housekeeping* and *Better Homes and Gardens.* She describes herself as both a "product of Hollywood upbringing" and her own "romanticism" and continually envisions herself smoothly slipping into the role guaranteed by popular culture. Whenever she meets a man who might potentially fulfill her dream, she anticipates the enviable comfort of "settling down." The scenario is always the same: "I would always wear pretty aprons and my son would play in the Little League. My husband would come home (he looked like Curly) and smoke his pipe in the den as I made cookies for the Scouts meeting," (*GT*, 127–28), or "We would live quietly in a pretty little house and I'd have another child, a girl, and the two children (whom he'd love equally) would climb over his knees and I would make three layer caramel cakes in my electric kitchen until they went off to college" (*GT*, 120). These glamorous dreams, of course, never quite materialize, but Angelou maintains a hopeful outlook an a determination to support and protect herself and her infant son. Her primary motivation during these early years of motherhood is to spare her son the insecurity and rejection she faced as a child. During these years, Angelou even works as an absentee madam and a prostitute, in hopes of achieving a regular family life and easing her unabiding sense of guilt over not being able to provide herself and her son with financial and familial security.

Yet Angelou understands that the hurdles she has to cross on her road to success are often higher than those set by her own expectations and standard of performance. Although she spends the first years of her son's life in California, both in the Bay Area and in San Diego, she often faces racial discrimination reminiscent of her childhood experiences in the South. At one point in *Gather Together*, when she suspects that her thriving business as a madam of a two-prostitute house will soon be uncovered by the police, Angelou returns to Stamps with her son, hoping to find the same comfort and protection she had known as a child. Specifically, she seeks her grandmother's "protective embrace" and her "courage" as well as the "shield of anonymity," but she soon realizes that the South is not ready to welcome her and that she has "outgrown" its "childhood protection." The five years she has spent in school and working in California have broadened her horizons and convinced her of her right to be accepted on the basis of her character and intelligence. But the South to which she returns is unchanged: "The town was halved by railroad tracks, the swift Red River and racial prejudice . . ." and "above all, the atmosphere was pressed down with the smell of old fears, and hates, and guilt" (*GT*, 61–63).

Not long after her arrival in Stamps, Angelou comes face to face with the double standards of racial discrimination during an unpleasant confrontation with a salesclerk in the white-owned general merchandise store. Although she attempts to explain to her grandmother why she refused to accept the clerk's humiliating insults, Momma warns her that her "principles" are too flimsy a protection against the unrestrained contempt of bigotry: "'You think 'cause you've been to California these crazy people won't kill you? You think them lunatic cracker boys won't try to catch you in the road and violate you? You think because of your all-fired principle some of the men won't feel like putting their white sheets on and riding over here to stir up trouble? You do, you're wrong'" (*GT*, 78–79). That same day, her grandmother sends her back to California where she and her son are somewhat more distanced from the lingering hatred of the South. Not until the filming of a segment of Bill Moyer's PBS series on creativity thirty years later does Angelou return to her childhood home.

Upon her return to the Bay Area and to her mother's home, she is more determined than ever to achieve independence and win the respect of others. Leaving her son in the care of baby-sitters, she works long hours first as a dancer and entertainer and then as a short-order cook in Stockton. But as is often the case, the reality of her situation falls far below her ideal, and Angelou eventually turns to marijuana as a temporary consolation: "The pot had been important when I was alone and lonely, when my present is dull and the future uncertain" (*GT*, 131). During this period, she also falls in love with an older man who is a professional gambler supported by prostitution. When his luck fails him, Angelou agrees to help him pay his debt by becoming a prostitute herself. She makes this sacrifice fully believing that after her man has regained his financial security, he will marry her and provide her with the fulfillment of her romantic dream. Rationalizing her decision, she compares prostitution to marriage: "There are married women who are more whorish than a street prostitute because they have sold their bodies for marriage licenses, and there are some women who sleep with men for money who have great integrity because they are doing it for a purpose" (*GT*, 135). But once again her dreams are disappointed, and she finds herself on her own at the end.

The second volume of her autobiography ends just before she decides to settle down with a man she pictures as an "ideal husband, " who is in fact a heroin addict and gambler. Before it is too late, Angelou learns that she is on the verge of embracing disaster and defeat. At the end, she regains her innocence through the lessons of a compassionate drug addict: "I had walked the precipice and seen it all; and at the critical moment, one man's generosity pushed me safely away from the edge. . . . I had given a promise and found my innocence, I swore I'd never lose it again" (*GT*, 181). With these words, ready to accept the challenge of life anew, Angelou brings the second volume of her life story to a close. In *Gather Together in My Name*, a title inspired by the Gospel of Matthew (18:20), she asks her family and readers to gather around her and bear witness to her past.

The third volume of Maya Angelou's autobiography, *Singin' and Swingin' and Gettin' Merry Like Christmas* (1976) concentrates on the early years of her career as professional dancer and singer, her related experience with racial prejudice, and with the guilt suffered through separation from her young son. During her childhood, her love for music grows through her almost daily attendance at the Colored Methodist Episcopal Church in Stamps and through her dance classes in California. Music in fact is her closest companion and source of moral support during her first few months back in the San Francisco area. She calls music her "refuge" during this period of her life and welcomes its protective embrace, into which she could "crawl into the spaces between the notes and curl (her) back to loneliness" (*SS*, 1). Without losing any time, she secures a job in sales and inventory at the Melrose Record Shop on Fillmore, which at the time served as a meeting place for musicians and music lovers of all description. In addition to earning enough money to quit her two previous jobs and bring her son home from the baby-sitter's in the evenings and on Sundays, Angelou also gains valuable exposure to the newest releases in blues and jazz and to an expansive circle of eccentric people.

Her sales position at the record shop is her first step into the world of entertainment. Her hours behind the cashier counter studying catalogs and helping customers make their selections bring her an easy familiarity with the newest stars and songs. Relying on her dance lessons and her trusted memory of popular lyrics, she later auditions for a position as a dancer at the

Garden of Allah, where she is eventually hired as the first black show girl. Unlike the three white women who are also featured in the nightly show, Angelou is not required to strip but rather earns her audiences' attention on the basis of her dance routines alone. All of the dancers, however, are instructed to supplement their regular salary by selling B-grade drinks and bottles of champagne on commission to interested customers. At first reluctant to put herself at the mercy of fawning, flirtatious spectators, she soon learns to sell more drinks than any of the others, simply by giving away the house secret on the composition of the ginger ale and Seven-Up cocktails and the details of the commission scale. But her success evokes the jealousy of the other women, and soon her first venture into professional entertainment comes to an end.

Through contracts established during her work at the Garden of Allah, Angelou auditions for an opening at the Purple Onion, a North Beach cabaret where she soon replaces Jorie Remus and shares the nightly bill with Phyllis Diller. After lessons with her drama coach, Lloyd Clark, who, incidentally, is responsible for coining her stage name, Maya Angelou, she polishes her style as an interpretative dancer and perfects a series of calypso songs that eventually comprise her regular act at the cabaret. Although the audience at the Purple Onion has never been entertained by a performer like Angelou, she quickly becomes extremely popular and gains much wider exposure than she did as a dancer at the Garden of Allah. Many professional stars and talent scouts, visiting San Francisco from New York and Chicago, drop in at the Purple Onion and some eventually invite her to audition for their shows. In 1954, for example, Leonard Sillman brought his Broadway hit *New Faces of 1953* to the Bay Area. When she learns through friends that Sillman needed a replacement for Eartha Kitt, who would be leaving for an engagement in Las Vegas, she jumps at the chance to work with a cast of talented performers. Even though she is invited to join the show, the management at the Purple Onion refuses to release her from her contract. Her first real show business break, therefore, does not come until after she goes to New York to try out for a new Broadway show called *House of Flowers*, staring Pearl Bailey and directed by Saint Subber. While there she is unexpectedly asked to join the company of *Porgy and Bess* in the role of Ruby, just as the troupe is finishing up its engagement in Montreal and embarking on its first European tour. She accepts, thereby launching her international career as a dancer-singer.

As her professional career in entertainment develops, Angelou worries about her responsibility to care for her young son and provide him with a secure family life. In *Singin' and Swingin'*, she continues to trace her pursuit of romantic ideals into the face of loneliness and disappointment. While working in the Melrose Record Shop, she meets Tosh Angelos, a sailor of Greek-American heritage, and later marries him. Her first impression of marriage could not have been more idealistic:

> At last I was a housewife, legally a member of that enviable tribe of consumers whom security made fat as butter and who under no circumstances considered living by bread alone, because their husbands brought home the bacon. I had a son, a father for him, a husband and a pretty home for us to live in. My life began to resemble a Good Housekeeping advertisement. I cooked well-balanced meals and molded fabulous jello desserts. My floors were dangerous with daily applications of wax and our furniture slick with polish. (*SS*, 26)

Unfortunately, after a year, Tosh and she begin to argue and recognize that their different attitudes stand in the way of true compatibility and trust. Her "Eden"-like homelife and "cocoon of safety" begin to smother her sense of integrity and independence. In her autobiography, she describes this difficult period as a time in which she felt a "sense of loss," which "suffused [her] until [she] was suffocating within the vapors" (*SS*, 37). When their marriage ends, Angelou again looks for a way to give her young child a stable home and a permanent sense of family security. Understandably, her son temporarily distrusts her and wonders whether she will stop loving him and leave him behind to be cared for by others.

Before she marries Tosh, she seriously questions the nature of interracial marriage and is advised by others, including her mother, to examine the relationship carefully. Throughout *Singin' and Swingin'*, she studies her attitude toward white people and explains her growing familiarity with their life-styles and their acceptance of her as an equal within the world of entertainment. When she first meets her future Greek-American husband, she suspects that her racial heritage precludes a possibility of any kind of permanent relationship. Her Southern childhood is too close, too vibrant in her memory: "I would never forget the slavery tales, or my Southern past, where all whites, including the poor and ignorant, had the right to speak rudely to and even physically abuse any Negro they met. I knew the ugliness of white prejudice" (*SS*, 23). Although she discounts her suspicion in her dealings with Tosh Angelos, her deeply rooted fears stay close to the surface as she comes to associate with a large number of white artists and entertainers during her career as a dancer: "I knew you could never tell about white people. Negroes had survived centuries of inhuman treatment and retained their humanity by hoping for the best from the pale-skinned oppressors but at the same time being prepared for the worst" (*SS*, 104). Later, during her role as Ruby in *Porgy and Bess*, which played throughout Europe, the Middle East, and North Africa, she observes the double standards of white people who readily accept black Americans in Europe because they are fascinated by their exotic foreignness, but who are equally quick to discriminate against other people of color. In North Africa, she witnesses yet another version of racial bigotry in the way members of the Arab elite mistreat their African servants, "not realizing that auction blocks and whipping posts were too recent in our history for us [black Americans] to be comfortable around slavish servants" (*SS*, 210).

While in Rome, Angelou decides to cut short her engagement with *Porgy and Bess*, not because she has witnessed the complexities of racial prejudice but rather because she realizes that her son has suffered during her extended absence. Throughout her European tour, she carries the burden of guilt, which comes to characterize her early years of motherhood. Although she recognizes the pattern of abandonment emerging in her son's life as it had in her own, she often sees no alternative than to accept a job and, with it, the pain of separation. Finally, upon learning that her son has developed a severe and seemingly untreatable rash in her absence, she decides to return to San Francisco. Once there, she assumes full responsibility for "ruining (her) beautiful son by neglect" and for the "devastation to his mind and body" (*SS*, 233). Shortly after her return, Guy recovers, and together they reach a new level of trust and mutual dependence based on the understanding that their separation is now over for good. *Singin' and Swingin'* comes to a close as mother and son settle into a Hawaiian beach resort where she has just opened a new engagement at a nightclub. She achieves a longed for peace of mind as she comes to treasure her "wonderful, dependently independent son" (*SS*, 242).

In *The Heart of a Woman* (1980), the fourth in the autobiographical series, Maya Angelou continues the account of her son's youth and, in the process, repeatedly returns to the story of her childhood. The references to her childhood serve partly to create a textual link for readers who might be unfamiliar with the earlier volumes and partly to emphasize the suggestive similarities between her childhood and her son's. Her overwhelming sense of displacement and instability is, ironically, her son's burden too. In a brief flashback in the second chapter, she reminds us of the displacement that characterized her youth and links this aspect of her past with her son's present attitude. When Guy is fourteen, Angelou decides to move to New York. She does not bring Guy to the East until she has found a place for them to live, and when he arrives after a one-month separation, he initially resists her attempts to make a new home for them:

> The air between us [Angelou and Guy] was burdened with his aloof scorn. I understood him too well.
>
> When I was three my parents divorced in Long Beach, California, and sent me and my four-year-old brother, unescorted, to our paternal grandmother. We wore wrist tags which informed anyone concerned that were Marguerite and Bailey Johnson, en route to Mrs. Annie Henderson in Stamps, Arkansas.
>
> Except for disastrous and mercifully brief encounters with each of them when I was seven, we didn't see our parents again until I was thirteen. (*HW*, 34–35)

From this and similar encounters with Guy, Angelou learns that the continual displacement of her own childhood is something she cannot prevent from recurring in her son's life.

In New York, Angelou begins to work as the Northern coordinator of the Southern Christian Leadership Conference and devotes most of her time to raising funds, boosting membership, and organizing volunteer labor, both in the office and in the neighborhoods. Throughout *Heart of a Woman*, she expands her own narrative by including anecdotes about well-known entertainers and political figures. Her account of a visit with Martin Luther King, Jr., at her SCLC office is just one example of this autobiographical technique. When Dr. King pays his first visit to the New York office during her tenure, she does not have advance notice of his presence and rushes into her office one day after lunch to find him sitting at her desk. They begin to talk about her background and eventually focus their comments on her brother, Bailey:

> "Come on, take your seat back and tell me about yourself."
>
> . . . When I mentioned my brother Bailey, he asked what he was doing now.
>
> The question stopped me. He was friendly and understanding, but if I told him my brother was in prison, I couldn't be sure how long his understanding would last. I could lose my job. Even more important, I might lose his respect. Birds of a feather and

> all that, but I took a chance and told him Bailey was in Sing Sing.
>
> He dropped his head and looked at his hands.
>
> . . . "I understand. Disappointment drives our young men to some desperate lengths." Sympathy and sadness kept his voice low. "That's why we must fight and win. We must save the Baileys of the world. And Maya, never stop loving him. Never give up on him. Never deny him. And remember, he is freer than those who hold him behind bars." (*HW*, 92–93)

Angelou appreciates King's sympathy and of course shares his hope that their work will make the world more fair and free. She recognizes the undeniable effects of displacement on Bailey's life and fervently hopes that her own son will be spared any further humiliation and rejection.

From time to time, Angelou sees marriage as the answer to her own sense of dislocation and fully envisions a perfect future with various prospective husbands. While in New York, she meets Vusumzi Make, a black South African freedom fighter, and imagines that he will provide her with the same domestic security she had hoped would develop from other relationships: "I was getting a husband, and part of that gift was having someone to share responsibility and guilt" (*HW*, 131). Yet her hopes are ever more idealistic than usual, inasmuch as she imagines herself participating in the liberation of South Africa as Vus Make's wife: "With my courage added to his own, he would succeed in bringing the ignominious white rule in South Africa to an end. If I didn't already have the qualities he needed, then I would just develop them. Infatuation made me believe in my ability to create myself into my lover's desire" (*HW*, 123). In reality, Angelou is only willing to go so far in recreating herself to meet her husband's desires and is all too soon frustrated with her role as Make's wife. He does not want her to work but is unable on his own to support his expensive tastes as well as his family. They are evicted from their New York apartment just before they leave for Egypt and soon face similar problems in Cairo. Their marriage dissolves after some months, despite Angelou's efforts to contribute to their financial assets by working as editor of the *Arab Observer*. In *Heart of a Woman*, she underscores the illusory nature of her fantasy about marriage to show how her perspective has shifted over the years and how much understanding she has gained about life in general. Re-creating these fantasies in her autobiography is a subtle form of truth telling and a way to present hard-earned insights about her life to her readers.

A second type of fantasy in *Heart of a Woman* is borne out in reality rather than in illusion, as is the case with her expectations of marriage. One of the most important uses of the second kind of fantasy involves a sequence that demonstrates how much she fears for Guy's safety throughout his youth. A few days after mother and son arrive in Accra, where they move when her marriage with Vus Make deteriorates, some friends invite them to a picnic. Although his mother declines, Guy immediately accepts the invitation in a show of independence. On the way home from the day's outing, her son is seriously injured in an automobile accident. Even though he has had very little experience driving, his intoxicated host asks Guy to drive. When their return is delayed, Angelou is terrified by her recurring fear for Guy's safety. Later, in the Korle Bu emergency ward, her familiar fantasy about harm endangering her son's life moves to the level of reality, as she relates the vulnerability she feels in her role as mother with full responsibility for the well-being of her only child. In a new country, estranged from her husband and with no immediate prospects for employment, she possesses very little control over her life or her son's safety. After the accident in Ghana, Guy is not only fighting for independence from his mother but also for life itself. The conclusion of *Heart of a Woman*, nevertheless, announces a new beginning for Angelou and hope for her future relationship with Guy.

Her most recent autobiography, *All God's Children Need Traveling Shoes* (1986), has swept Angelou to new heights of critical and popular acclaim. Her life story resumes exactly where it ended chronologically and geographically in *The Heart of a Woman*, with Guy's recovery from his automobile accident in Accra. Although only portions of two earlier volumes of her autobiographical narrative occur in Africa, her latest addition to the series takes place almost exclusively in Ghana. In *All God's Children Need Traveling Shoes*, however, Angelou focuses primarily on the story of her and many other black Americans' attempts in the early 1960s to return to the ancestral home in Africa. As in her four previous autobiographies, she explores the theme of displacement and the difficulties involved in creating a home for oneself, one's family, and one's people.

In choosing to live in Ghana following the deterioration of her marriage to Vus Make, Angelou hopes to find a place where she and her son can make a home for themselves, free at last from the racial bigotry she has faced throughout the United States, Europe, and parts of the Middle East. While Guy is recuperating from his injuries, she carefully evaluates her assets and concludes that since his birth, her only home has been wherever she and her son are together: "we had been each other's home and center for seventeen years. He could die if he wanted to and go off to wherever dead folks go, but I, I would be left without a home" (*TS*, 5). Her initial expectations, therefore, for feeling at ease and settling down in West Africa are, understandably, considerable:

"We had come home, and if home was not what we had expected, never mind, our need for belonging allowed us to ignore the obvious and to create real places or even illusory places, befitting our imagination" (*TS*, 19). Unfortunately, the Ghanian people do not readily accept Angelou, her son, and most of the black American community in Accra, and they unexpectedly find themselves isolated and often ignored.

Taken as a whole, *All God's Children Need Traveling Shoes* recounts the sequence of events that gradually brings the autobiographer closer to an understanding and eventually to an acceptance of the seemingly unbreachable distance between the Ghanians and the black American expatriates. Within the first few weeks of her stay in Ghana, Angelou suspects that she has mistakenly followed the misdirected footsteps of other black Americans who "had not come home, but had left one familiar place of painful memory for another strange place with none" (*TS*, 40). In time, she understands that their alienation is most likely based on the fact that they, unlike the Ghanians, are the descendants of African slaves, who painfully bear the knowledge that "not all slaves were stolen, nor were all slave dealers European'" (*TS*, 47). No one in the expatriate group can feel fully at ease in Africa as long as they carry the haunting suspicion that "African slavery stemmed mostly from tribal exploitation" (*TS*, 48) and not solely from European colonial imperialism.

Angelou, nevertheless, perseveres; she eventually settles into lasting friendships with both Americans and Africans and finds work through her talents as a journalist and a performer. With her professional and personal contacts, she meets many African political activists, as well as diplomats and artists from around the world. The acquaintances, in addition to a brief tour in Berlin and Venice with the original St. Mark's Playhouse company of Genet's *The Blacks*, enlarge Angelou's perspective on racial complexities and help her locate a place in Africa where she can live, albeit temporarily, at peace.

In *All God's Children Need Traveling Shoes*, Angelou continually reminds the reader that the quest for a place to call home is virtually endemic to the human condition. During her time in Ghana, she comes to understand that the search is seldom successful, regardless of the political or social circumstances involved. Toward the end of her personal narrative, Angelou sums up her conclusions about the struggle to find or create a home: "If the heart of Africa still remained allusive, my search for it had brought me closer to understanding myself and other human beings. The ache for home lives in all of us, the safe place where we can go as we are and not be questioned" (*TS*, 196). In a 1984 interview conducted during the period when she was completing an earlier draft of *All God's Children Need*

Traveling Shoes, Angelou voices the same illuminating insight:

> Neubauer: How far will the fifth volume go?
>
> Angelou: Actually, it's a new kind. It's really quite a new voice. I'm looking at the black American resident, me and the other black American residents in Ghana, and trying to see all the magic of the eternal quest of human beings to go home again. That is maybe what life is anyway. To return to the Creator. All of that naivete, the innocence of trying to. That awful rowing towards God, whatever it is. Whether it's to return to your village or the lover you lost or the youth that some people want to return to or the beauty that some want to return to.
>
> Neubauer: Writing autobiography frequently involves this quest to return to the past, to the home. Sometimes, if the home can't be found, it can't be located again, then that home or that love or that family, whatever has been lost, is recreated or invented.
>
> Angelou: Yes, of course. That's it! That's what I'm seeing in this trek back to Africa. That in so many cases that idealized home of course is non-existent. In so many cases some black Americans created it on the spot. On the spot. And I did too. Created something, looked, seemed like what we have idealized very far from reality.

Whatever vision of home Angelou creates for herself and her son in Ghana, she discovers a heightened sense of self-awareness and independence. By the end of her stay in West Africa, she has a renewed image of herself as a woman, lover, mother, writer, performer, and political activist. In her state of fortified strength, she decides to leave Africa and return to the country of her birth, however disturbing the memories of slavery and the reality of racial hatred. In fact, Angelou ends her sojourn in foreign lands to commit herself to Malcolm X's struggle for racial equality and social justice in the United States, by planning to work as an office coordinator for the Organization of Afro-American Unity. She has finally freed herself from the illusion of claiming an ancestral home in Africa. Ironically perhaps, with the writing of *All God's Children Need Traveling Shoes* and the brilliant clarity of the autobiographical present, "this trek back to Africa," Maya Angelou also decides to return to the South, and for the first time since her youth, make her home there. Although she has learned that "the idealized home of course is nonexistent," she leaves her readers to suspect that her traveling shoes are never really out of sight; if nothing else, we will soon find ourselves following her paths of autobiographical discovery once again.

Poetry

Most of the thirty-eight poems in Maya Angelou's *Just Give Me a Cool Drink of Water 'fore I Diiie* (1971) appeared several years earlier in a collection called *The Poetry of Maya Angelou*, published by Hirt Music. Among these are some of her best known pieces, such as "Miss Scarlett, Mr. Rhett and Other Latter Day Saints" and "Harlem Hopscotch." The volume is divided into two parts; the first deals with love, its joy and inevitable sorrow, and the second with the trials of the black race. Taken as a whole, the poems cover a wide range of settings from Harlem streets to Southern churches to abandoned African coasts. These poems contain a certain power, which stems from the strong metric control that finds its way into the terse lines characteristic of her poetry. Not a word is wasted, not a beat lost. Angelou's poetic voice speaks with a sure confidence that dares return to even the most painful memories to capture the first signs of loss or hate.

The first twenty poems of *Cool Drink* describe the whole gamut of love, from the first moment of passionate discovery to the first suspicion of painful loss. One poem, in fact, is entitled "The Gamut" and in its sonnet form moves from "velvet soft" dawn when "my true love approaches" to the "deathly quiet" of night when "my true love is leaving" (*CD*, 5). Two poems, "To a Husband" and "After," however, celebrate the joyous fulfillment of love. In the first, Angelou suggests that her husband is a symbol of African strength and beauty and that through his almost majestic presence she can sense the former riches of the exploited continent. To capture his vibrant spirit, she retreats to Africa's original splendor and conjures up images as ancient as "Pharoah's tomb":

> You're Africa to me
> At brightest dawn.
> The congo's green and
> Copper's brackish hue . . .

In this one man, she sees the vital strength of an entire race: "A continent to build / With Black Man's brawn" (*CD*,15). His sacrifice, reminiscent of generations of unacknowledged labor, inspires her love and her commitment to the African cause. "After" also speaks of the love between woman and man but is far more tender and passionate. The scene is the lovers' bed when "no sound falls / from the moaning sky" and "no scowl wrinkles / the evening pool." Here, as in "To a Husband," love is seen as strong and sustaining, even jubilant in its harmonious union, its peaceful calm. Even the "stars lean down / A stony brilliance" in recognition of their love (*CD*, 18). And yet there is certain absent emptiness in the quiet that hints of future loss.

In the second section, Angelou turns her attention to the lives of black people in America from the time of slavery to the rebellious 1960s. Her themes deal broadly with the painful anguish suffered by blacks forced into submission, with guilt over accepting too much, and with protest and basic survival.

"No No No No" is a poem about the rejection of American myths that promise justice for all but only guarantee freedom for a few. The powerfully cadenced stanzas in turn decry the immorality of American involvement in Vietnam,

> while crackling babies
> in napalm coats
> stretch mouths to receive
> burning tears . . .

as well as the insincere invitation of the Statue of Liberty, which welcomes immigrants who crossed "over the sinuous cemetery / of my many brothers," and the inadequate apologies offered by white liberals. The first stanza ends with the refrain that titles the complete collection of poems, "JUST GIVE ME A COOL DRINK OF WATER 'FORE I DIIIE." In the second half of the poem, the speaker identifies with those who suffered humiliation

> on the back porches
> of forever
> in the kitchens and fields
> of rejections

and boldly cautions that the dreams and hopes of a better tomorrow have vanished (*CD*, 40–43). Even pity, the last defense against inhumanity, is spent.

Two poems that embody the poet's confident determination that conditions must improve for the black race are "Times-Square-Shoeshine

Composition" and "Harlem Hopscotch." Both ring with a lively, invincible beat that carries defeated figures into at least momentary triumph. "Times-Square" tells the story of a shoeshine man who claims to be an unequaled master at his trade. He cleans and shines shoes to a vibrant rhythm that sustains his spirit in spite of humiliating circumstances. When a would-be customer offers him twenty-five cents instead of the requested thirty-five cents, the shoeshine man refuses the job and flatly renounces the insulting attempt to minimize the value of his trade. Fully appreciating his own expertise, the vendor proudly instructs his potential Times Square patron to give his measly quarter to his daughter, sister, or mamma, for they clearly need it more than he does. Denying the charge that he is a "greedy bigot," the shoeshine man simply admits that he is a striving "capitalist," trying to be successful in a city owned by the superrich.

Moving uptown, "Harlem Hopscotch" celebrates the sheer strength necessary for survival. The rhythm of this powerful poem echoes the beat of feet, first hopping, then suspended in air, and finally landing in the appropriate square. To live in a world measured by such blunt announcements as "food is gone" and "the rent is due," people need to be extremely energetic and resilient. Compounding the pressures of hunger, poverty, and unemployment is the racial bigotry that consistently discriminates against people of color. Life itself has become a brutal game of hopscotch, a series of desperate yet hopeful leaps, landing but never pausing long: "In the air, now both feet down. / Since you black, don't stick around." Yet in the final analysis, the words that bring the poem and the complete collection to a close triumphantly announce the poet's victory: "Both feet flat, the game is done. / They think I lost. I think I won" (*CD*, 50). These poems in their sensitive treatment of both love and black identity are the poet's own defense against the incredible odds in the game of life.

Within four years of the publications of *Just Give Me a Cool Drink 'fore I Diiie*, Maya Angelou completed a second volume of poetry, *Oh Pray My Wings Are Gonna Fit Me Well* (1975). By the time of its release, her reputation as a poet who transforms much of the pain and disappointment of life into lively verse had been established. During the 1970s her reading public grew accustomed to seeing her poems printed in *Cosmopolitan*. Angelou had become recognized not only as a spokesperson for blacks and women, but also for all people who are committed to raising the moral standards of living in the United States. The poems collected in *My Wings*, indeed, appear at the end of the Vietnam era and in some important ways exceed the scope of her first volume. Many question traditional American values and urge people to make an honest appraisal of the demoralizing rift between the ideal and the real. Along with poems about love and the oppressions of black people, the poet adds several that directly challenge Americans to reexamine their lives and to strive to reach the potential richness that has been compromised by self-interest since the beginnings of the country.

One of the most moving poems in *My Wings* is entitled "Alone," in which carefully measured verses describe the general alienation of people in the twentieth century. "Alone" is not directed at any one particular sector of society but rather is focused on the human condition in general. No one, the poet cautions, can live in this world alone. This message punctuates the end of the three major stanzas and also serves as a separate refrain between each and at the close of the poem:

> Alone, all alone
> Nobody, but nobody
> Can make it out here alone.

Angelou begins by looking within herself and discovering that her soul is without a home. Moving from an inward glimpse to an outward sweep, she recognizes that even millionaires suffer from this modern malaise and live lonely lives with "hearts of stone." Finally, she warns her readers to listen carefully and change the direction of their lives:

> Storm clouds are gathering
> The wind is gonna blow
> The race of man is suffering. (*MW,* 70)

For its own survival, the human race must break down barriers and rescue one another from loneliness. The only cure, the poet predicts, is to acknowledge common interests and work toward common goals.

A poem entitled "America" is no less penetrating in its account of the country's problems. Again Angelou pleads with the American people to "discover this country" and realize its full potential. In its two-hundred-year history, "the gold of her promise / has never been mined." The promise of justice for all has not been kept and in spite of "her crops of abundance / the fruit and the grain," many citizens live below the poverty line and never have enough food to feed their families. Similarly, racial bigotry has denied generations of Americans their full dignity and natural rights, while depriving them of the opportunity to contribute freely to the nation's strength. At the close of the poem, Angelou calls for the end of "legends untrue," which are perpetuated through history to "entrap" America's children (*MW,* 78–79). The only hope for the country is to discard these false myths once and for all and to guarantee that all people benefit from democratic principles.

In one poem, "Southeast Arkansia," the poet shifts her attention from the general condition of humanity to the plight of black people in America. The setting of this tightly structured poem is the locale where Angelou spent most of her childhood. At the end of the three stanzas, she poses a question concerning the responsibility and guilt involved in the exploitation of the slaves. Presumably, the white men most immediately involved have never answered for their inhumane treatment of "bartered flesh and broken bones." The poet doubts that they have ever even paused to "ponder" or "wonder" about their proclivity to value profit more than human life (*MW,* 99).

Any discussion of *My Wings* that did not address the poems written about the nature of love would be necessarily incomplete. The entire volume is dedicated to Paul du Feu, Angelou's husband from 1973 to 1980. One very brief poem, "Passing Time," speaks of a love that is finely balanced and delicately counterpoised. This love stretches over time, blanketing both the beginning and end of a day: "Your skin like dawn / Mine like dusk" (*MW,* 62). Together is reached a certain harmony that carries the lovers through the day, perfectly complementing each other's spirit. Equally economical in form is the poem "Greyday," which in nine short lines compares a lonely lover to Christ. While she is separated from her man, "the day hangs heavy / loose and grey." The woman feels as if she is wearing "a crown of thorns" and "a shirt of hair." Alone, she suffers in her solitude and mourns that

> No one knows
> my lonely heart
> when we're apart. (*MW,* 64)

Such is love in the world of *My Wings;* when all is going well, love sustains and inspires, but when love fades, loneliness and pain have free rein.

As the title of Maya Angelou's third volume of poetry, *And Still I Rise* (1978), suggests, this collection contains a hopeful determination to rise above discouraging defeat. These poems are inspired and spoken by a confident voice of strength that recognizes its own power and will no longer be pushed into passivity. The book consists of thirty-two poems, which are divided into the three sections, "Touch Me, Life, Not Softly," "Traveling," and "And Still I Rise." Two poems, "Phenomenal Woman" and "Just for a Time" appeared in *Cosmopolitan* in 1978. Taken as a whole, this series of poems covers a broader range of subjects than the earlier two volumes and shifts smoothly from issues such as springtime and aging to sexual awakening, drug addiction, and Christian salvation. The familiar themes of love and its inevitable loneliness and the oppressive climate of the South are still central concerns. But even more striking than the poet's careful treatment of these subjects is her attention to the nature of woman and the importance of family.

One of the best poems in this collection is "Phenomenal Woman," which captures the essence of womanhood and at the same time describes the many talents of the poet herself. As is characteristic of Angelou's poetic style, the lines are terse and forcefully, albeit irregularly, rhymed. The words themselves are short, often monosyllabic, and collectively create an even, provocative rhythm that resounds with underlying confidence. In four different stanzas, a woman explains her special graces that make her stand out in a crowd and attract the attention of both men and women, although she is not, by her own admission, "cut or built to suit a fashion model's size." One by one, she enumerates her gifts, from "the span of my hips" to "the curl of my lips," from "the flash of my teeth" to "the joy in my feet." Yet her attraction is not purely physical; men seek her for her "inner mystery," "the grace of (her) style," and "the need for (her) care." Together each alluring part adds up to a phenomenal woman who need not "bow" her head but can walk tall with a quiet pride that beckons those in her presence (*IR*, 121–23).

Similar to "Phenomenal Woman" in its economical form, strong rhyme scheme, and forceful rhythm is "Woman Work." The two poems also bear a thematic resemblance in their praise of woman's vitality. Although "Woman Work" does not concern the physical appeal of woman, as "Phenomenal Woman" does, it delivers a corresponding litany of the endless cycle of chores in a woman's typical day. In the first stanza, the long list unravels itself in forcefully rhymed couplets:

> I've got the children to tend
> The clothes to mend
> The floor to mop
> The food to shop
> Then the chicken to fry
> Then baby to dry.

Following the complete category of tasks, the poet adds four shorter stanzas, which reveal the source of woman's strength. This woman claims the sunshine, rain, and dew as well as storms, wind, and snow as her own. The dew cools her brow, the wind lifts her "across the sky," the snow covers her "with white / Cold icy kisses," all bringing her rest and eventually the strength to continue (*IR*, 144–45). For her, there is no other source of solace and consolation than nature and its powerful elements.

In two poems, "Willie" and "Kin," Angelou turns her attention from woman to her family. "Willie" tells the story of her paternal uncle, with whom she and her brother, Bailey, lived during their childhood in Stamps, Arkansas. This man, although "crippled and limping, always walking lame," knows the secret of survival. For years, he suffers humiliation and loneliness, both as a result of his physical affliction and his color. Yet from him, the child learns about the hidden richness of life and later follows his example to overcome seemingly insurmountable hardships. Willie's undying message echoes throughout the poem: "I may cry and I will die, / But my spirit is the soul of every spring" and "my spirit is the surge of open seas." Although he cannot personally change the inhumane way people treat their brothers and sisters, Willie's spirit will always be around; for as he says, "I am the time," and his inspiration lives on beyond him (*IR*, 141–42).

As in "Willie," the setting of "Kin" is the South, particularly Arkansas, and the subject is family. This powerful poem is dedicated to Bailey and is based on the painful separation of brother and sister during their adult years. As children, Marguerite and Bailey were constant companions and buffered each other somewhat from the continual awareness of what it meant to grow up black in the South. Then, she writes, "We were entwined in red rings / Of blood and loneliness . . ." Now, distanced by time and Bailey's involvement with drugs, the poet is left

> . . . to force strangers
> Into brother molds, exacting
> Taxations they never
> Owed or could pay.

Meanwhile, her brother slips further and further away and fights

> . . . to die, thinking
> In destruction lies the seed
> Of birth . . .

Although she cannot reach him in his "regions of terror," Angelou sinks through memory to "silent walks in Southern woods" and an "Arkansas twilight" and is willing to concede that her brother "may be right (*IR*, 149–50).

But ultimately, the poet challenges her readers to fight against the insipid invitation of destruction and death. Throughout *And Still I Rise*, the strong, steady rhythm of her poetic voice beckons whoever will listen to transcend beyond the level of demoralizing defeat and to grasp life on its own terms. The single strongest affirmation of life is the title poem, "And Still I Rise." In the face of "bitter, twisted lies," "hatefulness," and "history's shame," the poet promises not to surrender. Silently, she absorbs the power of the sun and moon and becomes a "black ocean, leaping and wide, / Welling and swelling I bear in the tide." Her inner resources, "oil wells," "gold mines," and "diamonds," nourish her strength and sustain her courage. Her spirit will soar as she transforms "the gifts that my ancestors gave" into poetry, and herself into "the dream and the hope of the slave" (*IR*, 154–55). Through all of her verse, Angelou reaches out to touch the lives of others and to offer them hope and confidence in place of humiliation and despair.

Her fourth volume of verse, *Shaker, Why Don't You Sing?* (1983), is dedicated to her son, Guy Johnson, and her grandson, Colin Ashanti Murphy Johnson. As do her three previous collections of poems, *Shaker* celebrates the power to struggle against lost love, defeated dreams, and threatened freedom, and to survive. Her poetic voice resonates with the control and confidence that have become characteristic of Angelou's work in general and of her determination that "life loves the person who dares to live it." The vibrant tone of these poems moves gracefully from the promise of potential strength to the humor of light satire, at all times bearing witness to a spirit that soars and sings in spite of repeated disappointment. Perhaps even more than in her earlier poems, Angelou forcefully captures the loneliness of love and the sacrifice of slavery without surrendering to defeat or despair.

More than half of the twenty-eight poems in *Shaker* concern the subject of love between woman and man, and of these, most deal with the pain, loss, and loneliness that typically characterize unrequited love. In many of these poems, a woman awakens at sunrise, with or without her lover by her side, wondering how much longer their dying relationship will limp along before its failure will be openly acknowledged. An underlying issue in these poignant poems about love is deception—not so much the intricate fabrication of lies to cover up infidelity but rather the unvoiced acquiescence to fading and failing love. In "The Lie," for example, a woman protects herself from humiliation when her lover threatens to leave her by holding back her anger and pretending to be unmoved, even eager to see her man go:

> I hold curses, in my mouth,
> which could flood your path, sear
> bottomless chasms in your road.

Deception is her only defense:

> I keep, behind my lips,
> invectives capable of tearing
> the septum from your
> nostrils and the skin from your back. (*SW*, 33)

Similarly, in the very brief poem, "Prelude to a Parting," a woman lying in bed beside her lover senses the imminent end when he draws away from her touch. Yet neither will acknowledge "the tacit fact" or face the "awful fear of losing," knowing, as they do without speaking, that nothing will "cause / a fleeing love / to stay" (*SW*, 25).

Not all of the love poems in this collection suggest deception or dishonesty, but most describe the seemingly inevitable loss of love. The title poem, "Shaker, Why Don't You Sing?," belongs to this second group. A woman, "evicted from sleep's mute palace" and lying awake alone in bed, remembers the "perfect harmonies" and the "insistent rhythm" of a lost love. Her life fills with silence now that love has withdrawn its music, its "chanteys" that "hummed / [her] life alive." Now she rests "somewhere / between the unsung notes of night" and passionately asks love to return its song to her life: "O Shaker, why don't you sing?" (*SW*, 42–43). This mournful apostrophe to love serves as a refrain in an unsung song and, in its second utterance, brings the poem to a close unanswered.

The same determined voice comes through in a number of other poems that relate unabiding anguish over the oppressions of the black race. Several of these poems deal specifically with the inhumane treatment of the slaves in the South. "A Georgia Song," for example, in its beautifully lyrical cadences, recalls the unforgotten memories of slavery, which linger like "odors of Southern cities" and the "great green / Smell of fresh sweat. / In Southern fields." Angelou deftly recounts the "ancient / Wrongs" and describes a South broken by injustice and sorrow. Now, "dusty / Flags droop their unbearable / Sadness." Yet the poet calls for a new dream to rise up from the rich soil of Georgia and replace the "liquid notes of / Sorrow songs" with "a new song. A Song / Of southern peace." (*SW*, 8–10). Although the memories of "ancient / Wrongs" can never be forgotten, the poem invites a renewal of Southern dreams and peace.

Perhaps the most powerful poem in this collection is "Caged Bird," which inevitably brings Angelou's audience full circle with her best-known autobiography, *I Know Why the Caged Bird Sings.* This poem tells the story of a free bird and a caged bird. The free bird floats leisurely on "trade winds soft through the sighing trees" and even "dares to claim the sky." He feeds on "fat worms waiting on a dawn-bright lawn" and soars to "name the sky his own." Unlike his unbound brother, the caged bird leads a life of confinement that sorely inhibits his need to fly and sing. Trapped by the unyielding bars of his cage, the bird can only lift his voice in protest against his imprisonment and the "grave of dreams" on which he perches. Appearing both in the middle and end of the poem, this stanza serves as dual refrain:

> The caged bird sings
> with a fearful trill
> of things unknown
> but longed for still
> and his tune is heard
> on the distant hill
> for the caged bird
> sings of freedom. (*SW,* 16–17)

Although he sings of "things unknown, " the bird's song of freedom is heard even as far as the "distant hill." His song is his protest, his only alternative to submission and entrapment. Angelou knows why the caged bird and all oppressed beings must sing. Her poems in *Shaker, Why Don't You Sing?* imply that as long as such melodies are sung and heard, hope and strength will overcome defeated dreams.

At the end of *All God's Children Need Traveling Shoes,* Angelou hints at her association with Tom Feelings, a young black American artist who lived in Ghana during the early 1960s. Angelou cites Malcolm X's introduction of this newcomer to the black American expatriate community: "'A young painter named Tom Feelings is coming to Ghana. Do everything you can for him. I am counting on you" (*HW,* 193). By introducing Feelings at the conclusion of her latest autobiography, she subtly sets the scene for her most recent publication, *Now Sheba Sings the Song* (1987), a single poem, illustrated by eighty-two of Feeling's drawing of black women, sketched throughout the world over a period of twenty-five years. Together the poem and the sepia-toned drawings royally celebrate the universal majesty of the black woman. In his introduction to the book, Feelings credits

Angelou as the "someone who shared a similar experience [with the women he drew], someone who traveled, opened up, took in, and mentally recorded everything observed. And most important of all, it [his collaborator] had to be someone whose *center* is woman" (*NS*, 6). Angelou's poem, in turn, glorifies the spiritual, physical, emotional, and intellectual powers of black women or what Feelings calls "Africa's beauty, strength, and dignity [which are] wherever the Black woman is" (*NS*, 6). Angelou affirms the black woman's "love of good and God and Life" (*NS*, 48) and beckons "he who is daring and brave" (*NS*, 54) to meet the open challenge of the radiant Queen of Sheba. Maya Angelou's songs, like Sheba's, testify to the creative powers inherent in the works of today's Southern women writers.

Chronology

1928 Maya Angelou is born Marguerite Johnson on April 4 in St. Louis, Missouri, the daughter of Bailey and Vivian Baxter Johnson.

1931 Her parents divorce; Angelou and her four-year-old brother are sent to live with their maternal grandmother, Annie Henderson, in Stamps, Arkansas.

1936 During a visit to her mother in St. Louis Angelou is raped by her mother's boyfriend. The man is beaten to death by her uncles and Angelou does not speak for almost five years. She returns to Stamps and discovers literature under the tutelage of an educated neighbor, Mrs. Flowers.

1940 Graduates from the eighth grade at the top of her class. Her mother, now a professional gambler, takes the children to live in San Francisco.

1940–44 Attends George Washington High School in San Francisco and takes dance and drama lessons at the California Labor School.

1945 While still in high school, becomes the first black woman streetcar conductor in San Francisco; graduates from Mission High School at age 16; one month later, gives birth to a son.

1946 Works as a cook for $75 per week at the Creole Cafe; with $200 she moves to San Diego.

1947 After becoming involved in prostitution as a madam, Angelou returns to Stamps. She upbraids a rude white store clerk; her grandmother, fearing reprisals from the Ku Klux Klan, sends her back to San Francisco.

1948 Joins a nightclub dance act; then works as a restaurant cook; spends several days as a prostitute, until her brother threatens violence if she continues.

1950 Marries Tosh Angelos; they divorce three years later.

1953 Angelou resumes her career as a dancer at the Purple Onion.

1954–55 Joins a twenty-two nation tour of *Porgy and Bess*, sponsored by the U.S. Department of State.

1955 Returns to care for her young son, Guy; becomes instructor of Modern Dance at the Rome Opera House and at Hambina Theatre, Tel Aviv.

1957 Appears in a play, *Calypso Heatwave*. Makes a commitment to become a writer and black civil rights activist; moves to Brooklyn and participates in the Harlem Writers Guild, a group that included John Henrik Clarke, Paule Marshall, James Baldwin, and social activist author John Killens.

1959–60 Succeeds Bayard Rustin as northern coordinator of Martin Luther King, Jr.'s, Southern Christian Leadership Conference.

1960 Appears in the Off-Broadway production of *The Blacks*; produces and performs Off-Broadway in Cabaret for Freedom, written with Godfrey Cambridge.

1961–62 Associate editor of the *Arab Observer*, an English-language newspaper in Cairo, Egypt.

1963-66 Assistant administrator of the School of Music and Drama at the University of Ghana's Institute of African Studies at Legon-

Accra, Ghana. Feature editor of the *African Review*; contributor to the Ghanian Broadcasting Company.

1964 Appears in *Mother Courage* at the University of Ghana.

1966 Appears in *Medea* and *The Least of These* in Hollywood; lecturer at the University of California, Los Angeles.

1970 Writer in residence at the University of Kansas; receives Yale University fellowship; *I Know Why the Caged Bird Sings* is published and nominated for a National Book Award.

1971 A volume of poetry, *Just Give Me a Cool Drink of Water 'fore I Diiie* is published and nominated for a Pulitzer Prize.

1972 Television narrator, interviewer, and host for African-American specials and theatre series.

1973 Receives a Tony Award nomination for her Broadway debut in *Look Away*. Marries Paul Du Feu in December; they divorce in 1981.

1974 *Gather Together in My Name* is published; directs the film *All Day Long*; appears in the adapted Sophocles play *Ajax* at the Mark Taper Forum; named distinguished visiting professor at Wake Forest University, Wichita State University, and California State University.

1975 A volume of poetry, *Oh Pray My Wings Are Gonna Fit Me Well*, is published; appointed by President Gerald R. Ford to the American Revolution Bicentennial Council; member of the National Commission on the Observance of International Women's Year; becomes member of the board of trustees of the American Film Institute; appointed Rockefeller Foundation scholar in Italy; receives honorary degrees from Smith College and Mills College.

1976 *Singin' and Swingin' and Gettin' Merry Like Christmas* is published; directs her play, *And I Still Rise*; named Woman of the Year in Communications; receives honorary degree from Lawrence University.

1977 Appears in the television film *Roots*, and receives a Tony Award nomination for best supporting actress.

1978 *And I Still Rise* is published.

1981 *The Heart of a Woman* is published. Angelou receives a lifetime appointment as Reynolds Professor of American Studies, Wake Forest University.

1983 *Shaker, Why Don't You Sing?*, a volume of poetry, is published. Angelou is named one of the Top 100 Most Influential Women by the *Ladies' Home Journal*; receives the Matrix Award.

1986 *All God's Children Need Traveling Shoes; Mrs. Flowers: A Moment of Friendship*; *Poems: Maya Angelou* are published.

1987 *Now Sheba Sings the Song* is published; receives the North Carolina Award in Literature.

1988 Directs Errol John's *Moon on a Rainbow Shawl* in London.

1990 A volume of poetry, *I Shall Not Be Moved*, is published.

1993 The inaugural poem *On the Pulse of Morning; Soul Looks Back in Wonder*, poems; and *Wouldn't Take Nothing for My Journey Now* are published. Angelou contributes poetry to the film *Poetic Justice*.

1994 *My Painted House, My Friendly Chicken, and Me* and *Phenomenal Women: Four Poems Celebrating Women* are published.

1995 *A Brave and Startling Truth* is published.

1996 *Kofi and His Magic*, a children's story, is published.

Contributors

HAROLD BLOOM is Sterling Professor of Humanities at Yale University and Professor of English at New York University. He is the author of *The Visionary Company*, *The Anxiety of Influence*, *Poetry and Repression*, and other volumes of literary criticism. His forthcoming study, *Freud, Transference and Authority*, considers all of Freud's major writings. A MacArthur Prize Fellow, Professor Bloom is general editor of five series of literary criticism published by Chelsea House.

SIDONIE ANN SMITH has written extensively on women's autobiography. Her works include two books: *Poetics of Women's Autobiography: Marginality and the Fictions of Self-Representation* and, co-edited with Julia Watson, a collection of essays, *De-Colonizing the Subject: The Politics of Gender in Women's Autobiography*.

GEORGE E. KENT was Professor of English at the University of Chicago and the author of *Blackness and the Adventure of Western Culture*.

CAROL E. NEUBAUER is a member of the Department of English and Foreign Languages at Bradley University. She has published extensively on Maya Angelou and other writers in journals such as *Black American Literature Forum*, *The Journal of Modern African Studies*, *MELUS*, *World Literature Written in English*, and *The Massachusetts Review*. Her recent work includes a study of Chinese women writers.

SONDRA O'NEALE is Associate Professor of the Women's Studies Department at the University of Wisconsin-La Crosse. She has published extensively in professional journals and edited texts on the works of African-

American slaves and on the works of African-American women and on the phenomenon of religion and biblical typology in modern American culture. *Jupiter Hammon and the Biblical Beginnings of African-American Literature* is her most recent book.

SELWYN R. CUDJOE is Professor of Africana studies at Wellesley College. He is the author of *Resistance and Caribbean Literature* and *V.S. Naipaul: A Materialist Reading*. He is editor of *Caribbean Women Writers: Essays from the First International Conference* and *Eric E. Williams Speaks*. His most recent works include the volume *C.L.R. James: His Intellectual Legacies*.

PRISCILLA R. RAMSEY is Associate Professor of Afro-American Studies at Howard University. Her published articles include *John A. Williams: The Black American Narrative and the City* and *The Critical Canon of Houston A. Baker: A Prodigy Scholar.*

CHRISTINE FROULA is associate professor of English at Yale University. She has published books and essays on modern literature, contemporary theory, and feminist criticism including *Modernism's Body: Sex, Culture, and Joyce*.

KENETH KINNAMON is a professor of English and Chairman of the Department at the University of Arkansas. He has published *The Emergence of Richard Wright: A Study in Literature and Society*, a monograph on James Baldwin, and edited *James Baldwin: A Collection of Critical Essays*, and *New Essays on Native Son*. With Joseph Benson, Michel Fabre, and Craig Werner, he is co-editor of *A Richard Wright Bibliography*; and with Richard K. Barksdale, *Black Writers of America*.

JOANNE M. BRAXTON is Frances L. and Edwin L. Cummings Professor of American Studies and English at the College of William and Mary. She is the author of *Black Women Writing Autobiography: A Tradition within a Tradition* and co-editor, with Andree N. McLaughlin, of *Wild Women in the Whirlwind: The Renaissance in Contemporary Afra-American Writing*.

FRANÇOISE LIONNET is Associate Professor of English at the University of Chicago and the author of *Blackness and the Adventure of Western Culture* and *Autobiographical Voices: Race, Gender, Self-Portraiture*. Her works include studies of Francophone and African-American women writers, French Caribbean and North African post-colonial literature, and issues of multi-cultural discourse.

MARY JANE LUPTON is a member of the English faculty at Morgan State University. She has published articles on African American women novelists in *Black American Literature Forum*, *CLA Journal*, *Southern Literary Journal*, and *The Zora Neale Hurston Forum*. She has also written about the psychological and cultural aspects of menstruation.

Bibliography

Arensberg, Liliane K. "Death as Metaphor of Self in *I Know Why the Caged Bird Sings*," *CLA Journal*, 20:2 (December 1976): 273–91.

Benson, Carol. "Out of the Cage and Still Singing," *Writer's Digest* (January 1975): 18–20.

Bertolino, James. "Maya Angelou Is Three Writers: *I Know Why the Caged Bird Sings*," *Censored Books: Critical Viewpoints*. Ed. Nicholas J. Karolides, Lee Burress, and John M. Kean. Metuchen, NJ: The Scarecrow Press, 1993. 299–305.

Bloom, Lynn Z. "Maya Angelou," *Dictionary of Literary Biography*, 38. Detroit: Gale, 1985. 3–12.

Butterfield, Stephen. *Black Autobiography in America*. Amherst: University of Massachusetts Press, 1974.

Chrisman, Robert. "*The Black Scholar* Interviews Maya Angelou," *Black Scholar* (January–February 1977): 44–52.

Cordell, Shirley J. "The Black Woman: A Focus on 'Strength of Character' in *I Know Why the Caged Bird Sings*," *Virginia English Bulletin*, 36:2 (Winter 1986): 36–39.

Demetrakopoulos, Stephanie A. "The Metaphysics of Matrilinearism in Women's Autobiography: Studies of Mead's *Blackberry Winter*, Hellman's *Pentimento*, Angelou's *I Know Why the Caged Bird Sings*, and Kingston's *The Woman Warrior*," in *Women's Autobiography: Essays in Criticism*. Ed. Estelle Jelinek. Bloomington: Indiana University Press, 1980. 180–205.

Elliott, Jeffrey M., ed. *Conversations with Maya Angelou*. Jackson: University Press of Mississippi, 1989.

Estes-Hicks, Onita. "The Way We Were: Precious Memories of the Black Segregated South," *African American Review*, 27:1 (Spring 1993): 9–18.

Foster, Frances. "Parents and Children in Autobiography by Southern Afro-American Writers," *Home Ground: Southern Autobiography*. Columbia: University of Missouri Press, 1992. 98–109.

Froula, Christine. "The Daughter's Seduction: Sexual Violence and Literary History," *Signs*, 11:4 (Summer 1986): 621–44.

Fulghum, Robert. "Home Truths and Homilies," *Washington Post Book World* (September 19, 1993): 4.

Georgoudaki, Ekaterini. *Race, Gender, and Class Perspectives in the Works of Maya*

Angelou, Gwendolyn Brooks, Rita Dove, Nikki Giovanni, and Audre Lorde. Thessaloniki: Aristotle University of Thessaloniki, 1991.

Gilbert, Susan. "Maya Angelou's *I Know Why the Caged Bird Sings:* Paths to Escape," *Mount Olive Review* 1:1 (Spring 1987): 39–50.

Goodman, G., Jr. "Maya Angelou's Lonely Black Outlook," *The New York Times* (March 24, 1972): 28.

Gottlieb, Annie. "Growing Up and the Serious Business of Survival," *New York Times Book Review* (June 16, 1974): 16, 20.

Gruesser, John C. "Afro-American Travel Literature and Africanist Discourse," *Black American Literature Forum*, 24:1 (Spring 1990): 5–20.

Hord, Fred Lee. "Someplace to Be a Black Girl," *Reconstructing Memory: Black Literary Criticism.* Chicago: Third World Press, 1991. 75–85.

Inge, Tonette Bond, ed. *Southern Women Writers: The New Generation.* Tuscaloosa: University of Alabama Press, 1990.

Kelly, Ernece B. [Review of *I Know Why the Caged Bird Sings*] *Harvard Educational Review* 40: 4 (November 1970): 681–82.

Kent, George E. "Maya Angelou's *I Know Why the Caged Bird Sings* and Black Autobiographical Tradition," *Kansas Quarterly*, 7 (1975): 72–78. Reprinted in *African American Autobiography: A Collection of Critical Essays.* Ed. William L. Andrews. Englewood Cliffs, NJ: Prentice-Hall, 1993. 162–70.

Kinnamon, Keneth. "Call and Response: Intertextuality in Two Autobiographical Works by Richard Wright and Maya Angelou," *Studies in Black American Literature, Vol. II: Belief vs. Theory in Black American Literary Criticism.* Ed. Joe Weixlmann and Chester J. Fontenot. Greenwood, FL: Penkevill Publishing Co., 1986. 121–34.

MacKethan, Lucinda H. "Mother Wit: Humor in Afro-American Women's Autobiography," *Studies in American Humor*, 4:1–2 (Spring 1985): 51–61.

McMurry, Myra K. "Role-Playing as Art in Maya Angelou's *Caged Bird,*" *South Atlantic Bulletin*, 41:2 (May 1976): 106–11.

McPherson, Dolly. *Order Out of Chaos: The Autobiographical Works of Maya Angelou.* New York: Peter Lang, 1990.

———. "Defining the Self through Place and Culture: Maya Angelou's *I Know Why the Caged Bird Sings,*" *MAWA Review*, 5:1 (June 1990): 12–14.

Megna-Wallace, Joanne. "Simone de Beauvoir and Maya Angelou: Birds of a Feather," *Simone de Beauvoir Studies* 6 (1986): 49–55.

Moore, Opal. "Learning to Live: When the Caged Bird Breaks From the Cage," *Censored Books: Critical Viewpoints.* Ed. Nicholas J. Karolides, Lee Burress, and John M. Kean. Metuchen, NJ: The Scarecrow Press, 1993. 306–16.

Phillips, Frank Lamont. Review of *Gather Together in My Name, Black World* 24:9 (July 1975): 52, 61.

Premo, Cassie. "When the Difference Becomes Too Great: Images of the Self and Survival in a Postmodern World," *Genre* 16 (1995): 183–91.

Redmond, Eugene B. "Boldness of Language and Breadth: An Interview with Maya Angelou," *Black American Literature Forum*, 22:2 (Summer 1988): 156–57.

Saunders, James Robert. "Breaking Out of the Cage: The Autobiographical Writings of Maya Angelou," *The Hollins Critic*, 28:4 (October 1991): 1–11.

Tate, Claudia, ed. *Black Women Writers at Work.* New York: Continuum, 1983. 1–11.

Tawake, Sandra Kiser. "Multi-Ethnic Literature in the Classroom: Whose Standards?" *World Englishes: Journal of English as an International and Intranational Language*, 10:3 (Winter 1991): 335–40.

Wall, Cheryl. "Maya Angelou," *Women Writers Talking*. Ed. Janet Todd. New York: Holmes & Meier, 1983. 59–67.

Vermillion, Mary. "Reembodying the Self: Representations of Rape in *Incidents in the Life of a Slave Girl* and *I Know Why the Caged Bird Sings*," *Biography*, 15:3 (Summer 1992): 243–60.

Weller, Sheila. "Work in Progress/Maya Angelou," *Intellectual Digest* (June 1973).

Acknowledgments

"The Song of a Caged Bird: Maya Angelou's Quest after Self-Acceptance" by Sidonie Ann Smith from *Southern Humanities Review* 7:4 (Fall 1973). © 1973 by Auburn University.

"Maya Angelou's *I Know Why the Caged Bird Sings* and Black Autobiographical Tradition" by George E. Kent from *African American Autobiography: A Collection of Critical Essays*. © 1993 by Prentice-Hall. Reprinted with permission of the publisher. Article originally appeared in *Kansas Quarterly* 7 (1975): 72–78.

"Displacement and Autobiographical Style in Maya Angelou's *The Heart of a Woman*" by Carol E. Neubauer from *Black American Literature Forum* 17:3 (Fall 1983). © 1983 by Indiana State University.

"Reconstruction of the Composite Self: New Images of Black Women in Maya Angelou's Continuing Autobiography" by Sondra O'Neale from *Black Women Writers (1950-1980)*, edited by Mari Evans. © 1983 by Mari Evans. Used by permission of Doubleday, a division of Bantam Doubleday Dell Publishing Group, Inc.

"Maya Angelou and the Autobiographical Statement" by Selwyn R. Cudjoe from *Black Women Writers (1950-1980)*, edited by Mari Evans. © 1983 by Mari Evans. Used by permission of Doubleday, a division of Bantam Doubleday Dell Publishing Group, Inc.

"Transcendence: The Poetry of Maya Angelou" by Priscilla R. Ramsey from *A Current Bibliography on African Affairs* 17:2 (1985). © 1985 by Baywood Publishing Co., Inc. Reprinted with permission of the author and the publisher.

"The Daughter's Seduction: Sexual Violence and Literary History" by Christine Froula from *Signs* 11:4 (Summer 1986). © 1986 by The University of Chicago Press. Reprinted with permission of the publisher and the author.

"Call and Response: Intertextuality in Two Autobiographical Works by Richard Wright and Maya Angelou" by Keneth Kinnamon from *Studies in Black American Literature, Vol. II: Beliefs vs. Theory in Black American Literary Criticism*, edited by Joe Weixlmann and Chester J. Fontenot. © 1986 by The Penkevill Publishing Co.

"A Song of Transcendence: Maya Angelou" by Joanne M. Braxton from *Black Women Writing Autobiography: A Tradition Within a Tradition* by Joanne M. Braxton. © 1989 by Temple University.

"Con Artists and Storytellers: Maya Angelou's Problematic Sense of Audience" by Françoise Lionnet from *Autobiographical Voices: Race, Gender, Self-Portraiture* by Françoise Lionnet. © 1989 by Cornell University.

"Singing the Black Mother: Maya Angelou and Autobiographical Continuity" by Mary Jane Lupton from *Black American Literature Forum* 24:2 (Summer 1990). © 1990 by Mary Jane Lupton.

"Maya Angelou: Self and a Song of Freedom in the Southern Tradition" by Carol E. Neubauer from *Southern Women Writers: The New Generation*, edited by Tonette Bond Inge. © 1990 by The University of Alabama Press. Used by permission of the publisher.

Index